P9-DIB-470

Learn C
on the

Macintosh®

INCLUDES
SPECIAL VERSION
OF SYMANTEC'S
THINK C

Dave Mark

Addison-Wesley Publishing Company, Inc.

Reading, Massachusetts • Menlo Park, California • New York
Don Mills, Ontario • Wokingham, England • Amsterdam
Bonn • Sydney • Singapore • Tokyo • Madrid • San Juan
Paris • Seoul • Milan • Mexico City • Taipei

Many of the designations used by manufacturers and sellers to distinguish their products are claimed as trademarks. Where those designations appear in this book and Addison-Wesley was aware of a trademark claim, the designations have been printed in initial capital letters.

Function descriptions in Appendix D copyright © 1989 Symantec Corporation and used with permission.

Library of Congress Cataloging-in-Publication Data

Mark, Dave.
    Learn C on the Macintosh : includes special version of Symantec's
Think C / Dave Mark.
                p.   cm.
    Includes bibliographical references and index.
    ISBN 0-201-56785-7
    1. Macintosh (Computer)—Programming.   2. C (Computer program
language)   I. Title.
QA76.8.M3M36773   1991
005.265—dc20   91-15354
                                                                    CIP

Copyright © 1991 by Dave Mark

All rights reserved. No part of this publication may be reproduced, stored in a retrieval system, or transmitted, in any form or by any means, electronic, mechanical, photocopying, recording, or otherwise, without the prior written permission of the publisher. Printed in the United States of America. Published simultaneously in Canada.

Sponsoring Editor: Julie Stillman
Project Editor: Elizabeth G. Rogalin
Cover design: Jean Seal
Set in 11.5-point Sabon by ST Associates

3 4 5 6 7 8 9 -MW- 95949392
Third printing, May 1992

This book is dedicated to Deneen J. Melander -
LFUEMIV,OK?...

Contents

Preface   *vii*

Chapter 1   Welcome Aboard   1
_____

What's in the Package?   3
Why Learn C?   4
What Should I Know to Get Started?   4
What Equipment Will I Need?   5
The Lay of the Land   6
The Chapters   6
Conventions Used in This Book   7
Strap Yourself In . . .   8

Chapter 2   Installing THIN C   11
_____

The Programming Process: A Quick Tour   14
Features of THIN C   20
What's Next?   22

Chapter 3   Programming Basics   25

Programming   28
How Computers Work   28
THIN C and the Project File   33
A Word About Memory   35
The Importance of Binary   39
What's Next?   40
Exercises   41

Chapter 4   C Basics: Functions   43

C Functions   45
Function Calling Examples   49
The Most Important Function   50
ANSI C and the Standard Library   51
Same Program, Two Functions   52
Generating Some Errors   56
What's Next?   59
Exercises   61

Chapter 5   C Basics: Variables and Operators   63

An Introduction to Variables   66
Operators   71
Using Parentheses ( )   78
Sample Programs   79
Sprucing Up Your Code   94
What's Next?   98
Exercises   99

Chapter 6   Controlling Your Program's Flow   101

Flow Control   104
Expressions   106
Statements   114
Sample Programs   129
What's Next?   138
Exercises   139

Chapter 7   Pointers and Parameters   141

What is a Pointer?   144
Pointer Basics   148
Function Parameters   155
What Does All This Have to do with Pointers?   160
Global Variables and Function Returns   164
Sample Programs   172
What's Next?   181
Exercises   183

Chapter 8   Variable Data Types   185

Other Data Types   188
Working With Characters   192
Characters and C   193
The ASCII Character Set   194
Arrays   200
Why Use Arrays?   202
Danger, Will Robinson!!!   211
Text Strings   212
A Text String in Memory   213

The Input Buffer   216
On With the Program   219
The #define   2221
#define Macros   224
What's Next?   230
Exercises   231

Chapter 9   Designing Your Own Data Structures   233

Structures   236
Model A: Three Ways   236
Model B: The Data Structure Approach   240
Allocating Your Own Memory   248
Keep Track of That Address!   250
Working With Linked Lists   251
Order in the Code   268
What's Next?   269
Exercises   271

Chapter 10 Working With Files   273

What is a File?   276
Working with Files, Part One   276
Working with Files, Part Two   283
What's Next?   298
Exercises   299

Chapter 11 Filling in the Gaps   303

What is Typecasting?   306
Unions   310
Function Recursion   314
A Recursive Approach   316
Binary Trees   319
Function Pointers   328
More on Strings   330
What's Next?   333
Exercises   335

Chapter 12 Adding the Macintosh Interface   339

The Macintosh User Interface   342
The Graphical User Interface   342
Getting Started With the Mac Toolbox   346
Inside Macintosh   347
The Macintosh C Programming Primer   348
Macintosh Programming Secrets   349

Appendices   351

Appendix A   Glossary   351
Appendix B   Complete Program Listings   361
Appendix C   Syntax Reference Section   401
Appendix D   Standard Library Functions   405
Appendix E   The Complete THINK C
              Development Environment   423
Appendix F   Answers to Selected Exercises   435
Appendix G   Bibliography   441

Preface

One of the best decisions I ever made was back in 1979 when I hooked up with my buddy Tom and learned C. At first, C was just a meaningless scribble of curly brackets, semicolons, and parentheses. Fortunately for me, Tom was a C guru, and with him looking over my shoulder, I learned C quickly.

Now it's your turn.

This time I'll be looking over *your* shoulder as you learn C. My goal is to present every aspect of C the way I would have liked it explained to me. I've saved up all the questions I had as I learned the language and tried to answer them here.

Learning to program in C will open a wide range of opportunities for you. C is one of the most popular programming languages in the world today. Recessions may come and go, but there's always a demand for good C programmers. Whether you want to start your own software company or just write programs for your own enjoyment, you will discover that C programming is its own reward. Most of all, C programming is fun.

I hope you enjoy the book. If you make it to MacWorld on either coast, stop by the Addison-Wesley booth and say hello. I'd love to hear from you. In the meantime, turn the page, and let's get started...

D. M.
Arlington, VA

Acknowledgments

I'd like to take a paragraph or two and thank some people whose names didn't make the cover, but who made this book possible. First of all, I'd like to thank Elizabeth Rogalin, Julie Stillman, and Mary Cavaliere from Addison-Wesley for all of their hard work in getting this book out the door.

Next, I'd like to thank Darrell LeBlanc from Symantec for the excellent job he did in producing THIN C, the development environment used throughout the book.

Thanks to Darrell LeBlanc and Joe Zobkiw for their perceptive and accurate technical comments. Thanks to Jackie Cowlishaw for a copyedit with flair (and absolutely no sarcasm. Not even a little. Really.). A very special thanks to Carlos Derr, Chuck Shankland, and Gerry Helldorfer, the DAFSA team. Thanks also to Philip Borenstein, Phil Shapiro, Susan Smith, and Steve LeBlanc for their support.

Thanks to my family (especially you, Stu), who stood behind me all the way.

Finally, I'd like to thank the man who was there at the beginning, the man who introduced me to the wonders of C, my good friend Tom Swartz. Thanks, Tom.

Chapter 1

Welcome Aboard

This Chapter
at a Glance

What's in the Package?
Why Learn C?
What Should I Know to Get Started?
What Equipment Will I Need?
The Lay of the Land
The Chapters
Conventions Used in This Book
Strap Yourself In . . .

WELCOME! BY PURCHASING THIS BOOK/DISK PACKAGE, you have taken the first step toward learning the C programming language. As you make your way through the book, you'll learn one of the most popular and powerful programming languages of all time.

You will be glad you took this step.

Before we start programming, there are a few questions worth addressing at this point.

What's in the Package?

Learn C on the Macintosh is a book/disk package. The book is filled with all kinds of interesting facts, figures, and programming examples all designed to teach you how to program in C.

In the back of the book is a Macintosh floppy disk, which contains all the software you'll need to run each of the book's programming examples on your own computer. Included on this disk is THIN C, a customized version of the leading Macintosh programming environment, THINK C, written especially for this book. The disk also includes each of the programs presented in the book, so you don't have to type the examples yourself. Such a deal!

Why Learn C?

There are many reasons for learning C. Perhaps the biggest reason is C's popularity as a programming language. C is probably the hottest programming language around. In fact, most of the best-selling Macintosh applications were written in C. If you are just getting started in programming, C is a great first programming language. If you already know a programming language, such as BASIC or Pascal, you'll find C a worthy addition to your language set.

C is everywhere. Almost every computer made today supports the C language. Once you learn C, you'll be able to create your own programs for fun and profit. With C, you can create utilities, games, and tools that do exactly what you want them to do. You can even write the next great spreadsheet, word processor, or utility. Who knows? You might even make $80 gazillion in the process!

Whatever your reasons, learning to program in C will pay you dividends the rest of your programming life.

What Should I Know to Get Started?

For the most part, the only prerequisite to using this book is a basic knowledge of the Macintosh. Do you know how to double-click on an application to start it up? Does the scrolling list in Figure 1.1 look familiar? Do you know how to use a word processor like MacWrite or Microsoft Word? If you can use the Macintosh to run programs and edit documents, you have everything you need to get started learning C.

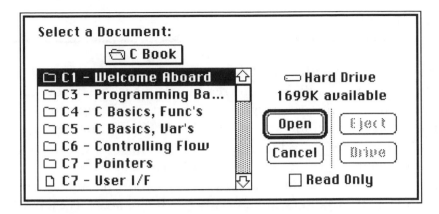

Figure 1.1   Scrolling through a list of documents.

If you know nothing about programming, don't worry. The first few chapters of this book will bring you up to speed. If you have some programming experience (or even a lot), you might want to skim the first few chapters, then dig right into the C fundamentals that start in Chapter 4.

What Equipment Will I Need?

While it is possible to learn C just by reading a book, you'll get the most out of this book if you run each example program as you read how it works. To do this, you'll need a Macintosh. If you don't have one, borrow a friend's. You'll need at least a Mac Plus with 1 megabyte of memory. The software accompanying this book will run with most Macintosh system software. It's even been tested with System 7.0!

For best results, run this software on a Macintosh with a hard disk drive. If you don't have access to a hard drive, you will at least want to use an external floppy drive, which will save you a lot of disk swapping.

The Lay of the Land

This book was designed with several different readers in mind. If you're new to programming, you'll want to read every chapter. If you get stuck, find a C buddy who can answer your questions. Try not to skip over material you don't understand. Ask. Most C programmers are friendly and are usually more than glad to help someone just getting started. Make a commitment to finish this book. You can do it!

If you have some programming experience, but know nothing about C, read Chapter 2, then skim through Chapter 3. If Chapter 3 is cake to you, jump right to Chapter 4. You'll probably find that the concepts presented in the first few chapters are pretty straightforward. Read at your own speed until you reach a comfortable depth. The farther into the book you get, the more complex the concepts.

The Chapters

This book is made up of 12 chapters and seven appendices. This chapter provides an overview of the book and gets you started down the right path.

Chapter 2 introduces the disk portion of this book/disk package. You'll learn about THIN C, the C programming environment designed especially for use with this book. You'll install THIN C on your hard drive or floppy-based Macintosh system and test the software to make sure it's installed properly. In Chapter 2, you'll run your first C program.

Regardless of any programming experience you already have, don't skip Chapter 2!

Chapter 3 is for those of you with little or no programming experience. Chapter 3 answers some basic questions, such as "Why write a computer program?" and "How do computer programs work?" We'll look at all the elements that come together to create a computer program, elements such as source code, a compiler, and the computer itself. Even if you're a seasoned Pascal programmer, you might want to read through this chapter, just to review the basics.

Chapter 4 opens the door to C programming. It focuses on one of the primary building blocks of C: the function. You'll run some sample programs, plus discover one of the cruelest, least-liked parts of programming: the syntax error.

Chapter 5 explores the foundation of C programming: variables and operators. When you finish this chapter you will have a fundamental understanding of programming. You'll know how to declare a variable and how to use operators to store data in the variable.

Chapter 6 introduces the concept of flow control. You'll learn how to use C programming constructs, such as `if`, `while`, and `for` to control the direction of your program. You'll learn how your program can be used to make decisions based on data in your program.

Chapter 7 starts off with the concept of pointers, also known as variable addresses. From this point on you'll use pointers in almost every C program you write. Pointers allow you to implement complex data structures, opening up a world of programming possibilities.

Chapter 8 introduces data types. You'll learn about arrays and strings and the common bond they share. At this point, you are in real danger of becoming a C guru. Careful!

Chapter 9 tackles data structures. You'll learn how to design and build the right data structure for the job. Your knowledge of pointers is sure to get a workout in this chapter.

Chapter 10 teaches you how to work with disk files. You'll learn how to open a file and read its contents into your program. You'll also learn how to write your program's data out to a file.

Chapter 11 is a potpourri of miscellaneous C programming issues. This chapter tries to clear up any programming loose ends. You'll learn about recursion, binary trees, and something not every C programmer knows about: C function pointers.

Chapter 12 prepares you for your next step along the programming path: the *Macintosh C Programming Primer*. You'll learn a little about what makes Macintosh programs special, plus find out how you can write your own programs that sport that special Macintosh look and feel.

Appendix A is a glossary of the technical terms used in this book.

Appendix B contains a complete listing of all the examples used in this book. This section will come in handy as a reference, as you write your own C programs. Need an example of an `if-else` statement in action? Turn to the examples in Appendix B.

Appendix C is another useful reference. It describes the syntax of each of the C statement types introduced in the book. Need an exact specification of a `switch` statement? Check out Appendix C.

Appendix D provides a description of the **Standard Library** functions introduced in this book. The Standard Library of functions is available as part of every standard C development environment, no matter what type of computer it's being used with. Need to know how to call one of the Standard Library functions introduced in the book? Use Appendix D.

Appendix E describes the differences between THIN C and THINK C. THINK C is the software development environment of choice in the Macintosh development community. THIN C provides a subset of THINK C's power and functionalism.

Appendix F provides answers to selected exercises presented at the end of each of the chapters. Some exercises were left unanswered to keep you on your toes.

Appendix G is a bibliography of useful programming titles.

Conventions Used in This Book

As you read this book, you'll encounter a few standard conventions intended to make the book easier to read. For example, technical terms appearing for the first time appear in **boldface**. You'll find most of these terms in the glossary in Appendix A.

By the Way _____

> Occasionally, you'll come across a block of text set off in its own little box, like this. These blocks are called **tech blocks,** and are intended to add technical detail to the subject currently being discussed. For the most part, each tech block will fit in one of three categories: "By the Way," "Important," and "Warning." As the names imply, "By the Way" tech blocks are intended to be informative but not crucial. "Important" tech blocks should be read beginning to end, and the information within tucked into a reasonably responsive part of your brain. "Warning" tech blocks are usually trying to caution you about a potentially disasterous programming problem you should be on the lookout for. Read and heed these warnings!

All of the source code examples in this book are presented using a special font, known as the `code font`. This includes source code fragments that appear in the middle of running text. Menu items, or items you'll click on, appear in **Chicago font**.

At the end of each chapter, you'll find a set of exercises designed to reinforce the concepts presented in that chapter. Go through each of the exercises. It will be time well spent. As mentioned earlier, Appendix F contains answers to selected chapter exercises.

Strap Yourself In...

That's about it. Let's get started... .

Chapter 2

Installing THIN C

This Chapter at a Glance

The Programming Process: A Quick Tour
  Installing THIN C
  Testing THIN C
  Opening the Project hello.π
  Running hello.π
Features of THIN C
What's Next?

BEFORE WE GET INTO THE DETAILS OF THIN C, IT HELPS TO have a basic understanding of the programming process. For you veteran programmers, hang in there! This will only take a minute.

Tucked into the back of *Learn C on the Macintosh* is a floppy disk containing THIN C, a sort of Swiss Army knife for programmers. THIN C provides you with all the tools you'll need to work with the programming examples presented in the book.

By the Way

THIN C was created especially for this book by a company called Symantec. Among Macintosh programming circles, Symantec is known best as the maker of THINK C, the programmer's choice in Macintosh programming environments.

The Programming Process: A Quick Tour

All programs start as something called **source code**. Source code is a set of instructions that tells your program what to do and when to do it. When you build a model airplane, you follow a set of instructions written in English. When your program runs, it follows a set of instructions written in a language it can understand. In our case, we'll write instructions to the computer in a language called C. This chapter won't get into the details of the C language. That's the purpose of the rest of the book. For now, just think of source code as a set of instructions that tells your program what to do.

Source code is created using a tool called a **text editor**. A text editor operates like a typical Macintosh word processor. You can **Open** existing files, make changes to the text, then **Save** the file back out to your disk. You can even start from scratch by creating a **New** file. You get the idea. You'll use THIN C's built-in text editor to open, edit, and save the source code examples provided on the disk accompanying this book.

Once your source code is written, you're ready for the **compiler**. The compiler translates your C source code from its textual form into a series of ones and zeros called **machine code**. Think of machine code as a streamlined version of your source code designed to maximize the efficiency of your computer.

As you might have guessed, THIN C comes with a built-in compiler. Once your source code is compiled (translated) into machine code, THIN C will even run your program for you.

As you read through this book, you'll become very familiar with the process of programming with THIN C. Before you can program with THIN C, however, you have to install it.

Installing THIN C

THIN C will work best on a Macintosh system with a hard disk drive. If your Mac doesn't have a hard drive, don't fret. You can run THIN C straight off a floppy disk. As you are probably aware, however, software tends to run slower on a floppy-based Mac.

Before you do anything else, make a backup copy of the THIN C disk and place the original disk in a safe place. From now on, only work with the backup of THIN C. That way, when your dog uses your backup disk as a teething ring, you'll have the original stored safely away and can make another backup.

If your Macintosh doesn't have a hard disk drive, you can run THIN C directly off the backup disk you just made (you did make a backup, didn't you?). Just make sure your backup disk is unlocked. All the files you'll need are located inside the folder named `Development` on the floppy disk.

If your Macintosh does have a hard drive, copy the folder named `Development` from the floppy disk onto your hard drive. All the files you'll need are inside this folder.

Testing THIN C

Now that you've installed THIN C, you're ready to take it for a test drive. On your hard drive or floppy disk (depending on where you have THIN C installed) open the folder `Development`. You'll see a folder called `Projects` which contains all the source code presented in the book. For the most part, you'll only be interested in the files in the `Projects` folder.

Open the `Projects` folder. You'll see a scrolling list of folders. There is one folder for every sample program in the book. Notice that the folders are in alphabetical order, sorted by the name of the sample program. Scroll down the list until you find a folder named `hello`. Open the folder named `hello`. (Make sure you don't accidentally open the folder named `hello2`. That's for later.) If you have problems running THIN C under System 7, make sure your computer is set to 24-bit mode.

Figure 2.1 shows the files in the `hello` folder. One file is named `hello.π` and the other is `hello.c`. Each of these files is necessary to run the example program called `hello`.

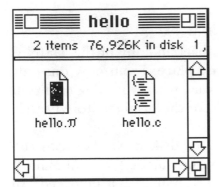

Figure 2.1   The hello folder.

The file hello.c contains the source code for the program hello. The file hello.π is an administrative file, collecting information relevant to the hello program. In THIN C lingo, hello.π is known as a **project file.** Together, these two files make up the hello project.

Important

Throughout the remainder of the book, sample programs are referred to as projects. The term "project" is specific to THIN C, so your C-coding friends may not be familiar with it. Outside of the THIN C world, just use the term "program."

Throughout the book, project file names will always end with the character ".π" and source code file names with the character ".c".

Opening the Project hello.π

Just to make sure THIN C is installed properly, let's open hello.π. Double-click on the hello.π icon. The THIN C application should start running and a **project window** for the hello.π project should appear (see Figure 2.2). The project window is the focal point for the project. The project window's title reflects the name of the project; in this case, hello.π.

Inside the project window is a list of the files that make up the project. The project hello.π makes use of the two files ANSI.lib and hello.c. The file hello.c contains the source code for the project. The file ANSI.lib is a special file you'll find in each of the book's sample projects. We'll talk about ANSI.lib later in the book.

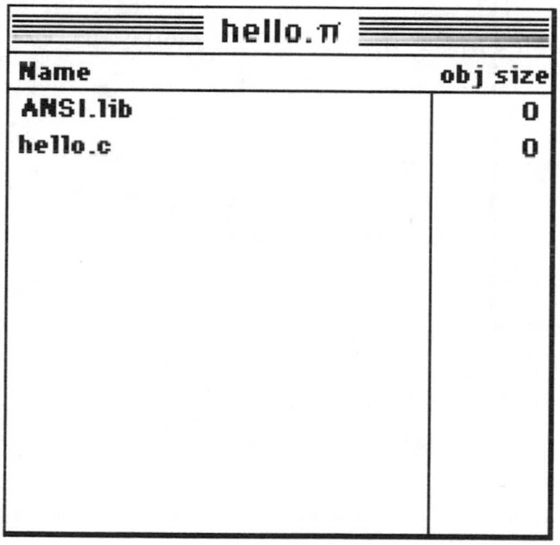

Name	obj size
ANSI.lib	0
hello.c	0

Figure 2.2   The project window for hello.π.

Wheel your mouse over to the project window and double-click on the name `hello.c`. The first click causes the name `hello.c` to be highlighted (see Figure 2.3). The second click opens an editing window showing the source code contained in the file `hello.c`. You can use the standard Macintosh text-editing techniques (clicking, dragging, and typing) to edit the source code in this window. You'll have plenty of editing opportunities later in the book. For now, close the source code window, leaving the source code as you found it.

Figure 2.3   The project window with `hello.c` highlighted.

By the Way _____

As the more adventurous of you may have already discovered, the file `ANSI.lib` is not a source code file. If you double-click on the name `ANSI.lib` in the project window, you'll see the dialog box shown in Figure 2.4.

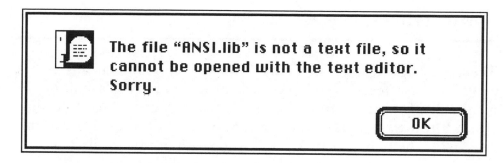

Figure 2.4 Hey! `ANSI.lib` is not a text file!

Running hello.π

Now try running the program whose source code you just looked at. Select **Run** from the **Project** window. THIN C will compile then run your program. A new window should appear on the screen, similar to the one shown in Figure 2.5. Hit the return key on your keyboard to exit the program. If you encounter problems running `hello.π`, try recopying the files from the original floppy disk.

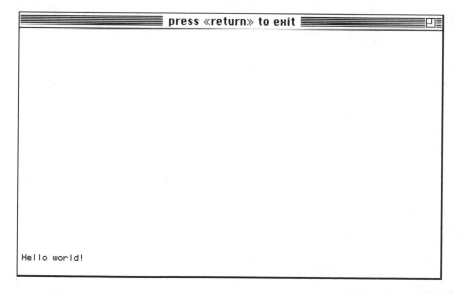

Figure 2.5 Running `hello.π`.

Features of THIN C

There are a few features of THIN C worth mentioning at this point. Most of these features are accessed through THIN C's pull-down menus. Look at the **File** menu (as shown in Figure 2.6). Selecting **New**, **Open...**, or **Close** will create, open, or close a text file. For the most part, the only text files you'll work with are the project source code files. Since these files already exist, you probably won't have much need for the **New** command. Since you can open a source code file by double-clicking its name in the project window, and close the file by clicking on the window's close box, you probably won't have much need for either **Open...** or **Close**. On the other hand, it's nice to know these options are there.

The rest of the **File** menu is fairly straightforward. **Save** and **Save As...** are useful for saving your source code once you've made changes to it. **Revert** reverts the open file back to the last saved version. **Page Setup...** and **Print...** are useful for printing a copy of your source code. **Quit** exits THIN C and returns you to the desktop.

```
┌─────────────┐
│ File        │
├─────────────┤
│ New      ⌘N │
│ Open...  ⌘O │
│ Close       │
│·············│
│ Save     ⌘S │
│ Save As...  │
│ Revert      │
│·············│
│ Page Setup..│
│ Print...    │
│·············│
│ Quit     ⌘Q │
└─────────────┘
```

Figure 2.6   THIN C's **File** menu.

The **Edit** menu (Figure 2.7) starts with the Macintosh standards **Undo**, **Cut**, **Copy**, **Paste**, and **Clear**. The **Set Tabs & Font...** item brings up a dialog box (Figure 2.8) that allows you to set the font and tabs for the source code files in the current project. The number in the **Tabs** field determines how many characters wide a tab character is. Use the font and font size pop-up menus to set the font for the project's source code.

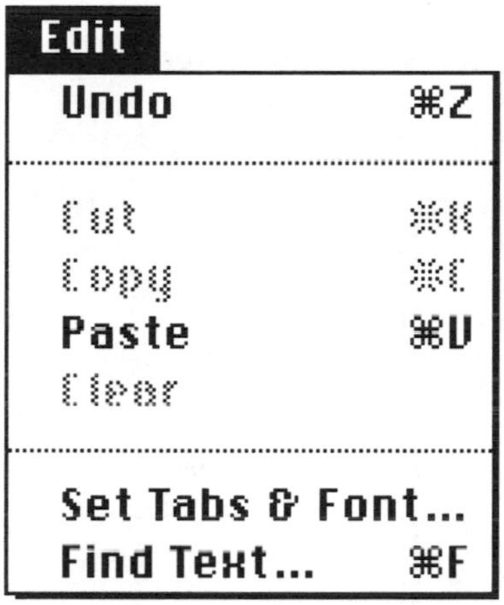

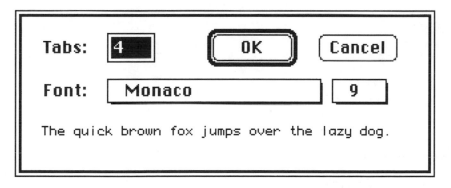

Figure 2.7   The **Edit** menu.

Figure 2.8   The **Set Tabs & Font...** dialog box.

The **Find Text...** item brings up a dialog box (Figure 2.9) that lets you search through your source code for a specific text string.

The **Project** menu (Figure 2.10) is perhaps the most-used menu in THIN C. If no project is open, the **Open Project...** item prompts you for a project to open. **Close Project** closes the currently open project. **Remove Objects** is useful for compacting project files (and therefore saving disk space). When THIN C compiles your source code, it saves the newly created machine code (also known as **object code**) inside the project file. This makes the project file bigger, taking up precious disk space. **Remove Objects** deletes the object code from the project file, saving you some disk space.

Figure 2.9   The **Find Text...** dialog box.

Figure 2.10   The **Project** menu.

By the Way _____

> Normally, once you've compiled a project, you can run the project again and again without recompiling. Two things will force THIN C to recompile your code: making a change to your source code or performing a **Remoue Objects**.
>
> Since **Remoue Objects** does save you disk space, it's a good idea to **Remoue Objects** once you finish exploring a project.

The final item on the **Project** menu is by far the most useful. Selecting **Run** asks THIN C to run your program for you.

What's Next?

That's about it for our THIN C intro. Are you ready to get started with C? Get comfortable and turn the page. Here we go... .

Chapter 3

Programming Basics

This Chapter at a Glance

Programming
How Computers Work
    The Parts of a Computer
    Creating a Computer Program
    The Life of a Program
    Source Code
THIN C and the Project File
A Word About Memory
    Binary, Bits, and Bytes
    Can a Byte Be Negative
The Importance of Binary
What's Next?
Exercises

BEFORE WE DIG INTO THE SPECIFICS OF C PROGRAMMING, we'll spend a few minutes reviewing the basics of computer programming. We'll answer such basic questions as "Why write a computer program?" and "How do computer programs work?" We'll look at all of the elements that come together to create a computer program, such as source code, a compiler, and the computer itself. Finally, we'll look inside the computer, focusing on the computer's memory, the silicon chips that hold your programs and data.

If you've already done some programming, skim through this chapter. If you feel comfortable with the material, skip ahead to Chapter 4. Most of the issues covered in this chapter will be C-independent.

Programming

Why write a computer program? There are many reasons. Some programs are written in direct response to a problem too complex to solve by hand. For example, you might write a program to calculate the constant π to 5000 decimal places, or to determine the precise moment to fire the boosters that will bring the space shuttle home safely.

Other programs are written as performance aids, allowing you to perform a regular task more efficiently. You might write a program to help you balance your checkbook, keep track of your baseball card collection, or lay out this month's issue of *Dinosaur Today*.

Whatever their purpose, each of these examples share a common theme. They are all examples of the art of programming.

How Computers Work

Before you can program a computer, it helps to have a basic understanding of how computers operate. Computers range in size from the huge mainframe computers that require their own air-conditioning systems, down to personal computers (also called PCs) that fit on your desk. All of these computers operate in basically the same way. They are all constructed of tiny slivers of silicon, called **integrated circuits** or **ICs**. Figure 3.1 shows a three-dimensional drawing of an integrated circuit.

The body of the integrated circuit is made up of extremely thin (much thinner than the finest human hair) layers of silicon. A laser beam is used to strategically place impurities into the silicon, a process called **doping**. Doping produces a predetermined effect on voltages applied to the legs of the IC. The point to remember about ICs is that scientists create them to serve a specific purpose. One type of IC might be designed to operate the fuel injector in your car. Another might operate your microwave oven. Most important, there are several ICs inside your computer making it work.

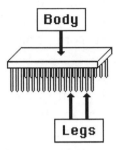

Figure 3.1 An integrated circuit, or IC, drawn fairly close to actual size. The brains of the IC are in the body. The body is connected to the rest of the computer via the legs.

The most important IC in your computer is called the **Central Processing Unit,** or **CPU.** The CPU functions as the brains inside your computer. It sends out instructions to all the different parts of your computer, telling each what to do and when to do it. The CPU inside every Macintosh was designed by a company called Motorola. They are all part of Motorola's 68000 series of CPU ICs. The Macintosh Plus, Macintosh Classic, and Macintosh SE all use a 68000 CPU. The Macintosh II uses a 68020 CPU. The Macintosh IIci uses a 68030 CPU. In general, the higher the CPU's model number, the faster and more powerful the machine will be.

The Parts of a Computer

At the center of every computer is its **motherboard.** The motherboard is a large rectangle, made of plastic and strips of metal, designed to house the CPU and related ICs. Sockets are built into the surface of the motherboard, designed to hold the legs of an integrated circuit. The legs of an IC are made of a stiff metal and plug into IC sockets in much the same way as an electrical plug slides into a wall socket.

Once the CPU is plugged into the motherboard it can communicate with other devices attached to the motherboard. There are several types of such devices. Perhaps the most important is the **console**, which enables you to communicate with your computer. On a Mac, the console consists of a screen, a keyboard, and a mouse. (The screen is the bright glowing object you spend an awful lot of time staring at.)

In computer terms, the screen is called an **output device**, because it's the primary device used by the computer to get information out to you. The keyboard and mouse are known as **input devices**. They are the primary devices you use to get information into the computer. You use the mouse to point and click, telling the computer which document to open or which application to run. You type on your keyboard, sending the characters to the computer. The characters might be part of a memo to your boss, or perhaps part of the name you'd like to save the memo as.

Most computers also have storage devices attached to the motherboard. Storage devices allow you to store data for later retrieval. On the Mac, your data will consist of the documents and applications you use every day. Typical Mac storage devices are hard disk drives and floppy disk drives. If you buy an application, such as Microsoft Word, chances are you will open the box, take the floppy disks out of the package, pop a floppy disk into the floppy disk drive, and copy the application onto your hard disk drive. Most people use floppy disks to transport data between larger storage devices, such as hard disk drives.

Most storage devices have a storage limit. The newer Macintosh floppy disk drives allow a maximum of approximately 1.4 million characters per floppy. A typical hard disk drive holds at least 40 million characters. Some hard drives hold as much as a billion characters!

There is one more important part of your computer. Every computer has it. Some computers have more than others. We're talking about your computer's **memory**. Computer memory consists of a set of integrated circuits, designed to hold data on a temporary basis. When you turn your computer off, its memory is erased. The computer's memory is only useful when it is turned on.

Typically, computer memory is used to hold a copy of the data you are currently working on. For example, when you want to edit a letter to your cousin Lou using your word processor, you tell the computer to fetch a copy of your letter from your hard disk drive (or from a floppy).

The computer will copy the letter into its memory. As you click and type, editing the letter, you're actually changing the *copy* in the computer's memory. When you're done editing, you tell the computer to save the copy of Lou's letter it has in memory, back onto your hard drive (or floppy). If you turn off the computer without saving the letter to some longer-term storage device — poof! — the letter in memory (as well as your changes) is gone.

Creating a Computer Program

The previous section took you on a brief tour of your computer. The tour focused on the hardware (the physical elements) that makes a computer a computer. Now we'll take a look at the programming process, focusing on the elements involved in creating a computer program. We'll start with a quick overview of the chain of events that lead up to a finished program, then go back and review the process in more detail.

The Life of a Program

As mentioned in Chapter 2, most computer programs start as source code. Your source code will consist of a sequence of statements that tells the computer what to do. Source code is written in a specific programming language, such as C or Pascal. Each programming language has a specific set of rules that defines what is and isn't "legal" in that language.

Your mission in reading this book is to learn how to create useful, efficient, and, best of all, legal C source code.

You'll store your source code in a file, as though it were a letter created in a word processor. Unfortunately, computers don't understand such programming languages as C and Pascal. Computers only speak one language, a language made up of ones and zeros, called machine code. You'll write your programs in C, then translate the C source code into machine code your computer will understand.

The process of translating your source code into machine code is called compilation. The tool that accomplishes this is a **compiler**. The program you installed in Chapter 2, THIN C, is a compiler. You will use THIN C to translate the sample programs in this book from C into machine code.

Once you have machine code, you're ready to **run** your program. In the Macintosh world you run a program by double-clicking on its icon. When you ran THIN C, you double-clicked your mouse on the THIN C icon. Running an application prompts the application to do its thing: You run a compiler to compile source code; you run a word processor to edit a memo.

THIN C has a built-in program runner. In one step you can ask THIN C to compile and then run your C program. We'll do this a lot. As you run your program, you might notice a feature or two that you want to change. You do this by editing your source code. You guessed it — THIN C has a built-in **source code editor,** as well.

Once you edit your source code you'll want to compile it, then run it again to make sure it does what you want. Sometimes you'll get a program to behave exactly the way you planned the first time you run it. More frequently, it will take a few (sometimes several) tries before you get it just right.

Let's look at some of these steps in more detail, starting with source code.

Source Code

If you were programming using everyday English, your source code might look like this:

```
Hi, Computer!
Do me a favor. Ask me for five numbers, add them together,
then tell me the sum.
```

If you wanted to run this program, you'd need a compiler able to translate English source code into machine code. Since THIN C only understands C source code, let's look at a C program that does the same thing:

```
main()
{
  int    i, num, sum;

  sum = 0;

  for ( i=1; i<=5; i++ )
  {
        printf( "Enter number %d --->", i );
        scanf( "%d", &num );
        sum = sum + num;
  }

  printf( "The sum of these numbers is %d.", sum );
}
```

If this program doesn't mean anything to you, don't panic. Just keep reading. By the time you finish reading this book, you'll be writing C code like a pro.

As we said before, a compiler is used to translate the source code from its textual form into machine code. Source code is for you, machine code is for your computer.

Next, we'll look at how THIN C handles the translation from source code to machine code.

THIN C and the Project File

Each program you build using THIN C will be based on something called a project file. Each THIN C project file contains all the information THIN C needs to edit, compile, and run your program.

In Chapter 2, you used THIN C to open a sample program called hello.π. When THIN C opened hello.π, a project window appeared.

Figure 3.2 The project window for hello.π

The project window is shown in Figure 3.2. Notice that the project window is titled with the name of the project, hello.π. The project window lists all of the files needed to compile this particular project. The file ANSI.lib is a special file we'll talk about in Chapter 4. You'll see ANSI.lib in all of your THIN C projects.

The file hello.c contains the source code for this project. If you double-click on the name hello.c in the project window, an editing window will appear, allowing you to make changes to hello.c. The numbers to the right of each file name (both zeros in this case) keep track of the amount of source code that has been translated into machine code.

Machine code is also known by the name **object code**. When a file's object size (the number to the right of the name in the project window) is zero, the file hasn't been compiled yet.

Don't concern yourself too much with the specifics of THIN C project files. We'll work through each example in the book, step by step, so you won't get lost. Understanding how to write C source code is far more important than the intricacies of the THIN C project file.

By the Way

> Since THIN C stores the object or machine code inside the project file on your hard drive, your project files will take up more room with a compiled program than with an uncompiled program. To save space, select **Remove Objects** from the **Project** menu when you are done with a project. This item tells THIN C to delete any object code it may have created for the project. Don't worry, **Remove Objects** won't affect your source code. It'll just slim down your project file a bit.

A Word About Memory

Before we move on to the specifics of the C language, there's one more topic we need to cover. Inside every computer, from Apple to Zenith, you'll find something called **RAM**, which stands for **Random Access Memory**. This memory is extremely important to programmers (especially C programmers), so pay close attention.

The standard unit of measurement in the memory world is the **byte**. A standard Macintosh Plus comes with one megabyte of memory, which is equal to 2^{20} bytes (a little more than one million bytes). One million bytes sounds like a lot, but it can get used up in a hurry. That million bytes is divvied up between the Mac's operating system, the Finder, and any applications that are running. There are some applications that require more than one megabyte just to run.

Figure 3.3 shows the Finder's Info box for Microsoft Word 4.0. (To bring up this window, select an application's Finder icon, then select **Get Info** from the Finder's **File** menu.) At the bottom of the window you'll see the application's memory size. This is the minimum memory required by the application to run successfully. In this case, Microsoft Word requires at least 512K ($1K = 2^{10} = 1024$ bytes, so 512K = 524,288 bytes). That's half the memory of a Mac Plus!

Binary, Bits, and Bytes

What do you do with all of these bytes? Almost every line of source code you write will use up some of your precious bytes. As you'll see in Chapter 5, you'll use storage containers called **variables** to hold your program's data.

For example, if you were writing a game program, you might create a variable called currentScore to keep track of a player's current score. As the player's score changes, the byte or bytes of memory associated with the name currentScore will change in value. Part of learning to program in C is learning to change (or read) the value of your program's variables. This means changing or reading the value of the bytes of memory associated with these variables. Let's take a closer look at the byte.

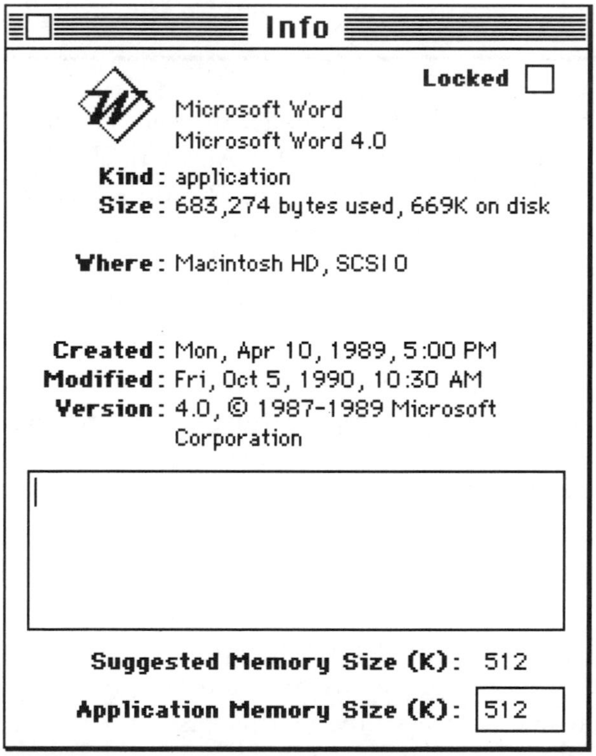

Figure 3.3   Microsoft suggests you run Word with at least 512K bytes of memory.

Each byte of computer memory is made up of 8 **bits**. Each bit has a value of either 1 or 0. Figure 3.4 shows a byte holding the value 00101011. The value 00101011 is said to be the **binary** representation of the value of the byte. Look closer at Figure 3.4. Notice that each bit is numbered (the bit numbers are above each bit in the figure), with bit 0 on the extreme right side to bit 7 on the extreme left. This is a standard bit-numbering scheme used in most computers.

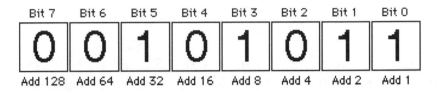

Figure 3.4   A byte holding the binary value 00101011.

Notice also the labels that appear beneath each bit in the figure (Add 1, Add 2, etc.). These labels are the key to binary numbers. Memorize them. (It's easy — each bit is worth twice the value of its right neighbor.) These labels are used to calculate the value of the entire byte. Here's how it works:

- Start with a value of 0.
- For each bit with a value of 1, add the label value below the bit.

That's all there is to it! In the byte pictured in Figure 3.4, you'd calculate the byte's value by adding 1 + 2 + 8 + 32 = 43. Where did we get the 1, 2, 8, and 32? They're the bottom labels of the only bits with a value of 1. Try another one.

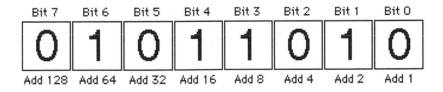

Figure 3.5   What's the value of this byte?

What's the value of the byte pictured in Figure 3.5? Easy, right? 2 + 8 + 16 + 64 = 90. Right! How about the byte in Figure 3.6?

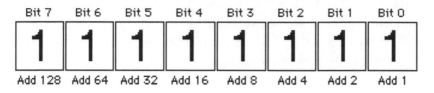

Figure 3.6   Last one: What's the value of this byte?

This is an interesting one: 1 + 2 + 4 + 8 + 16 + 32 + 64 + 128 = 255. This example demonstrates the largest value that can fit in a single byte. Why? Because every bit is turned on. We've added everything we can add to the value of the byte.

The smallest value a byte can have is 0 (00000000). Since a byte can range in value from 0 to 255, a byte can have 256 possible values.

Can a Byte Be Negative?

There will be times when you'll want a byte to represent negative, as well as positive, numbers. Most computers solve this problem by using **two's complement notation.**

Don't worry about the details of binary representation and arithmetic. What's important to remember is that the computer uses one notation for positive-only numbers and a different notation for numbers that can be positive or negative. Both notations allow a byte to take on one of 256 different values. The positives-only scheme allows values ranging from 0 to 255. The two's complement scheme allows values ranging from -128 to 127. This concept will come up again when we start talking about variables later in the book.

Important _____

> To represent a negative number using two's complement notation:
>
> - Start with the positive version of the number
> - Complement all the bits (turn the 1s into 0s and the 0s into 1s)
> - Add 1 to the result.
>
> For example, the binary notation for the number 9 is 00001001. The two's complement for -9 would be 11110110 + 1 = 11110111.
>
> The binary notation for the number 2 is 00000010. The two's complement for -2 would be 11111101 + 1 = 11111110. Notice that in binary addition, when you add 01 + 01 you get 10. Just as in regular addition, you carry the 1 to the next column.

The Importance of Binary

Inside your Macintosh, thousands of wires carry signals among the computer's various components. Most of these signals spend their existence toggling between two voltage levels. A shift to the lower of the two voltage levels signals a 0, while a shift to the higher voltage signals a 1. For all its complexity, this primitive mechanism is just about the only way two parts of a computer can communicate: ones and zeroes. Binary.

Your computer's memory works much the same way. Each bit of memory corresponds to a tiny physical region on a memory chip. If that region maintains an electrical charge, that bit has a value of 1. If the region loses its charge, the bit falls to 0. Ones and zeroes. Binary.

Your computer thinks in binary. To communicate with it, you need to speak its language. In prehistoric times — oh, around 1960 — people programmed computers by setting bits in memory using physical switches, one switch per bit. Mighty inefficient!

As computers evolved, new techniques were developed for communicating with them. Today we use compilers that translate our English-like source code into machine code. The machine code contains the ones and zeroes that allow our instructions to reach the computer, allowing it to do our bidding.

What's Next?

This chapter covered some of the fundamental concepts behind programming. We're now ready to explore the mysteries of the C programming language. Get out your programming gloves — we're about to go to code!

Exercises

Convert the following numbers to binary:
1) 26   2) 30   3) 12   4) 99
5) 127   6) 19   7) 47   8) 100

Convert the following numbers to two's complement binary:
9) -1   10) -26   11) -30   12) -127
13) -99   14) -19   15) -13   16) 0

Convert these two's complement numbers to decimal:
17) 11111111   18) 10101010
19) 10001111   20) 10000000
21) 11000000   22) 10000001
23) 11100011   24) 10000100

Thoughts on upcoming topics:

25) Define a scheme for representing positive and negative numbers using 2 bytes instead of just 1 byte.

26) What is the range of this 2-byte representation?

Chapter 4

C Basics:
Functions

This Chapter
at a Glance

C Functions
  Titles and Bodies
  Syntax Errors and Algorithms
Function Calling Examples
The Most Important Function
ANSI C and the Standard Library
Same Program, Two Functions
  Opening hello2.π
  Running hello2.π
Generating Some Errors
  C is Case Sensitive
What's Next?
Exercises

EVERY PROGRAMMING LANGUAGE IS DESIGNED TO follow strict rules that define the language's source code structure. The C programming language is no different. These next few chapters will explore the syntax of C.

Chapter 3 discussed some fundamental programming topics, including the process of translating source code into machine code through a tool called the compiler. This chapter focuses on one of the primary building blocks of C programming, the **function**.

C Functions

C programs are made up of functions. A function is a chunk of source code that accomplishes a specific task. You might write a function that adds a list of numbers, or one that calculates the radius of a given circle. Here's an example:

```
main()
{
    printf( "Welcome to my program!" );
}
```

This function, called `main()`, prints a welcome message in a window.

Important

> Throughout this book, we'll refer to a function by placing a pair of parentheses after its name. This will help distinguish between variable names and function names. For example, the name `doTask` refers to a variable (variables are covered in Chapter 5), while `doTask()` refers to a function.

Titles and Bodies

Functions start with a **title**, in this case:

```
main()
```

The title consists of the name of the function, followed by a pair of parentheses. As we'll see later, you can pass data to and from a function by adding **parameters** between the parentheses. It is perfectly acceptable to write functions without parameters, as we did with `main()`.

Following the title comes the body of the function. The body is always placed between a pair of curly brackets: "{" and "}". These brackets are known in programming circles as "left-curly" and "right-curly". Here's the body of `main()`:

```
{
    printf( "Welcome to my program!" );
}
```

The body of a function consist of a series of one or more **statement**s, each followed by a semicolon (;). If you think of a computer program as a detailed set of instructions for your computer, a statement is one specific instruction. The `printf()` featured in the body of `main()` is a statement. It instructs the computer to display some text on the screen.

As you make your way through this book, you'll learn C's rules for creating efficient, compilable statements.

Creating efficient statements will make your programs run faster with less chance of error. The more you learn about programming (and the more time you spend at your craft) the more efficient you'll be at making code.

Syntax Errors and Algorithms

Creating compilable code is another story. While compiling your code, if the compiler reaches a statement it doesn't understand, there it will sit. The compiler will not let you run your program until every line of source code compiles.

As you learn C, you'll find yourself making two types of mistakes. The simplest type, called a **syntax error**, prevents the program from compiling. The syntax of a language is the set of rules that determines what will and will not be read by the compiler. Many syntax errors are the result of a mistyped letter, or **typo**. Another common syntax error occurs when you forget the semicolon at the end of a statement.

The second type of mistake is a flaw in your program's **algorithm**. An algorithm is the approach used to solve a problem. You use algorithms all the time. For example, here's an algorithm for sorting your mail:

1) Start by taking the mail out of the mailbox.
2) If there's no mail, you're done! Go watch TV.
3) Take a piece of mail out of the pile.
4) If it's junk mail, throw it away, then go back to step 2.
5) If it's a bill, put it with the other bills, then go back to step 2.
6) If it's not a bill and not junk mail, read it, then go back to step 2.

This algorithm completely describes the process of sorting through your mail. Notice that the algorithm works, even if you didn't get any mail. Notice also that the algorithm always ends up at step 2, with the TV on.

Figure 4.1 shows a pictorial representation of the mail-sorting algorithm, commonly known as a **flow chart**. Some programmers like to use a flow chart to flesh out a program's algorithm before they actually start writing the program. Here's how this works.

This flow chart uses two types of boxes. The rectangular box portrays an action, such as taking mail out of the mailbox or throwing junk mail in the trash. The diamond-shaped box always poses a yes/no question. Action boxes have a single arrow leading out of them and on to the next box to read, once you've finished taking the appropriate action. Question boxes have two arrows leading out of them. One shows the path to take if the answer to the question is yes, the other shows the path to take if the answer is no. Follow the flow chart through, comparing it to the algorithm described above.

In the C world, a well-designed algorithm results in a well-behaved program. On the other hand, a poorly designed algorithm can lead to unpredictable results. Suppose, for example, you wanted to write a program that added three numbers together, printing the sum at the end. If you accidentally printed one of the numbers instead of the sum

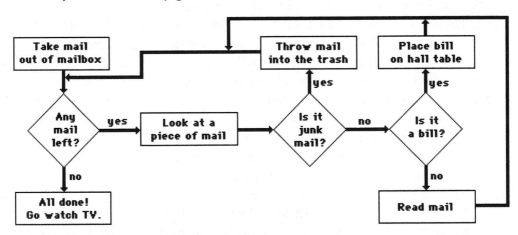

Figure 4.1   An algorithm for sorting the mail.

of the numbers, your program would still compile and run. The result of the program would be in error, however (you printed one of the numbers instead of the sum), because of a flaw in your program's algorithm.

The efficiency of your source code, referred to earlier, is a direct result of good algorithm design. Keep the concept of algorithm in mind as you work your way through the examples in the book.

Function-Calling Examples

In Chapter 2, you ran hello, a program with a single function, main(). As a refresher, here's the source code from hello:

```
main()
{
    printf( "Hello, world!" );
}
```

You ran hello by selecting **Run** from the **Project** menu. Then THIN C started by executing the first line in the function named main(). In this case, the first line in main() was the **call** to the function printf(). Whenever your source code calls a function, each of the statements in the *called* function is executed before the next statement of the *calling* function is executed.

Confused? Look at Figure 4.2. In this example, main() starts with a call to the function MyFunction(). This call to MyFunction() will cause each of the statements inside MyFunction() to be executed. Once the last statement in MyFunction() is executed, control is returned to main(). Now, main() can call AnotherFunction().

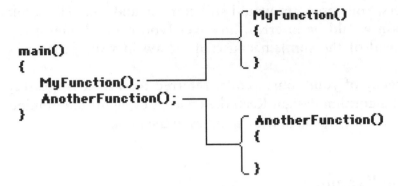

Figure 4.2   When `main()` calls `MyFunction()`, all of the statements inside `MyFunction()` get executed before `main()` calls `AnotherFunction()`.

The Most Important Function

The most important function in the C universe is one you write yourself: the `main()` function. Every C program you write will have a `main()` function. Your program will start running with the first line in `main()` and, unless something unusual happens, end with the last line in `main()`. Along the way `main()` may call other functions which may, in turn, call other functions and so on.

THIN C comes with a set of built-in functions you can use in your own programs. One of these functions is `printf()`. The `printf()` function opens THIN C's special text window on the screen (if it's not already open) and draws text in the window. The text `printf()` draws is specified by the text you place between `printf()`'s parentheses. For example, `hello`'s call to `printf()` looks like this:

```
printf( "Hello, world!" );
```

This call asks `printf()` to print the string `"Hello, world!"` in the text window.

There are many other built-in functions that come with THIN C. THIN C's set of built-in functions is known as the **Standard Library**.

By the Way _____

> In C, a string is a series of text characters inside a pair of double quotes ("). You'll learn more about strings in Chapter 8.

ANSI C and the Standard Library

The American National Standards Institute (ANSI) established a standard for the C programming language. We call this standard **ANSI C**. Part of this standard is a specific definition of the syntax of the C language. As we stated earlier, the syntax of a language gives programmers a set of rules that rigidly defines the format of their source code. For example, ANSI C tells you when you can and can't use a semicolon. ANSI C tells you to use a pair of parentheses after the name of your function, regardless of whether your function has any parameters. You get the idea. The greatest benefit to having a national standard for C is portability. ANSI C on one computer is identical to ANSI C on another computer. When you finish with this book, you'll be able to program in C on any computer that has an ANSI C compiler.

Another part of the ANSI C standard is the Standard Library. The Standard Library is a set of functions available to every ANSI C programmer. As you may have guessed, the `printf()` function is part of the Standard Library.

By the Way

> There's a boatload of useful functions in the Standard Library. We'll describe some of the more useful ones as we go along. The documentation that comes with your compiler should also provide a detailed description of each of the functions in the Standard Library. For example, the THINK C (not THIN C) compiler comes with a separate manual called the *Standard Libraries Reference* that covers THINK C's version of the Standard Library.

Same Program, Two Functions

As you start writing your own programs, you'll find yourself designing many individual functions. You might need a function that puts a form up on the screen for the user to fill out. You might need a function that takes a list of numbers as input, providing the average of those numbers in return. Whatever your needs, you will definitely be creating a lot of functions. Let's see how it's done.

Our first program, hello, consisted of a single function, main(), that passed the text string "Hello, world!" to printf(). Our second program, hello2, captures that functionalism in a new function, called SayHello().

Opening hello2.π

Start up THIN C by double-clicking on its icon in the Finder. THIN C will prompt you for a project file to open (Figure 4.3). Go into the folder called Projects (you'll have to go up one level to find it), then into the subfolder named hello2, and open the file named hello2.π.

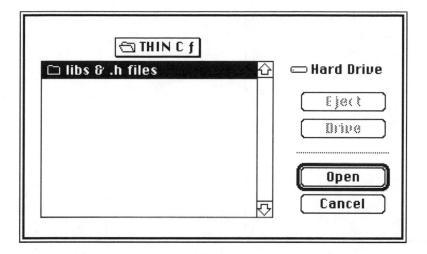

Figure 4.3   THIN C prompting you for a project file to open.

At this point, a hello2.π project window will appear, as shown in Figure 4.4. If you double-click on the name hello2.c in the project window, a source code editing window will appear, containing source code remarkably similar to this:

```
SayHello()
{
    printf( "Hello, world!" );
}

main()
{
    SayHello();
}
```

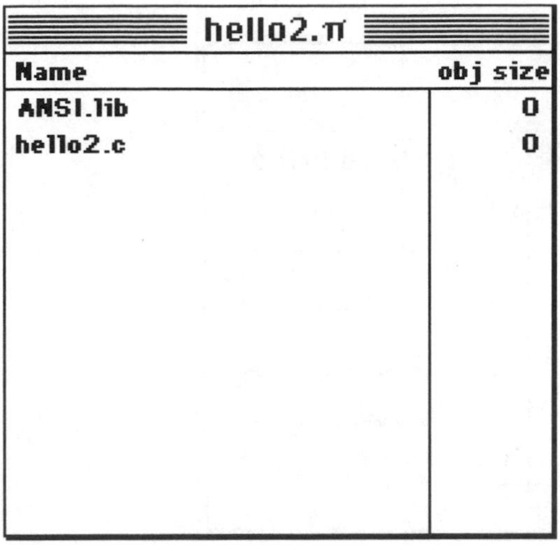

```
====================== hello2.π ======================
Name                                        obj size
ANSI.lib                                          0
hello2.c                                          0
```

Figure 4.4   Project window for hello2.π.

In hello, main() called printf() directly. In hello2, main() calls a function which calls printf(). This extra layer of functionalism demonstrates a basic C programming technique, taking code from one function and using it to create a new function. This example took this line of code:

```
printf( "Hello, world!" );
```

and used it to create a new function called SayHello(). This function is now available for use by the rest of the program. Every time we call the function SayHello(), it's as if we executed the line of code:

```
printf( "Hello, world!" );
```

SayHello() may be a simple function, but it demonstrates an important concept. Wrapping a chunk of code in a single function is a powerful technique. Suppose you create an extremely complex function, say, 100 lines of code in length. Now suppose you call this function in five different places in your program. With 100 lines of code, plus the five function calls, you are essentially achieving 500 lines' worth of functionalism. That's a pretty good return on your investment!

Let's watch hello2 in action.

Running hello2.π

Select **Run** from the **Project** menu. You should see something similar to Figure 4.5. Remember to type a carriage return to exit from the program. Notice that, even though we embedded our printf() inside the function SayHello(), hello2 ran the same as hello1.

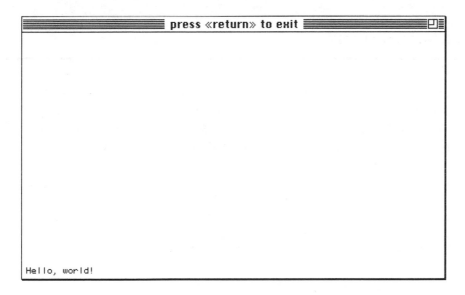

Figure 4.5 THIN C's text window, waiting for a carriage return.

By the Way _____

> THIN C maintains a special text window for your convenience. When your program starts running, the text window is hidden. If you don't call any of the Standard Library routines that print in the special text window, such as `printf()`, you'll never see the text window. Before THIN C allows your program to exit, it checks to see if the text window is visible. If it is, THIN C asks you to type a carriage return before allowing your program to exit (see Figure 4.5).

Generating Some Errors

Before we move on to variables in the next chapter, let's see how the compiler responds to errors in our source code. Place a semicolon at the end of the first line of code. The semicolon should appear just after the right parenthesis (in the source code below, the changed line is in boldface):

```
SayHello();
{
    printf( "Hello, world!" );
}

main()
{
    SayHello();
}
```

Select **Run** from the **Project** menu. THIN C can tell if you've made any changes to your source code file. Since you have, THIN C will automatically attempt to recompile your program. In this case, the compilation will fail. The dialog box shown in Figure 4.6 will appear just below the menu bar at the top of your screen.

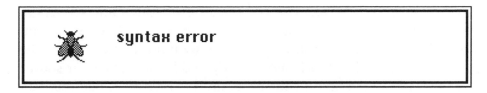

Figure 4.6   The dreaded **syntax error** message.

Get used to this message — you will see it a lot. Basically, THIN C is trying to tell you that it found an error in your source code. Dismiss the window by clicking in it (or by typing a carriage return). Now take a look at your source code window. THIN C tried to place the edit cursor as close to the syntax error as it could (Figure 4.7). THIN C will always place the cursor at the beginning of a line of text. In this case, THIN C placed the cursor at the beginning of the line following the error.

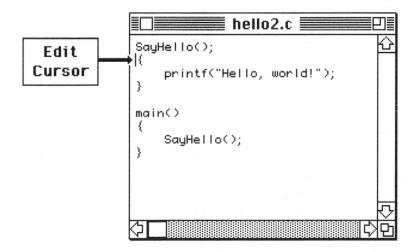

Figure 4.7   THIN C places the cursor as close to the syntax error as it can.

Use the mouse and the delete key to delete the offending semicolon at the end of the first line of code. Select **Run** from the **Project** menu again. This time, the code should compile without a hitch. Once the code is compiled, THIN C will ask you if you'd like to save your source code changes before running your program (Figure 4.8). Click the **Yes** button to save your changes.

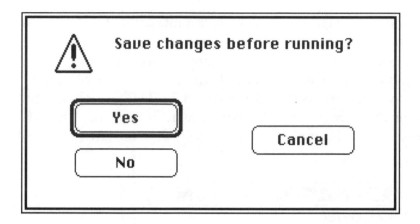

Save changes before running?

Yes

Cancel

No

Figure 4.8   THIN C asks if you'd like to save your source code changes.

C is Case Sensitive

There are many different types of errors possible in C programming. One of the most common results from the fact that C is a **case-sensitive** language. In a case-sensitive language, there is a big difference between lower- and upper-case letters. This means you can't refer to printf() as Printf() or even PRINTF(). If you do you'll see the error message shown in Figure 4.9a when you try to run your program. The **link failed** error message tells you that THIN C can't locate one of the functions you've referenced. The offending function is listed in the **Link Errors** window that appears just below the **link failed** dialog box. As you can see in Figure 4.9b, THIN C couldn't find a function named Printf(). To fix this problem, just change Printf() to printf() and recompile.

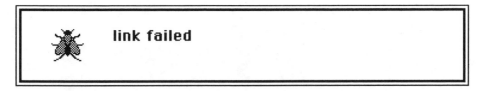

Figure 4.9a   The **link failed** error message.

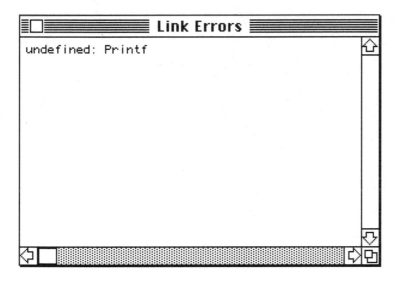

Figure 4.9b   The **Link Errors** window.

What's Next?

Congratulations! You've made it through basic training. You know how to open a project, how to compile your code, and even how to create an error message or two. You've learned about the most important function: main(). You've also learned about printf() and the Standard Library.

Now you're ready to dig into the stuff that gives a C program life: variables and operators.

Exercises

Open the project `hello2.π`, edit `hello2.c` as described in each exercise, and describe the error that results:

1) Change the line:

    ```
    SayHello()
    ```

    to say:

    ```
    SayHello
    ```

2) Change things back. Now change the line:

    ```
    main()
    ```

    to say:

    ```
    musthavemain()
    ```

3) Change things back. Now delete the { after the line:

    ```
    main()
    ```

4) Change things back. Now change the line:

    ```
    printf("Hello, world!");
    ```

    to say:

    ```
    printf("Hello, world!")
    ```

Chapter 5

C Basics: Variables and Operators

This Chapter at a Glance

An Introduction to Variables
   Working with Variables
   The Size of a Type
Operators
   The +, −, ++, and − − Operators
   The +=, and −= Operators
   The *, /, *=, and /= Operators
Using Parentheses ( )
Sample Programs
   Opening operator.π
     Stepping Through the Source Code
   Opening postfix.π
     Stepping Through the Source Code
   Opening slasher.π
     Stepping Through the Source Code
Sprucing Up Your Code
   Source Code Spacing
   Comment Your Code
What's Next?
Exercises

AT THIS POINT, YOU SHOULD FEEL PRETTY COMFORTABLE with the THIN C environment. You should know how to open a project and how to edit a project's source code. You should also feel comfortable running a project and (heaven forbid) fixing any syntax errors that may have occurred along the way.

On the programming side, you should recognize a function when you see one. When you think of a function you should first think of `main()`, the most important function. You should remember that functions are made up of statements separated by semicolons.

With these things in mind, we're ready to explore the foundation of C programming: **variables** and **operators**. Variables and operators are the building blocks you'll use to construct your program's statements.

An Introduction to Variables

A large part of the programming process involves working with data. You might need to add together a column of numbers or sort a list of names alphabetically. The tricky part of this process is representing your data in a program. This is where variables come in.

Variables can be thought of as containers for your program's data. Imagine a table with three containers sitting on it. Each container is labeled. One container is labeled cup1, one labeled cup2, and the third cup3. Now imagine you have three pieces of paper. Write a number on each piece of paper and place one piece inside each of the three containers. Figure 5.1 shows a picture of what this might look like.

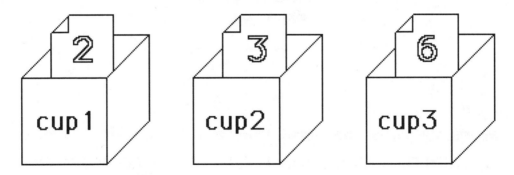

Figure 5.1   Three cups, each with its own value.

Now imagine asking a friend to reach into the three cups, pull out the number in each one, and add the three values together. You can ask your friend to place the sum of the three values in a fourth container created just for this purpose. The fourth container is labeled sum and can be seen in Figure 5.2.

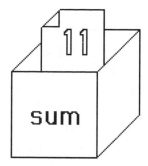

Figure 5.2   A fourth container, containing the sum of the other three containers.

This is exactly how variables work. Variables are containers for your program's data. You create a variable and place a value in it. You then ask the computer to do something with the value in your variable. You can ask the computer to add three variables together, placing the result in a fourth variable. You can even ask the computer to take the value in a variable, multiply it by 2, and place the result back into the original variable.

Getting back to our example, now imagine that you changed the values in cup1, cup2, and cup3. Once again, you could call on your friend to add the three values, updating the value in the container sum. You've reused the same variables, using the same formula, to achieve a different result. Here's the C version of this formula:

```
sum = cup1 + cup2 + cup3;
```

Every time you execute this line of source code, you place the sum of the variables cup1, cup2, and cup3 into the variable named sum. At this point, it's not important to understand exactly how this line of C source code works. What is important is to understand the basic idea behind variables. Each variable in your program is like a container with a value in it. This chapter will teach you how to create your own variables and how to place a value in a variable.

Working With Variables

Variables come in a variety of flavors, called **types**. A variable's type determines the type of data that can be stored in that variable. You determine a variable's type when you create the variable. (We'll discuss creating variables in just a second.) Some variable types are useful for working with numbers. Other variable types are designed to work with text. In this chapter, we'll work strictly with variables of one type, a numerical type called `int` (in Chapter 8 we'll get into other variable types). A variable of type `int` can hold a numerical value, such as 27 or -589.

Working with variables is a two-stage process. First you create a variable, then you use the variable. In C, you create a variable by **declaring** it. Declaring a variable tells the compiler, "Create a variable for me. I need a container to place a piece of data in." When you declare a variable, you have to specify the variable's type as well as its name. In our earlier example, we created four containers. Each container had a label. In the C world, this would be the same as creating four variables with the names `cup1`, `cup2`, `cup3`, and `sum`. In C, if we want to use the value stored in a variable, we use the variable's name. We'll show you how to do this later in the chapter.

Here's an example of a variable declaration:

```
int myVariable;
```

This declaration tells the compiler to create a variable of type `int` (remember, `int`s are useful for working with numbers) with the name `myVariable`. The type of the variable (in this case, `int`) is extremely important. As you'll see, variable type determines the type and range of values a variable can be assigned.

By the Way

You may have noticed the unusual spelling of the variable name `myVariable`. Here are a few rules to follow when you create your own variable names:

- Always start your variable names with a lower-case letter. This yields variable names like `number` or `digit`.
- It's OK to create a variable name of more than one word. Simply start each successive word in the variable name with an upper-case letter. This yields variable names like `myVariable` or `howMany`.

The Size of a Type

When you declare a variable, the compiler reserves a section of memory for the exclusive use of that variable. When you assign a value to a variable, you are actually modifying the variable's dedicated memory to reflect that value. The number of bytes assigned to a variable is determined by the variable's type. For example, an `int` always gets 2 bytes of memory. The variable declaration:

```
int myInt;
```

reserves 2 bytes of memory for the exclusive use of the variable `myInt`. If you later assign a value to `myInt`, that value is stored in those 2 bytes. If you ever refer to `myInt`'s value, you'll be referring to those 2 bytes. As you'll see, you don't need to know too much about those 2 bytes. The compiler handles all the memory manipulation for you.

The one thing you do need to understand is the importance of type *size*. Every type has a specific size. As we said, the size of an `int` is always 2 bytes. As you learn about different C data types (see Chapter 8), you'll also learn about the size of each type.

Why is the size of a type important? The size of a type determines the range of values that type can handle. As you might expect, a type that's 4 bytes in size can hold a wider range of values than a type that's only 1 byte in size.

Think back to Chapter 3. In the section on binary, we discovered that 1 byte (8 bits) of memory can hold one of $2^8 = 256$ possible values. By extension, 2 bytes (16 bits) of memory can hold one of $2^{16} = 65,536$ possible values. If the 2 bytes are **unsigned** (never allowed to hold a negative value) they can hold values ranging from 0 to 65,535. If the 2 bytes are **signed** (allowed to hold both positive and negative values) they can hold values ranging from -32,768 to 32,767.

By default, all C data types are signed (allowed to hold both positive and negative values). This means that a variable declared as follows:

```
int myInt;
```

is signed and can hold values ranging from -32,768 to 32,767.

When you compile your program, the compiler makes a list of all the memory needed for your program's variables. When you declared myInt to be of type int, the compiler reserved 2 bytes of memory for the exclusive use of myInt.

Important

To declare a variable as unsigned, precede its declaration with the unsigned qualifier. Here's an example:

```
unsigned int       myInt;
```

This version of myInt can hold values ranging from 0 to 65,535.

By the Way _____

> int is short for **integer.** As any math hound will tell you, integers are whole numbers, like 1, -26, or 3,876,560. The number 3.14159 is not an integer!

Now that you've defined the type of variable your program will use (in this case, int), you can assign a value to your variable.

Operators

One way to assign a value to a variable is with the **= operator.** An operator is a special character (or set of characters) that represents a specific computer operation. The = operator tells the computer to compute the value of the right side of the = and assign that value to the left side of the =. Take a look at this line of source code:

```
myInt = 237;
```

This statement causes the value 237 to be placed in the 2 bytes allocated for myInt.

By the Way _____

> As we just illustrated, you can use numerical constants (such as 237) directly in your code. In the C world, these constants are called **literals**. Just as there are different types of variables, there are also different types of literals. You'll see more on this topic later in the book.

Look at this example:

```
main()
{
    int myInt, anotherInt;

    myInt = 503;
    anotherInt = myInt;
}
```

Notice we've declared two variables in this program. One way to declare multiple variables is the way we did here, separating the variables by a comma (,). There's no limit to the number of variables you can declare using this method.

We could have declared these variables using two separate declaration lines:

```
int myInt;
int anotherInt;
```

Either way is fine. As you'll see, C is an extremely flexible language. However, there is one rule you must remember. Within a function, you must declare all variables before any other type of statement occurs. Consider this example:

```
main()
{
    int myInt;

    myInt = 503;

    int anotherInt;

    anotherInt = myInt;
}
```

This program will not compile. Why? A variable (anotherInt) was declared after a nondeclaration statement (myInt = 503). Here's the corrected version:

```
main()
{
    int myInt;
    int anotherInt;

    myInt = 503;
    anotherInt = myInt;
}
```

This program starts by declaring two ints (allocating a total of 4 bytes of memory, 2 bytes for each int):

```
    int myInt;
    int anotherInt;
```

Next, the program assigns the value 503 to the 2 bytes of memory allocated to myInt:

```
    myInt = 503;
```

Finally, the value in myInt's 2 bytes is copied into the 2 bytes allocated to anotherInt:

```
    anotherInt = myInt;
```

At this point, the variable anotherInt contains the value 503.

Why go to all this effort just to assign a value to a variable? Think of it as learning to walk before you can fly. As we cover more and more of the C language, you'll start to see some of the fantastic things you can accomplish. At the beginning of this chapter, we looked at an example that took the values from three containers, added them together, and placed the result in a fourth container. That's what this is all about. C variables and operators allow you to manipulate and manage data inside a program. The data might represent your baseball card collection or the flight path of the Mars lander. Variables and operators allow you to massage the data to get the results you want. Have patience, and keep reading.

Let's look at some other operators.

The +, -, ++, and -- Operators

The + and - operators each take two values and reduce them to a single value. For example, the statement:

```
myInt = 5 + 3;
```

will first resolve the right side of the = by adding the numbers 5 and 3 together. Once that's done, the resulting value (8) is assigned to the variable on the left side of the =. This statement assigns the value 8 to the variable myInt. Assigning a value to a variable means copying the value into the memory allocated to that variable.

Here's another example:

```
myInt = 10;
anotherInt = 12 - myInt;
```

The first statement assigns the value 10 to myInt. The second statement subtracts 10 from 12 to get 2, then assigns the value 2 to anotherInt.

The ++ and -- operators operate on a single value only. ++ **increments** (raises) the value by 1 and -- **decrements** (lowers) the value by 1. Take a look:

```
myInt = 10;
myInt++;
```

The first statement assigns `myInt` a value of 10. The second statement changes `myInt`'s value from 10 to 11. Here's a `--` example:

```
myInt = 10;
--myInt;
```

This time the second line of code left `myInt` with a value of 9. You may have noticed that the first example showed the ++ following `myInt`, while the second example showed the `--` preceding `myInt`.

The position of the ++ and `--` operators determines when their operation is performed in relation to the rest of the statement. Placing the operator on the right side of a variable or expression (**postfix notation**) tells the compiler to resolve all values before performing the increment (or decrement) operation. Placing the operator on the left side of the variable (**prefix notation**) tells the compiler to increment (or decrement) first, then continue evaluation. Confused? The following examples should make this point clear:

```
myInt = 10;
anotherInt = myInt--;
```

The first statement assigns `myInt` a value of 10. In the second statement, the `--` operator is on `myInt`'s right side. This use of postfix notation tells the compiler to assign `myInt`'s value to `anotherInt` before decrementing `myInt`. This example leaves `myInt` with a value of 9 and `anotherInt` with a value of 10.

Here's the same example, written using prefix notation:

```
myInt = 10;
anotherInt = --myInt;
```

This time, the `--` is on the left side of `myInt`. In this case, the value of `myInt` is decremented before being assigned to `anotherInt`. The result? `myInt` and `anotherInt` are both left with a value of 9.

By the Way

> This use of prefix and postfix notation shows both a strength and a weakness of the C language. On the plus side, C allows you to accomplish a lot in a small amount of code. In the previous examples, we changed the value of two different variables in a single statement. C is powerful.
>
> On the down side, C code written in this fashion can be extremely cryptic, difficult to read for even the most seasoned C programmer.
>
> Write your code carefully.

The += and -= Operators

In C, you can place the same variable on both the left and right sides of an assignment statement. For example, the statement:

```
myInt = myInt + 10;
```

increases the value of `myInt` by 10. The same results can be achieved using the += operator:

```
myInt += 10;
```

is the same as:

```
myInt = myInt + 10;
```

In the same way, the -= operator can be used to decrement the value of a variable. The statement:

```
myInt -= 10;
```

decrements the value of `myInt` by 10.

The *, /, *=, and /= Operators

The * and / operators each take two values and reduce them to a single value, much the same as the + and - operators do. The statement:

```
myInt = 3 * 5;
```

multiplies 3 and 5, leaving myInt with a value of 15. The statement:

```
myInt = 5 / 2;
```

divides 5 by 2 and, assuming myInt is declared as an integer type, assigns the integral (truncated) result to myInt. The number 5 divided by 2 is 2.5. Since myInt can only hold integer values, the value 2.5 is truncated and the value 2 is assigned to myInt.

The *= and /= operators work much the same as their += and -= counterparts. The statement:

```
myInt *= 10;
```

is identical to the statement:

```
myInt = myInt * 10;
```

The statement:

```
myInt /= 10;
```

is identical to the statement:

```
myInt = myInt / 10;
```

> The / operator doesn't perform its truncation automatically.
> The accuracy of the result is limited by the data type of the
> operands. If the division is performed using `int`s, the result
> will be an `int`, and is truncated to an integer value.
>
>   There are several data types (such as `float`, introduced
> in Chapter 8) which support floating point division using
> the / operator.

Using Parentheses ()

Sometimes the expressions you create can be evaluated in several ways.
Here's an example:

```
myInt = 5 + 3 * 2;
```

You can add 5 + 3, then multiply the result by 2 (giving you 16).
Alternatively, you can multiply 3 * 2 and add 5 to the result (giving you
11). Which is correct?

C has a set of built-in rules for resolving the order of operators. As
it turns out, the * operator has a higher precedence than the + operator,
so the multiplication will be performed first, yielding a result of 11.

Don't write code that depends on these rules. That's why the C gods
gave us parentheses! Use parentheses in pairs to define the order in
which you want your operators performed. The statement:

```
myInt = ( 5 + 3 ) * 2;
```

will leave `myInt` with a value of 16. The statement:

```
myInt = 5 + ( 3 * 2 );
```

will leave `myInt` with a value of 11. You can use more than one set of parentheses in a statement, as long as they occur in pairs — one left parenthesis associated with each right parenthesis. The statement:

```
myInt = ( ( 5 + 3 ) * 2 );
```

will leave `myInt` with a value of 16.

Sample Programs

So far in this chapter, we've discussed variables (mostly of type `int`) and operators (mostly mathematical). The program examples on the following pages combine variables and operators into useful C statements. We'll also learn about a powerful part of the Standard Library, the `printf()` function.

Opening operator.π

Our first program, `operator.π`, provides a testing ground for some of the operators covered in the previous sections.

Start up THIN C by double-clicking on its icon in the Finder. THIN C will prompt you for a project file to open. Go into the folder called `Projects`, into the subfolder called `operator`, then open the project called `operator.π`. The project window for `operator.π` should appear (Figure 5.3).

Run `operator.π` by selecting **Run** from the **Projects** menu. THIN C will first attempt to compile `operator.c`. Assuming you haven't mucked around with the source code, things should proceed smoothly, resulting in a clean compile. Once the code compiles, THIN C will run `operator.π`.

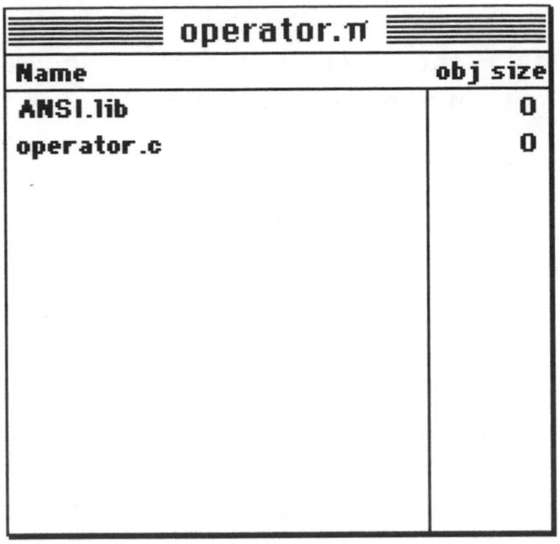

Figure 5.3   Project window for operator.π.

The first clue you'll have that operator.c is running will be the appearance of a standard Macintosh window bearing the title **press «return» to exit**. This window is called the **console** window (Figure 5.4). The function printf() allows you to display text and numbers in the console window, making it easy to track your program's progress.

operator.c declares a variable (myInt) and uses a series of statements to change the value of the variable. By including a printf() after each of these statements, operator.c makes it easy to follow the variable, step by step, as its value changes.

Once the console window appears, a series of six lines of text will scroll into view, starting at the bottom of the window and moving up, one line at a time. Compare your console with the window in Figure 5.5.

Press the return key on your keyboard to return to THIN C.

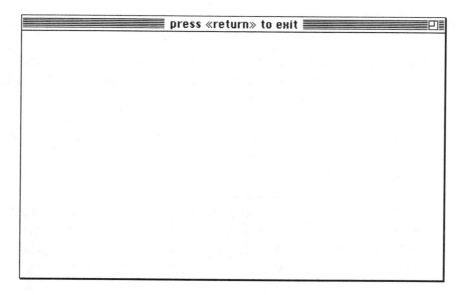

Figure 5.4 THIN C's console window.

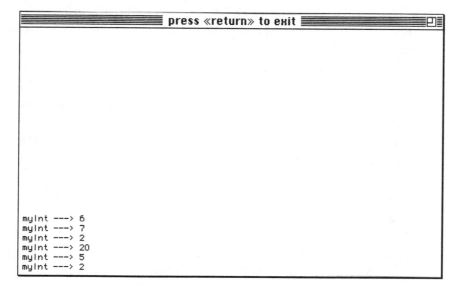

Figure 5.5 `operator.c` in action.

By the Way

In ancient times, programmers used character-based displays to communicate with their machines. These displays were called consoles. A typical console screen supported 24 rows of text, each up to 80 columns wide. When the computer wanted to communicate with you, it displayed some characters on your console. To respond to the computer, you'd type at your keyboard. The characters you typed would also appear on your console.

Programmers love character-based displays because they're simple. To display text on a window-based system (like the Macintosh), you have to worry about things like text font, size, and style. You have to worry about lining all your text up just right.

With a character-based display, you didn't worry about things like that. Typically, you just sent the text out to the display, one line at a time. When you reached the bottom of the screen, the display would scroll the text automatically. So easy!

THIN C offers you the best of both worlds. THIN C supports all the elements specific to the Macintosh, such as pull-down menus, scroll bars, windows, and icons. (Once you feel comfortable with C, get a copy of the *Macintosh C Programming Primer*. It will teach you all about Mac-specific programming.)

THIN C also supports a specialized, character-based window, called the console window. The console window is essentially a 24-line, 80-column display console in a Macintosh window. Since the ANSI C standard was created with this simpler, character-based display in mind, we'll make extensive use of the console window as we learn C.

Stepping Through the Source Code

Before we walk through the source code in `operator.c`, you might want to bring the source code up on your screen. You can do this by double-clicking on the name `operator.c` in the project window. A new window will appear, listing the project's source code.

`operator.c` consists of a single function, `main()`, and a single variable, `myInt`.

```
main()
{
    int     myInt;
```

At this point in the program (after `myInt` has been declared but before any value has been assigned to it), `myInt` is said to be **uninitialized**. Since `myInt` was declared to be of type `int`, 2 bytes of memory were reserved exclusively for `myInt`'s use. Since we haven't placed a value in those 2 bytes yet, they could contain any value at all. Some compilers place a value of 0 in a newly allocated variable, some do not. The key is, don't depend on a variable being preset to some specific value. If you want a variable to contain a specific value, assign the value to the variable yourself!

The next line of code uses the * operator to assign a value of 6 to `myInt`. Following that, we use `printf()` to display the value of `myInt` in the console window.

```
    myInt = 3 * 2;
    printf( "myInt ---> %d\n", myInt );
```

By the Way _____

> In computerese, the term **initialization** refers to the process of establishing a variable's value for the first time. A variable that has been declared, but that has not had a value assigned to it, is said to be **uninitialized**. You initialize a variable the first time you assign a value to it.

The code between `printf()`'s left and right parentheses is its **parameters** or **arguments**. The parameters that you place between the parentheses when you call a function are automatically provided to the called function. If you place a variable or text string between the parentheses, the called function can use the variable or text string to determine its next course of action. Placing a parameter between a function's parentheses is known as **passing** the parameter. Passing parameters to a function allows you to customize that function's operation. For example, you could write a function called `MakeWindow()` that creates a new window on the screen. You might design `MakeWindow()` to take a parameter specifying the title of the window. A call to `MakeWindow()` might look like this:

```
MakeWindow( "My Window" );
```

The window produced by this call might look something like the one in Figure 5.6. Notice that the text string passed as a parameter to `MakeWindow()` was used as the title of the window. We'll dig into the details of functions and function parameters later in the book. For the moment, let's talk about `printf()` and the parameters used by this Standard Library function.

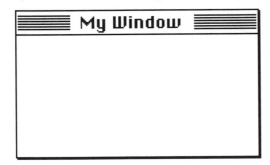

Figure 5.6   A window created by a call to `MakeWindow( "My Window" )`.

By the Way _____

> Some of the more eagle-eyed among you may have noticed that the text passed as a parameter to `MakeWindow()` had a pair of double quotes (") around it, and that these quotes never made it to the title of the window in Figure 5.6. Good for you! Keep reading and you'll see the important role that the double-quote character plays in the C language.

The first parameter passed to `printf()` defines what will be drawn in the console window. The simplest call to `printf()` uses a quoted text string as its only parameter. A quoted text string consists of a pair of double-quote characters (") with zero or more characters between them. For example, this call of `printf()`:

```
printf( "Hello!" );
```

will draw the characters `Hello!` in the console window. Notice that the double-quote characters are not part of the text string.

You can request that `printf()` draw a variable's value in the midst of the quoted string. Do this by embedding the two characters %d within the first parameter. The % character tells `printf()` where in the quoted string to place the variable's value (the value will replace the %d). The d following the % tells `printf()` that the variable you'd like included in the quoted string is of type `int`. This line of code:

```
printf( "...%d...", myInt );
```

tells `printf()` to print the value of the variable `myInt` in the midst of a series of dots. If `myInt` had the value 47, the printed line would look like this:

```
...47...
```

printf() uses a different letter for each C data type (there's a complete description of these later in the book). printf() always expects the variable whose value you'd like printed to be the second parameter, immediately following the quoted string. For example, this code:

```
int myVar;

myVar = 5;
printf( "myVar = %d", myVar );
```

will draw the text

```
myVar = 5
```

in the console window. You can place any number of % specifications in the first parameter, as long as you follow the first parameter by the appropriate number of variables. Here's another example:

```
int var1, var2;

var1 = 5;
var2 = 10;
printf( "var1 = %d, var2 = %d", var1, var2 );
```

will draw the text

```
var1 = 5, var2 = 10
```

in the console window. As you learn about more C data types, you'll want to use them with printf() as well.

Let's get back to our source code. These two lines:

```
myInt = 3 * 2;
printf( "myInt ---> %d\n", myInt );
```

will assign myInt a value of 6, then print the line:

```
myInt ---> 6
```

in the console window. Notice that the two characters \n weren't echoed in the console window. That's because the \ (known in programming circles as the **backslash**) has a special meaning when used inside a quoted string. The \ combines with the next character in the quoted string (in this case, the n) to form a **backslash sequence**. Each backslash sequence represents a special character, not easily represented by a single letter.

For example, the \n combination tells the compiler to generate a **newline** character, which causes the next character printed to appear in the left margin of the next line of the console window (similar to the carriage return on a typewriter). To get a feel for the newline character, try removing the \n characters from operator.c. You can edit the source code by clicking and typing in the operator.c source code window you opened earlier. To delete the \n characters, use the mouse to select them in the window, then hit the delete key on your keyboard.

Now select **Run** from the **Project** menu to run the project again. THIN C will recompile your program (since you made changes to it). Your output will appear to be one long line, instead of several short lines. Try it! Our version is shown in Figure 5.7.

We'll talk about some of the other \ character combinations later in the chapter. The next line of operator.c increments myInt from 6 to 7, and prints the new value in the console window.

```
myInt += 1;
printf( "myInt ---> %d\n", myInt );
```

The next line decrements myInt by 5, and prints its new value of 2 in the console window.

```
myInt -= 5;
printf( "myInt ---> %d\n", myInt );
```

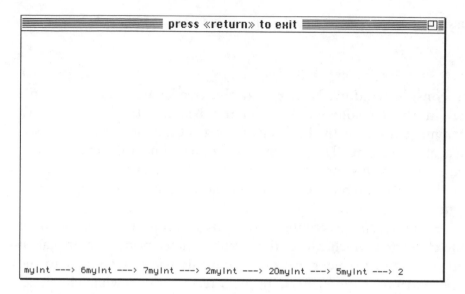

Figure 5.7   `operator.c` without the \n characters.

Next, `myInt` is multiplied by 10, and its new value of 20 is printed in the console window.

```
myInt *= 10;
printf( "myInt ---> %d\n", myInt );
```

Next, `myInt` is divided by 4, resulting in a new value of 5.

```
myInt /= 4;
printf( "myInt ---> %d\n", myInt );
```

Finally, `myInt` is divided by 2. Since 5 divided by 2 is 2.5 (not a whole number), a truncation is performed and `myInt` is left with a value of 2.

```
myInt /= 2;
printf( "myInt ---> %d", myInt );
}
```

Opening postfix.π

Our next program demonstrates the difference between postfix and prefix notation (the ++ and -- operators defined earlier in the chapter). Select **Close Project** from the **Project** menu to close operator.π. When prompted for a new project to open, go back to the Projects folder, open the subfolder named postfix, and select postfix.π from the scrolling list.

Take a look at the source code for postfix.c and try to predict the values in the two calls to printf() when you run the program. Remember, you can open a source code listing for postfix.c by double-clicking on the name postfix.c in the project window. Careful, this one's tricky.

Once your guesses are locked in, select **Run** from the **Project** menu. How'd you do? Compare your two guesses with the output in Figure 5.8. Let's look at the source code.

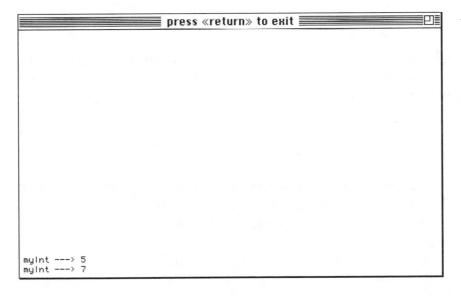

```
press «return» to exit
```

```
myInt ---> 5
myInt ---> 7
```

Figure 5.8 postfix.c in action. Was this what you expected?

Stepping Through the Source Code

The first half of postfix.c is pretty straightforward. Once again, myInt is declared to be of type int. Then, myInt is initialized to a value of 5. Next comes the tricky part.

```
main()
{
    int      myInt;

    myInt = 5;
```

The first call to printf() actually has a statement embedded in it. This is another great feature of the C language. Where there's room for a variable, there's room for an entire statement. Sometimes it's convenient to perform two actions within the same line of code. For example, this line of code:

```
printf( "myInt ---> %d\n", myInt = myInt * 3 );
```

first triples the value of myInt, then passes the result (the tripled value of myInt) on to printf(). The same could have been accomplished using two lines of code:

```
myInt = myInt * 3;
printf( "myInt ---> %d\n", myInt );
```

In general, when the compiler encounters an assignment statement where it expects a variable, it first completes the assignment, then passes on the result of the assignment as if it were a variable. Let's see this technique in action.

In postfix.c, our friend the postfix operator emerges again. Just prior to the two calls of printf(), myInt has a value of 5. The first of the two printf()'s increments the value of myInt using postfix notation:

```
printf( "myInt ---> %d\n", myInt++ );
```

The use of postfix notation means that the value of `myInt` will be passed on to `printf()` before `myInt` is incremented. This means that the first `printf()` will accord `myInt` a value of 5. However, when the statement is finished, `myInt` will have a value of 6.

The second `printf()` acts in a more rational (and preferable) manner. The prefix notation guarantees that `myInt` will be incremented (from 6 to 7) before its value is passed on to `printf()`.

```
    printf( "myInt ---> %d", ++myInt );
}
```

The purpose of demonstrating the vagaries of postfix and prefix operators is twofold. On one hand, it's extremely important that you understand exactly how these operators work from all angles. This will allow you to write code that works and will aid you in making sense of other programmers' code.

On the other hand, embedding prefix and postfix operators within function parameters may save you lines of code but, as you can see, may prove a bit confusing.

Opening slasher.π

The last program in Chapter 5, `slasher.π`, demonstrates several different backslash combinations. Select **Close Project** from the **Project** menu to close `postfix.π`. When prompted for a new project to open, go back to the `Projects` folder, open the subfolder named `slasher`, and select `slasher.π` from the scrolling list.

Run `slasher.π` by selecting **Run** from the **Project** menu. You should see something like the console window shown in Figure 5.9. Here's how we did it...

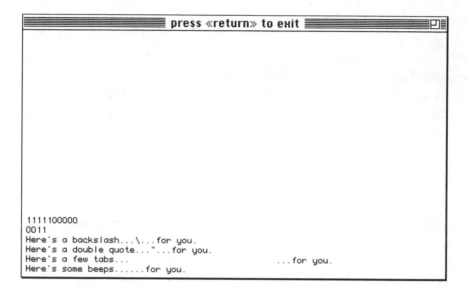

Figure 5.9   Slasher.c in action.

Stepping Through the Source Code

slasher.c consists of a series of printf()s, each of which demon-strates a different backslash combination. The first printf() prints a series of ten zeros, followed by the \r combination. The \r combination generates a carriage return without a line feed, leaving the cursor at the beginning of the current line (unlike \n, which leaves the cursor at the beginning of the next line down).

```
main()
{
    printf( "0000000000\r" );
```

The next printf() prints five 1s over the first five 0s, as if someone had printed the text string "1111100000". The \n at the end of this printf() moves the cursor to the beginning of the next line in the console window.

```
printf( "11111\n" );
```

The next `printf()` demonstrates \b, the backspace backslash combination. \b tells `printf()` to back up one character so that the next character printed replaces the last character printed. This `printf()` sends out four 0s, backspaces over the last two, then prints two 1s. The result is as if you had printed the string "0011".

```
printf( "0000\b\b11\n" );
```

The \ can also be used to cancel a character's special meaning within a quoted string. For example, the backslash combination \\ generates a single \ character. The difference is, this \ loses its special backslash powers. It doesn't affect the character immediately following it.

The backslash combination \" generates a " character, taking away the special meaning of the ". Without the \ before it, the " character would mark the end of the quoted string. The \ allows you to include a " inside a quoted string.

The backslash combinations \\ and \" are demonstrated in the next two `printf()`s:

```
printf( "Here's a backslash...\\...for you.\n" );
printf( "Here's a double quote...\"...for you.\n" );
```

The \t combination generates a single tab character. The console window has a tab stop every eight spaces. Here's a `printf()` example:

```
printf( "Here's a few tabs...\t\t\t\t...for you.\n" );
```

While the Mac offers a host of sound options, most text-based computer consoles offer one: the beep. While a beep isn't quite as interesting as a Clank! or a Boing!, it can still serve a useful purpose. The \a backslash combination provides a simple way to make your Mac beep.

```
printf( "Here are some beeps...\a\a\a\a...for you." );
}
```

That's all the sample programs for this chapter. Before we move on, however, I'd like to talk to you about something personal. It's about your coding habits.

Sprucing Up Your Code

You are now in the middle of your C learning curve. You've learned about variables, types, functions, and bytes. You've learned about an important part of the ANSI Standard Library, the function `printf()`. It's at this point in the learning process that programmers start developing their coding habits.

Coding habits are the little things programmers do that make their code a little bit different (and hopefully better!) than anyone else's. Before you get too set in your ways, here are a few coding habits you can, and should, add to your arsenal.

Source Code Spacing

You may have noticed the tabs, spaces, and blank lines scattered throughout the sample programs. These are known in C as **white space**. White space is ignored by C compilers. Believe it or not, this program:

```
main()
{
    int myInt;myInt




=
5
;
printf("myInt=%d",myInt);}
```

is equivalent to this program:

```
main()
{
    int myInt;

    myInt = 5;
    printf( "myInt = %d", myInt );
}
```

as far as the C compiler goes. The C compiler doesn't care if you put five statements per line, or if you put 20 carriage returns between your statements and your semicolons. About the only thing the compiler won't let you do is place white space in the middle of a word, such as a variable or function name. For example, this line of code:

```
my  Int = 5;
```

won't compile. Other than that, you're free to develop your own white-space style. Here are a few hints...

- Place a blank line between your variable declarations and the rest of your function's code. Also, use blank lines to group related lines of code.
- Sprinkle single spaces throughout a statement. Compare this line:

  ```
  printf("myInt=",myInt);
  ```

  with this line:

  ```
  printf( "myInt =", myInt );
  ```

  The spaces make the second line easier to read.

- When in doubt, use parentheses. Compare this line:

  ```
  myInt=var1+2*var2+4;
  ```

  with this line:

  ```
  myInt = (var1 + 2) * (var2 + 4);
  ```

  What a difference parentheses and spaces make!

- Always start variable names with a lower-case letter, using an upper-case letter at the start of each subsequent word in the name. This yields variable names such as `myVar`, `areWeDone`, and `employeeName`.

- Always start function names with an upper-case letter, using an upper-case letter at the start of each subsequent word in the name. This yields function names such as `DoSomeWork()`, `HoldThese()`, and `DealTheCards()`.

These hints are merely suggestions. Use a set of standards that make sense for you and the people with whom you work. The object here is to make your code as readable as possible.

Comment Your Code

One of the most critical elements in the creation of a computer program is clear and comprehensive documentation. When you deliver your award-winning graphics package to your customers, you'll want to have two sets of documentation. One set is for your customers, who'll need a clear set of instructions that guide them through your wonderful new creation.

The other set of documentation consists of the comments you'll weave throughout your code. Source code comments act as a sort of narrative, guiding a reader through your source code. You'll include comments that describe how your code works, what makes it special, and what to look out for when changing it. Well-commented code includes a comment at the beginning of each function that describes the function, the function parameters, and the function's variables. It's also a good idea to sprinkle individual comments among your source code statements, explaining the role each line plays in your program's algorithm. How do you add a comment to your source code? Take a look...

All C compilers recognize the sequence /* as the start of a comment and will ignore all characters until they hit the sequence */ (the end of comment characters). Here's some commented code:

```
main()
{
    int numPieces;   /* Number of pieces of pie left */

    numPieces = 8;   /*  We started with 8 pieces  */

    numPieces--;     /*  Marge had a piece  */
    numPieces--;     /*  Lisa had a piece  */
    numPieces -= 2;  /*  Bart had two pieces!!  */
    numPieces -= 4;  /*  Homer had the rest!!!  */

    printf( "Slices left = %d", numPieces );  /*  How about
                                                  some cake
                                                  instead?  */
}
```

Notice that, although most of the comments fit on the same line, the last comment was split between three lines. The above code will compile just fine.

Since each of the programs in this book are examined in detail, line by line, the comments were left out. This was done to make the examples as simple as possible. In this instance, do as we say, not as we do. Comment your code. No excuses!

What's Next?

This chapter introduced the concepts of variables and operators, tied together in C statements, separated by semicolons. We looked at several examples, each of which made heavy use of the Standard Library function `printf()`. We learned about the console window, quoted strings, and backslash combinations.

Chapter 6 will increase our programming options significantly, introducing C control structures such as the `for` loop and the `if ...` `then ...` `else` statement. Get ready to expand your C-programming horizons. See you in Chapter 6.

Exercises

1) Find the error in each of the following code fragments:

a. `printf( Hello, world );`

b. `int myInt   myOtherInt;`

c. `myInt =+ 3;`

d. `printf( "myInt = %d" );`

e. `printf( "myInt = ", myInt );`

f. `printf( "myInt = %d\", myInt );`

g. `myInt + 3 = myInt;`

h.
```
main()
{
    int    myInt;
    myInt = 3;
    int    anotherInt;

    anotherInt = myInt;
}
```

2)   Compute the value of `myInt` after each code fragment is executed:

    a.
```
myInt = 5;
myInt *= (3+4) * 2;
```

    b.
```
myInt = 2;
myInt *= ( (3*4) / 2 ) - 9;
```

    c.
```
myInt = 2;
myInt /= 5;
myInt--;
```

    d.
```
myInt = 25;
myInt /= 3 * 2;
```

    e.
```
myInt = (3*4*5) / 9;
myInt -= (3+4) * 2;
```

    f.
```
myInt = 5;
printf( "myInt = %d", myInt = 2 );
```

    g.
```
myInt = 5;
myInt = (3+4) * 2;
```

    h.
```
myInt = 1;
myInt /= (3+4) / 6;
```

Chapter 6

Controlling Your Program's Flow

This Chapter
at a Glance

Flow Control
    The if Statement
Expressions
    TRUE and FALSE
    Comparative Operators
    Logical Operators
    Compound Expressions
Statements
    The Curly Braces { }
    Where to Place the Semicolon
    The Loneliest Statement
    The while Statement
    The for Statement
    The do Statement
    The switch
    Breaks in Other Loops
Sample Programs
    IsOdd.π
      Stepping Through the Source Code
    nextPrime.π
      Stepping Through the Source Code
What's Next?
Exercises

SO FAR, YOU'VE LEARNED QUITE A BIT ABOUT THE C
language. You know about functions (especially one named `main()`),
which are made up of statements, which are separated by semicolons.
You know about variables, which have a name and a type. Up to this
point, you've dealt with variables of type `int`.

You also know about operators, such as =, +, and +=. You've learned about postfix and prefix notation, and the importance of writing clear, easy-to-understand code. You've learned about an important programming tool, the console window. You've learned about the ANSI Standard Library, a set of functions that comes as standard equipment with every ANSI C programming environment. You've also learned about `printf()`, an invaluable component of the Standard Library.

Finally, you've learned a few housekeeping techniques to keep your code fresh, sparkling, and readable. Comment your code, because your memory isn't perfect, and insert some white space to keep your code from getting too cramped.

Flow Control

One thing you haven't learned about the C language is **flow control**. The programs we've written so far have all consisted of a straight-forward series of statements, one right after the other. Every statement is executed in the order it occurred.

Flow control is the ability to control the order in which your program's statements are executed. The C language provides several keywords you can use in your program to control your program's flow. One of these is the keyword "**if**."

The if Statement

The keyword `if` allows you to choose between several options in your program. In English, you might say something like this:

```
If it's raining outside I'll bring my umbrella; otherwise I won't.
```

In this sentence, you're using if to choose between two options. Depending on the weather, you'll do one of two things. You'll bring your umbrella or you won't bring your umbrella. C's `if` statement gives you this same flexibility. Here's an example:

```
main()
{
    int myInt;

    myInt = 5;

    if ( myInt == 0 )
        printf( "myInt is equal to zero." );
    else
        printf( "myInt is not equal to zero." );
}
```

This program declares `myInt` to be of type `int` and sets the value of `myInt` to 5. Next, we use the `if` statement to test whether `myInt` is equal to 0. If `myInt` is equal to 0 (which we know is not true), we'll print one string. Otherwise, we'll print a different string. As expected, this program prints the string `"myInt is not equal to zero."`

`if` statements come two ways. The first, known as plain old `if`, fits this pattern:

```
if ( expression )
    statement
```

An `if` statement will always consist of the word `if`, a left parenthesis, an expression, a right parenthesis, and a statement. (We'll define both expression and statement in a minute.) This first form of `if` executes the statement if the expression in parentheses is true. An English example of the plain `if` might be:

```
If it's raining outside, I'll bring my umbrella.
```

Notice that this statement only tells us what will happen if it's raining outside. No particular action will be taken if it is not raining.

The second form of `if`, known as `if-else`, fits this pattern:

```
if ( expression )
    statement
else
    statement
```

An `if-else` statement will always consist of the word `if`, a left parenthesis, an expression, a right parenthesis, a statement, the word `else`, and a second statement. This form of `if` executes the first statement if the expression is true, and executes the second statement if the expression is false. An English example of an `if-else` statement might be:

```
If it's raining outside, I'll bring my umbrella, otherwise
I won't.
```

Notice that this example tells us what will happen if it is raining outside (I'll bring my umbrella) and if it isn't raining outside (I won't bring my umbrella). The example programs presented later in the chapter demonstrate the proper use of both `if` and `if-else`.

Our next step is to define the terms **expression** and **statement**.

Expressions

In C, an expression is anything that has a value. For example, a variable is a type of expression, since variables always have a value. (Even uninitialized variables have a value—we just don't know what the value is!) The following are all examples of expressions:

- `myInt + 3`

- `( myInt + anotherInt ) * 4`

- `myInt++`

An assignment statement is also an expression. Can you guess the value of an assignment statement? Think back to Chapter 5. Remember when we passed an assignment statement as a parameter to `printf()`? The value of an assignment statement is the value of its left side. Check out the following code fragment:

```
myInt = 5;
myInt += 3;
```

Both of these `statements` qualify as expressions. The value of the first expression is 5. The value of the second expression is 8 (because we added 3 to `myInt`'s previous value).

Literals can also be used as expressions. The number 8 has a value. Guess what? Its value is 8. All expressions, no matter what their type, have a numerical value.

TRUE and FALSE

Earlier, we defined the `if` statement as follows:

```
if ( expression )
    statement
```

We then said the statement gets executed if the expression is true. In the previous section, we stated that all expressions, no matter their type, have a numerical value. In C, even true and false have a numerical value. Let's look at C's concept of truth.

Everyone has an intuitive understanding of the difference between true and false. I think we'd all agree that the statement:

```
5 equals 3
```

is false. We'd also agree that the statement:

```
5 and 3 are both greater than 0
```

is true. This intuitive grasp of true and false carries over into the C language. In the case of C, however, both true and false have numerical values. Here's how it works.

In C, any expression that has a value of 0 is said to be FALSE. Any expression with a value other than 0 is said to be TRUE. As stated earlier, an if statement's statement gets executed if its expression is TRUE. To put this more accurately:

- *An if statement's statement gets executed if (and only if) its expression has a value other than 0.*

Here's an example:

```
myInt = 1;

if ( myInt )
    printf( "myInt is not equal to 0" );
```

The if statement in this piece of code first tests the value of myInt. Since myInt is not equal to 0, the printf() gets executed.

Comparative Operators

C expressions have a special set of operators, called **comparative operators.** Comparative operators compare their left sides with their right sides and produce a value of either TRUE (1) or FALSE (0), depending on the relationship of the two sides.

Important

As stated earlier, an expression with a value other than 0 is said to be TRUE. By default, when THIN C wants to represent the value TRUE, it uses a value of 1.

For example, the operator == determines whether the expression on the left is equal in value to the expression on the right. The expression:

```
myInt == 5
```

is said to be TRUE (1) if myInt is equal to 5, and is said to be FALSE (0) if myInt is not equal to 5. Here's an example of the == operator at work:

```
if ( myInt == 5 )
    printf( "myInt is equal to 5" );
```

If myInt is equal to 5, the expression myInt == 5 is TRUE and resolves to 1. Since its expression resolved to 1, the if statement executes its statement, in this case a call to printf().

If myInt is not equal to 5, the expression myInt == 5 is FALSE (resolves to 0) and the printf() is skipped. Remember, the key to triggering an if statement is an expression that resolves to a value other than 0.

Figure 6.1 shows some of the other comparative operators. You'll see some of these operators in the example programs later in the chapter.

Operator	Resolves to 1 if...
==	left side is equal to right
<=	left side is less than or equal to right
>=	left side is greater than or equal to right
<	left side is less than right
>	left side is greater than right
!=	left side is not equal to right side

Figure 6.1   Comparative operators.

Logical Operators

Thin C provides a set of literals, namely TRUE and FALSE, you can use directly in your code. As you might have guessed, TRUE has a value of 1 and FALSE has a value of 0. These two literals come in handy when dealing with our next set of operators, the **logical operators.**

The set of logical operators are modeled on the mathematical concept of truth tables. If you don't know much about truth tables (or are just frightened by mathematics in general), don't panic. Everything you need to know is outlined in the next few paragraphs.

The first of the set of logical operators is the ! operator. The ! operator turns TRUE into FALSE and FALSE into TRUE. Figure 6.2 shows the truth table for the ! operator. In this table, T stands for TRUE and F stands for FALSE. The letter A in the table represents an expression. If the expression A is TRUE, applying the ! operator to A yields the value FALSE. If the expression A is FALSE, applying the ! operator to A yields the value TRUE. The ! operator is commonly referred to as the NOT operator. !A is also known as "NOT A".

Here's a piece of code that demonstrates the ! operator:

```
int myFirstInt, mySecondInt;

myFirstInt = FALSE;
mySecondInt = ! myFirstInt;

if ( mySecondInt )
    printf( "mySecondInt must be TRUE" );
```

Figure 6.2   Truth table for the ! operator.

First, we declare two `int`s. We assign the value `FALSE` to the first `int`, then use the `!` operator to turn the `FALSE` into a `TRUE` and assign it to the second `int`. At this point, `mySecondInt` has a value of `TRUE`, which is the same thing as saying that `mySecondInt` has a value of 1. Either way, `mySecondInt` will cause the `if` to fire, and the `printf()` will get executed.

The `!` operator is a **unary** operator. Unary operators operate on a single expression (the expression on the right side of the operator). The other two logical operators, `&&  and  ||`, are **binary** operators. Binary operators, such as the `==` operator presented earlier, operate on two expressions, one on the left side and one on the right side of the operator.

The `&&` operator is commonly referred to as the `and` operator. The result of an `&&` operation is `TRUE` if, and only if, both the left side and the right side are `TRUE`. Here's an example:

```
int wealthy, generous;

wealthy = TRUE;
generous = TRUE;

if ( generous && wealthy )
    printf( "Here, have some money - I've got lots" );
else
    printf( "I'm either stingy or poor or both" );
```

This example uses two variables. One indicates whether the program is wealthy, the other whether the program is generous. All philosophical issues aside (can programs be wealthy?), the question of the moment is, which of the two `printf()`'s will fire? Since both sides of the `&&` were set to `TRUE`, the first `printf()` will be called. If either one (or both) of the variables were set to `FALSE`, the second `printf()` would be called. By the way, notice the use here of the second form of `if`, the `if-else` statement.

The || operator is commonly referred to as the or operator. The result of a || operation is TRUE if either the left side or the right side, or both sides, of the || are TRUE. Put another way, the result of a || is FALSE if, and only if, both the left side and the right side of the || are FALSE. Both the && and the || operators are summarized in the table in Figure 6.3.

A	B	A && B	A || B
T	T	T	T
T	F	F	T
F	T	F	T
F	F	F	F

Figure 6.3   Truth table for the && and || operators.

By the Way

You type an & character by holding down the shift key and typing a 7. You type a | character by holding down the shift key and typing a \ (backslash). Don't confuse the | with the letter l, i, or with the ! character.

Compound Expressions

All of the examples presented so far have consisted of relatively simple expressions. Here's an example that combines several different operators:

```
int myInt;

myInt = 7;

if ( (myInt >= 1) && (myInt <= 10) )
    printf( "myInt is between 1 and 10" );
else
    printf( "myInt is not between 1 and 10" );
```

This example tests whether a variable is in the range between 1 and 10. The key here is the expression:

```
(myInt >= 1) && (myInt <= 10)
```

that lies between the if statements parentheses. This expression uses the && operator to combine two smaller expressions. Notice that the two smaller expressions were surrounded by parentheses to avoid any ambiguity. If we left out the parentheses, like so:

```
myInt >= 1 && myInt <= 10
```

the expression might not be interpreted as we intended. Once again, use parentheses for safe computing.

Statements

At the beginning of the chapter, we defined the `if` statement as:

```
if ( expression )
    statement
```

We've covered expressions pretty thoroughly. Now, we'll turn our attention to the statement.

At this point in the book, you probably have a pretty good intuitive model of the statement. You'd probably agree that this:

```
myInt = 7;
```

is a statement. But is this:

```
if ( isCold )
    printf( "Put on your sweater!" );
```

one statement or two? Actually, the previous code fragment is a statement within another statement. The `printf()` is one statement, residing within a larger statement, the `if` statement.

The ability to break your code out into individual statements is not a critical skill. Getting your code to compile, however, is critical. As new types of statements are introduced, such as `if` and `if-else` introduced in this chapter, pay attention to the statement syntax. And pay special attention to the examples. Where do the semicolons go? What distinguishes this type of statement from all other types?

As you build up your repertoire of statement types, you'll find yourself using one type of statement within another. That's perfectly acceptable in C. In fact, every time you create an `if` statement, you'll use at least two statements, one within the other. Take a look at this example:

```
if ( myVar >= 1 )
    if ( myVar <= 10 )
        printf( "myVar is between 1 and 10" );
```

This example used an `if` statement as the statement for another `if` statement. This example calls the `printf()` if both if expressions are TRUE; that is, if `myVar` is greater than or equal to 1 and less than or equal to 10. You could have accomplished the same result with this piece of code:

```
if ( ( myVar >= 1 ) && ( myVar <= 10 ) )
        printf( "myVar is between 1 and 10" );
```

The second piece of code is a little easier to read. There are times, however, when the method demonstrated in the first piece of code is preferred. Take a look at this example:

```
if ( myVar != 0 )
    if ( ( 1 / myVar ) < 1 )
        printf( "myVar is in range" );
```

One thing you don't want to do in C is divide a number by 0. Any number divided by zero is infinity, and infinity is a foreign concept to the C language. If your program ever tries to divide a number by 0, your program is likely to crash. The first expression in this example tests to make sure `myVar` is not equal to zero. If `myVar` is equal to zero, the second expression won't even be evaluated! The sole purpose of the first `if` is to make sure the second `if` never tries to divide by zero. Make sure you understand this point. Imagine what would happen if we wrote the code this way:

```
if ( (myVar != 0) && ((1 / myVar) < 1) )
        printf( "myVar is in range" );
```

Some compilers (if not all) would evaluate the entire expression, even if `myVar` were equal to zero. This would result in a division by zero and, possibly, a crash.

The Curly Braces { }

Earlier in the book, you learned about the curly braces that surround the body of every function. These braces also play an important role in statement construction. Just as parentheses can be used to group terms of an expression together, curly braces can be used to group multiple statements together. Here's an example:

```
onYourBack = TRUE;

if ( onYourBack )
{
    printf( "Flipping over" );
    onYourBack = FALSE;
}
```

In the example, if `onYourBack` is `TRUE`, both of the statements in curly braces will be executed. A pair of curly braces can be used to combine any number of statements into a single super-statement. You can use this technique anywhere a statement is called for.

Where to Place the Semicolon

So far, the statements we've seen fall into two categories. Function calls, such as calls to `printf()`, and assignment statements are called **simple statements**. Always place a semicolon at the end of a simple statement, even if it is broken over several lines, like this:

```
printf( "%d%d%d%d", var1,
                    var2,
                    var3,
                    var4 );
```

Statements made up of several parts, including, possibly, other statements, are called **complex statements**. Complex statements obey some pretty strict rules of syntax. The `if` statement, for example, always looks like this:

```
if ( expression )
    statement
```

Notice there are no semicolons in this definition. The statement part of the `if` can be a simple statement or a complex statement. If the statement is simple, follow the semicolon rules for simple statements and place a semicolon at the end of the statement. If the statement is complex, follow the semicolon rules for that particular type of statement.

Notice that using "curlies" to build a super-statement out of smaller statements does not require the addition of a semicolon.

The Loneliest Statement

Guess what? A single semicolon qualifies as a statement, albeit a somewhat lonely one. For example, this code fragment:

```
if  ( bored )
      ;
```

is a legitimate (and thoroughly useless) `if` statement. If `bored` is `TRUE`, the semicolon statement gets executed. The semicolon by itself doesn't do anything but fill the bill where a statement was needed. There are times where the semicolon by itself is exactly what you need.

The while Statement

The `if` statement uses the value of an expression to decide whether to execute or skip over a statement. If the statement is executed, it is executed just once. Another type of statement, the `while` statement, repeatedly executes a statement as long as a specified expression is `TRUE`. The `while` statement follows this pattern:

```
while ( expression )
    statement
```

The `while` statement is also known as the `while` **loop**, because once the statement is executed, the `while` loops back to reevaluate the expression. Here's an example of the `while` loop in action:

```
int i;

i=0;

while ( ++i < 3 )
    printf( "%d\n", i );

printf( "We are past the while loop." );
```

This example starts by declaring a variable, `i`, to be of type `int`. `i` is then initialized to 0. Next comes the `while` loop. The first thing the `while` loop does is evaluate its expression. The `while` loop's expression is:

```
++i < 3
```

Before this expression is evaluated, `i` has a value of 0. The prefix notation used in the expression (`++i`) increments the value of `i` to 1 before the remainder of the expression is evaluated. The evaluation of the expression results in TRUE since 1 is less than 3. Since the expression is TRUE, the while loop's statement is executed. The printf() prints the value of i (in this case, 1) followed by a newline:

```
1
```

Next, the while loops back and reevaluates its expression. Once again, the prefix notation increments i, this time to a value of 2. Since 2 is less than 3, the expression evaluates to TRUE, and the printf() is executed. The printf() prints the value of i (2) below its previous line:

```
1
2
```

Once the printf() completes, it's back to the top of the loop to reevaluate the expression. Will this never end? Once again, i is incremented, this time to a value of 3. Aha! This time, the expression evaluates to FALSE, since 3 is not less than 3. Once the expression evaluates to FALSE, the while loop ends and control passes to the next statement, the second printf() in our example:

```
printf( "We are past the while loop." );
```

The while loop was driven by three factors: **initialization, modification,** and **termination**. Initialization is any code that affects the loop, but occurs before the loop is entered. In our example, the critical initialization occurred when the variable i was set to 0.

By the Way

Frequently, you'll use a variable in a loop that changes value each time through the loop. In our example, the variable i was incremented by 1 each time through the loop. The first time through the loop, i had a value of 1. The second time, i had a value of 2. Variables that maintain a value based on the number of times through a loop are known as **counters**.

Traditionally, programmers have given counter variables simple names like i, j, or k. Use these names for your counter variables only. Name all other program variables with names that clearly identify their purpose (i.e., names like employeeNumber, lastBinChecked, or currentBalance).

Modification is any code occurring within the loop that affects the value of the loop's expression. In our example, the modification occurred within the expression itself when the counter, i, was incremented.

Termination is any condition that causes the loop to terminate. In our example, termination occurs when the expression has a value of FALSE. This occurs when the counter, i, has a value that is not less than 3. Take a look at this example:

```
int i;

i=1;

while ( i < 3 )
{
    printf( "%d\n", i );
    i++;
}

printf( "We are past the while loop." );
```

This example produces the same results as the previous example. This time, however, the initialization and modification conditions have changed slightly. In this example, i starts with a value of 1 (instead of 0). In the previous example, the ++ operator was used to increment i at the very *top of the loop*. This example modifies i at the *bottom of the loop*.

Both of these examples show different ways to accomplish the same end. The phrase, "There's more than one way to eat an Oreo," sums up the situation perfectly. There will always be more than one solution to any programming problem. Don't be afraid to do things your own way. Just make sure your code works properly and is easy to read.

The for Statement

Nestled inside the C toolbox, right next to the while statement, is the for statement. The for statement is similar to the while statement, following the basic model of initialization, modification, and termination. Here's the pattern for a for statement:

```
for ( expression1 ; expression2 ; expression3 )
    statement
```

The first expression represents the for statement's initialization. Typically, this expression consists of an assignment statement, setting the initial value of a counter variable. This first expression is evaluated once, at the beginning of the loop.

The second expression is identical in function to the expression in a while statement, providing the termination condition for the loop. This expression is evaluated each time through the loop, before the statement is executed.

Finally, the third expression provides the modification portion of the for statement. This expression is evaluated at the bottom of the loop, immediately following execution of the statement.

The `for` loop can also be described in terms of a `while` loop:

```
expression1;
while ( expression2 )
{
    statement
    expression3;
}
```

By the Way ───────────────────────────────────────

> Since you can always rewrite a `for` loop as a `while` loop, why introduce the `for` loop at all? Sometimes, a programming idea fits more naturally into the pattern of a `for` statement. If the `for` loop makes for more readable code, why not use it? As you write more and more code, you'll develop a sense for when to use the `while` and when to use the `for`.

Here's an example of a `for` loop:

```
int i;

for ( i = 1; i < 3; i++ )
    printf( "%d\n", i );

printf( "We are past the for loop." );
```

This example is identical in functionalism to the `while` loops presented earlier. Note the three expressions on the first line of the `for` loop. Before the loop is entered, the first expression is evaluated (remember, assignment statements make great expressions):

```
i = 1
```

Once the expression is evaluated, i has a value of 1. We are now ready to enter the loop. At the top of each pass through the loop, the second expression is evaluated:

```
i < 3
```

If the expression evaluates as TRUE, the loop continues. Since i is less than 3, we can proceed. Next, the statement is executed:

```
printf( "%d\n", i );
```

The printf() prints the value of i (in this case, 1) followed by a newline:

```
1
```

Having reached the bottom of the loop, the for evaluates its third expression:

```
i++
```

This changes the value of i to 2. Back to the top of the loop. Evaluate the termination expression:

```
i < 3
```

Since i is still less than 3, the loop continues. Once again, the printf() prints the value of i (2) followed by a newline. The console window looks like this:

```
1
2
```

Next, the for evaluates expression3:

```
i++
```

incrementing the value of i to 3. Back to the top of the loop. Evaluate the termination expression:

```
i < 3
```

Lo and behold! Since i is no longer less than 3, the loop ends and the second `printf()` in our example is executed:

```
printf( "We are past the for loop." );
```

As was the case with `while`, `for` can take full advantage of a pair of curly braces:

```
for ( i = 0; i < 10; i++ )
{
    DoThis();
    DoThat();
    DanceALittleJig();
}
```

In addition, both `while` and `for` can take advantage of the loneliest statement, the lone semicolon. This example:

```
for ( i = 0; i < 1000; i++ )
    ;
```

does nothing 1,000 times. Actually, the example does take some time to execute. The initialization expression is evaluated once, and the modification and termination expressions are each evaluated 1,000 times. Here's a `while` version of the loneliest loop:

```
i = 0;

while ( i++ < 1000 )
    ;
```

By far, the `while` and `for` statements are the most common types of C loops. For completeness, however, we'll cover the remaining loop, a little-used gem called the `do` statement.

The do Statement

The do statement is a while statement that evaluates its expression at the bottom of its loop, instead of at the top. Here's the pattern a do statement must match:

```
do
    statement
while ( expression ) ;
```

Here's a sample:

```
i = 1;

do
{
    printf( "%d\n", i );
    i++;
}
while ( i < 3 );

printf( "We are past the do loop." );
```

The first time through the loop, i has a value of 1. The printf() prints a 1 in the console window, then the value of i is bumped to 2. It's not until this point that the expression (i < 3) is evaluated. Since 2 is less than 3, a second pass through the loop occurs.

During this second pass, the printf() prints a 2 in the console window, then the value of i is bumped to 3. Once again, the expression (i < 3) is evaluated. Since 3 is not less than 3, we drop out of the loop to the second printf().

The important thing to remember about do loops is this: Since the expression is not evaluated until the bottom of the loop, the body of the loop (the statement) is always executed at least once. Since for and while loops both check their expressions at the top of the loop, it's possible for either to drop out of the loop before the body of the loop is executed.

Let's move on to a completely different type of statement, known as the switch.

The switch

The switch statement uses the value of an expression to determine which of a series of statements to execute. Here's an example that should make this concept a little clearer:

```
switch ( theYear )
{
    case 1066:
        printf( "Battle of Hastings" );
        break;
    case 1492:
        printf( "Columbus sailed the ocean blue" );
        break;
    case 1776:
        printf( "Declaration of Independence\n" );
        printf( "A very important document!!!" );
        break;
    default:
        printf( "Don't know what happened during this year" );
}
```

The switch is constructed of a series of cases, each based on a specific value of theYear. If theYear has a value of 1066, execution continues with the statement following that case's colon, in this case, the line:

```
printf( "Battle of Hastings" );
```

Execution continues, line after line, until either the bottom of the switch (the right curly-brace) or a break statement is reached. In this case, the next line is a break statement.

The break statement comes in handy when you are working with switches and loops. The break tells the computer to jump immediately to the next statement after the end of the loop or switch.

Continuing with the example, if theYear has a value of 1492, the switch jumps to the lines:

```
printf( "Columbus sailed the ocean blue" );
break;
```

A value of 1776 jumps to the lines:

```
printf( "Declaration of Independence\n" );
printf( "A very important document!!!" );
break;
```

Notice that this case has two statements before the break. There is no limit to the number of statements a case can have. One is OK, 653 is OK. You can even have a case with no statements at all.

The original example also contains a default case. If the switch can't find a case that matches the value of its expression, the switch looks for a case labeled default. If the default is present, its statements are executed. If no default is present, the switch completes without executing any of its statements.

Here's the pattern the switch tries to match:

```
switch ( expression )
{
    case constant:
        statements
    case constant:
        statements
    default:
        statements
}
```

Important

> Why would you want a `case` with no statements? Here's an example:
>
> ```
> switch ( myVar )
> {
>     case 1:
>     case 2:
>         DoSomething();
>         break;
>     case 3:
>         DoSomethingElse();
> }
> ```
>
> In this example, if `myVar` has a value of 1 or 2, the function `DoSomething()` is called. If `myVar` has a value of 3, the function `DoSomethingElse()` is called. If `myVar` has any other value, nothing happens. Use a `case` with no statements when you want two different `case`s to execute the same statements.

At the heart of each `switch` is its expression. Most `switch`es are based on single variables but, as we mentioned earlier, assignment statements make perfectly acceptable expressions.

Each `case` is based on a **constant**. Numbers (like 47 or -12,932) are valid constants. Variables, such as `myVar`, are not. As you'll see later, single-byte characters (like `'a'` or `'\n'`) are also valid constants. Multiple-byte character strings (like `"Gummy-bear"`) are not.

The statements following a `case`'s colon represent zero or more statements. If your `switch` uses a `default case`, make sure you use it as shown in the pattern above. Don't include the word `case` before the word `default`.

Breaks in Other Loops

The break statement has other use besides the switch statement. Here's an example of a break used in a while loop:

```
i=1;

while ( i <= 9 )
{
    PlayAnInning( i );
    if ( ItsRaining() )
        break;
    i++;
}
```

This sample tries to play nine innings of baseball. As long as the function ItsRaining() returns with a value of FALSE, the game continues uninterrupted. If ItsRaining() returns a value of TRUE, the break statement is executed and the program drops out of the loop, interrupting the game.

The break statement allows you to construct loops that depend on multiple factors. The termination of the loop depends on the regular expression found at the top of the loop, as well as on any outside factors that might trigger an unexpected break.

Sample Programs

Are you ready for some programming? This chapter's sample programs focus on the if and if-else statements: the while, for, and do loops, and the switch statement. Get your Mac turned on, take care of any pressing personal problems, and let's get to it.

isOdd.c

Start up THIN C by double-clicking on its icon in the Finder. When prompted for a project to open, go into the projects folder, then into the isOdd folder and open the project called isOdd.π. The isOdd.π project loops through the integers from 1 through 20. isOdd tells you if each number is odd or even, and if the number is a multiple of 3.

Run isOdd.π by selecting **Run** from the **Project** menu. You should see something like the console window shown in Figure 6.4. You should see a line for each number from 1 through 20. Each of the numbers will be described as either odd or even. Each of the multiples of 3 will have additional text describing them as such. Here's how the program works:

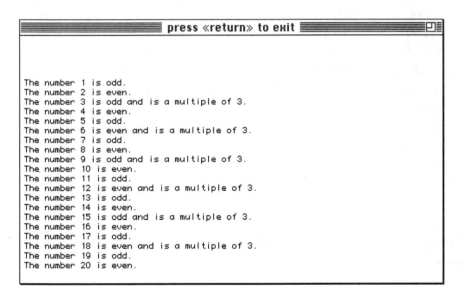

Figure 6.4   Running isOdd.π.

Stepping Through the Source Code

isOdd.π consists of the single function main(), which declares a single variable, an int (called i), used as a counter in a for loop.

```
main()
{
    int i;
```

Our goal here is to step through each of the numbers from 1 to 20. For each number, we want to check to see if the number is odd or even. We also want to check whether the number is evenly divisible by 3. Once we've analyzed a number, we'll use printf() to print a description of the number in the console window.

By the Way _____

> The scheme that defines the way a program works is called the program's algorithm. It's a good idea to try to work out the details of your program's algorithm **before writing one line of source code.**

As you might expect, the next step is to set up a for loop using i as a counter. i is initialized to 1. The loop will keep running as long as the value of i is less than or equal to 20. This is the same as saying the loop will exit as soon as the value of i is found to be greater than 20. Every time the loop reaches the bottom, the third expression, i++, will be evaluated, incrementing the value of i by 1. This is a classic for loop.

```
    for ( i = 1; i <= 20; i++ )
    {
```

Now we're inside the `for` loop. Our goal is to print a single line for each number (i.e., one line each time through the `for` loop). If you check back to Figure 6.4, you'll notice that each line starts with the phrase:

```
The number x is
```

where x is the number being described. That's the purpose of this first `printf()`:

```
printf( "The number %d is ", i );
```

Notice that this `printf()` wasn't part of an `if` statement. We want this `printf()` to print its message every time through the loop. The next sequence of `printf()`s are a different story altogether.

The next chunk of code determines whether `i` is even or odd, then uses `printf()` to print the appropriate word in the console window. Because the last `printf()` didn't end with a newline character (`'\n'`), the word "even" or "odd" will appear immediately following:

```
The number x is
```

on the same line in the console window.

```
if ( (i / 2) * 2 == i )
    printf( "even" );
else
    printf( "odd" );
```

Because `i` is an `int`, all division using `i` results in a whole number. For example, in the real world, when you divide 9 by 2, you get 4.5. Not so in the world of integer arithmetic. In expressions involving `int`s, the result is always truncated: 4.5 becomes 4, 7.2 becomes 7.

What does this have to do with evens and odds? If you divide an even number by 2, then multiply it by 2, you'll always end up with your original number. If you do the same with an odd number, you'll always end up with 1 less than your original number.

Here are a few examples. Using integer arithmetic, 9 divided by 2 is 4, 4 times 2 is 8, which is 1 less than 9. On the even side, 10 divided by 2 is 5, and 5 times 2 is 10, our original number.

The expression:

```
( i / 2 ) * 2 == i
```

will have a value of TRUE if and only if i is even. If i is even, we print the word "even" in the console window. If i is odd, we print the word "odd".

Important _____

> Remember this technique. Programmers use it all the time to determine whether one number is evenly divisible by another.

```
if ( (i / 3) * 3 == i )
    printf( " and is a multiple of 3" );
```

The next chunk of code uses the same technique to determine if i is evenly divisible by 3. The expression:

```
(i / 3) * 3 == i
```

will have a value of TRUE if and only if i is evenly divisible by 3. In this case, we add the phrase:

```
" and is a multiple of 3"
```

to the end of the current line. Finally, we add a period "." and a newline "\n" to the end of the current line, placing us at the beginning of the next line of the console window.

```
    printf( ".\n" );
```

The program ends with a pair of right curly-braces. The first one ends the `for` loop. The second one marks the end of `main()`.

```
    }
}
```

nextPrime.π

Our next program focuses on the mathematical concept of **prime numbers**. A prime number is any number whose only factors are 1 and itself. For example, 6 is not a prime number because its factors are 1, 2, 3, and 6. The number 5 is prime because its factors are limited to 1 and 5. The number 12 isn't prime — its factors are 1, 2, 3, 4, 6, and 12.

Our next program will find the next prime number greater than a specified number. For example, if we set our starting point to 14, the program would find the next prime, 17.

Close the project `isOdd.π` by selecting **Close Project** from the **Project** menu. When prompted for a new project to open, go back up to the `projects` folder, then into the `nextPrime` folder and open the project called `nextPrime.π`. We set up `nextPrime.π` to look for the next prime number after 19. Lock in your guesses before we reveal the answer.

Run `nextPrime.π` by selecting **Run** from the **Project** menu. You should see something like the console window shown in Figure 6.5. As you can see, the next prime number after 19 is (drum roll, please...) 23. Here's how the program works:

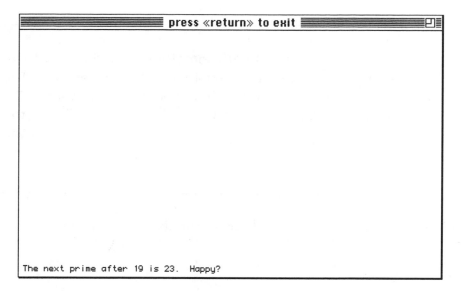

The next prime after 19 is 23. Happy?

Figure 6.5 Running nextPrime.π.

Stepping Through the Source Code

nextPrime.c starts by setting a variable called candidate to the first number under consideration as a prime number. Inside a while loop, candidate is incremented by one, then checked for primeness. The while loop exits as soon as a prime is found and the prime is printed in the console window.

Within the while loop, a for loop is used to check if candidate is a prime number. The for loop steps through every number from 2 to candidate - 1, looking for a number that divides evenly into candidate. If such a factor is found, the candidate is not a prime number and the while loop continues.

```
#include <stdio.h>
```

Important

> nextPrime.c **starts off with something called a** #include. **The** #include **includes a special file in the current file. The file** stdio.h **contains the definitions of the constants** TRUE **and** FALSE. **Chapter 9 covers the** #include **in detail. For the moment, think of this line as a mechanism for defining the constants** TRUE **and** FALSE.

nextPrime.c makes use of five different variables, all of them ints.

```
main()
{
    int     startingPoint, candidate, i;
    int     done, foundFactor;
```

startingPoint holds the number we want to start with, in this case, 19. candidate is the number currently under consideration as a prime. candidate starts off equal to startingPoint and is incremented each time through the while loop. i is used as a counter in the for loop, counting from 2 to candidate - 1.

```
    done = FALSE;
    startingPoint = 19;
    candidate = startingPoint;
```

done is initialized to FALSE. done represents the terminating condition of the while loop. The while loop will continue until done is set to TRUE, which will happen when a prime number is found.

startingPoint is initialized to 19. Remember, we want the next prime number after startingPoint. Although startingPoint's value is copied into candidate, candidate is incremented at the beginning of the while loop. This means that the first candidate we look at is 20.

```
while ( ! done )
{
    candidate++;
```

The `while` loop exits as soon as `done` is set to TRUE.

```
foundFactor = FALSE;
for ( i = 2; i < candidate; i++ )
{
    if ( (candidate / i) * i == candidate )
        foundFactor = TRUE;
}
```

`foundFactor` is set to FALSE each time through the `while` loop. The `for` loop ranges from 2 to `candidate` - 1. Each possible factor of `candidate` is tested using the technique demonstrated in `isOdd.c`. If a number is found that divides into `candidate` exactly, `foundFactor` is set to TRUE. If we get all the way through the `for` loop without finding a factor, `foundFactor` will still be FALSE, and we've found ourselves a prime number.

```
    done = (foundFactor == FALSE);
}
```

`done` is set to TRUE if `foundFactor` is FALSE. In English, this line means we're done if the candidate we just looked at had no factors between 1 and itself. The curly brace closes the `while` loop.

By the Way _____

> The line:
>
> ```
> done = (foundFactor == FALSE);
> ```
>
> could also have been written:
>
> ```
> done = ( ! foundFactor );
> ```
>
> Use whichever version you find easier to read.

```
    printf( "The next prime after %d is %d. Happy?",
                startingPoint, candidate );
}
```

Once we drop out of the `while` loop, we use `printf()` to print both the starting point and the first prime number greater than the starting point.

If you are interested in prime numbers, play around with this program. See if you can modify the code to print all the prime numbers from 1 to 100. How about the first 100 prime numbers?

What's Next?

Congratulations! You've made it through some tough concepts. You've learned about the C statements that allow you to control your program's flow. You've learned about C expressions and the concept of `TRUE` and `FALSE`. You've also learned about the logical operators based on the values `TRUE` and `FALSE`. You've learned about the `if`, `if-else`, `for`, `while`, `do`, `switch`, and `break` statements. In short, you've learned a lot!

Our next chapter introduces the concept of **pointers**.

A pointer to a variable is really the address of the variable in memory. If you pass the value of a variable to a function, the function can make use of the variable's value, but can't *change* the variable's value. If you pass the address of the variable to the function, the function can also change the value of the variable. Chapter 7 will tell you why.

Chapter 7 will also discuss function parameters in detail. As usual, plenty of code fragments and sample applications will be presented to keep you busy. See you there.

Exercises

1) What's wrong with each of the following code fragments?

a.
```
if  i
    i++;
```

b.
```
for ( i=0; i<20; i++ )
    i--;
```

c.
```
while ( )
    i++;
```

d.
```
do  ( i++ )
    until ( i == 20 );
```

e.
```
switch ( i )
{
    case "hello":
    case "goodbye":
        printf( "Greetings." );
        break;
    case default:
        printf( "Boring." );
}
```

```
f.   if ( i < 20 )
        if ( i == 20 )
            printf( "Lonely..." );
```

```
g.   while ( done = TRUE )
        done = ! done;
```

```
h.   for ( i=0; i<20; i*20 )
        printf( "Modification..." );
```

2) Modify `nextPrime.c` to compute the prime numbers from 1 to 100.

3) Modify `nextPrime.c` to compute the first 100 prime numbers.

Chapter 7

Pointers and Parameters

This Chapter at a Glance

What is a Pointer?
Why Use Pointers?
Checking Out of the Library
Pointer Basics
Variable Addresses
The & Operator
Declaring a Pointer Variable
Function Parameters
What are Function Parameters?
Variable Scope
How Function Paramters Work
Parameters are Temporary
What Does All This Have to do with Pointers?
Global Variables and Function Returns
Global Variables
Adding Globals to Your Programs
When to Use Globals
Function Returns
Danger! Avoid Uninitialized Return Values
To Return or Not to Return
Sample Programs
listPrimes.π
Stepping Through the Source Code
power.π
Running power.π
Stepping Through the Source Code
What's Next?
Exercises

YOU'VE COME A LONG WAY. YOU'VE MASTERED VARIABLE basics, operators, and statements. You're about to add some powerful, new concepts to your programming toolbox.

For starters, we'll introduce the concept of **pointers**, also known as variable addresses. From now on, you'll use pointers in almost every C program you write. Pointers allow you to implement complex data structures, opening up a world of programming possibilities.

What is a Pointer?

In programming, pointers are references to other things. When someone calls your name to get your attention, they're using your name as a pointer. Your name is one way people refer to you.

Your name and address can combine to serve as a pointer, telling the mail carrier where to deliver the new Sears catalog. Your address distinguishes your house from all the other houses in your neighborhood and your name distinguishes you from the rest of the people living in your house.

When you declare a variable in C, memory is allocated to the variable. This memory has an address. C pointers are special variables, specifically designed to hold one of these addresses. Later in the chapter, you'll learn how to create a pointer, how to make it point to a specific variable, and how to use the pointer to change the variable's value.

Why Use Pointers?

Pointers can be extremely useful, allowing you to access your data in ways that ordinary variables just don't allow. Here's a real-world example of "pointer flexibility."

When you go to the library in search of a specific title, chances are you start your search in a card catalog. Card catalogs contain thousands of index cards, one for every book in the library. Each index card contains information about a specific book, including such information as the author's name, the book's title, and the copyright date.

Most libraries have two card catalogs. One lists all the books, sorted alphabetically by subject. The other lists all the books, sorted alphabetically by author. In the subject card catalog, a book can be listed more than once. For example, a book about Thomas Jefferson might be listed under "Presidents, U.S.," "Architects," or even under "Inventors" (Jefferson was quite an inventor).

Figure 7.1 shows a catalog card for Albert Einstein's famous book on relativity, called *The Meaning of Relativity*. The card was listed in the subject catalog under the subject "RELATIVITY (PHYSICS)." Take a minute to look the card over. Pay special attention to the catalog information located on the left side of the card. The catalog number for this book is 530.1. This number tells you exactly where to find the book among all the other books on the shelves. The books are ordered numerically, so you'll find this book in the 500 shelves, between 530 and 531.

Important _____

> In this example, the library bookshelves are like your computer's memory, with the books acting as data. The catalog number is the address of your data (a book) in memory (on the shelf).

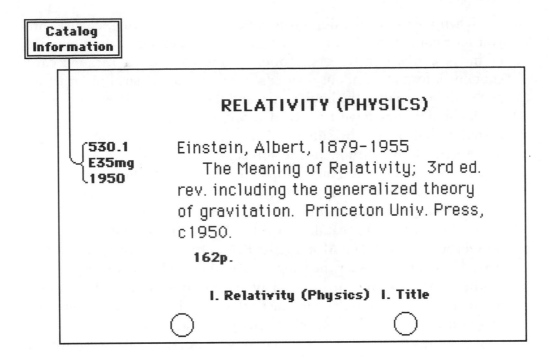

Figure 7.1   Catalog card for a rather famous book. Note the catalog information on the left side of the card.

As you might have guessed, the catalog number acts as a pointer. The card catalogs use these pointers to rearrange all the books in the library, without moving a single book. Think about it. In the subject card catalog, all the books are arranged by subject. Physically, the book arrangements have nothing to do with subject. Physically, the books are arranged numerically, by catalog number. By adding a layer of pointers between you and the books, the librarians achieve an extra layer of flexibility.

In the same way, the author card catalog uses a layer of pointers to arrange all the books by author. By using pointers, all the books in the library are arranged three different ways without ever leaving the shelves. The books are arranged physically (sorted by catalog number) and logically (sorted in one catalog by author, and in another by subject). Without the support of a layer of pointers, these logical book arrangements would be impossible.

By the Way _____

> Adding a layer of pointers is also known as "adding a level of indirection." The number of levels of indirection is the number of pointers you have to use to get to your library book (or to your data).

Checking Out of the Library

So far, we've talked about pointers in terms of library catalog numbers. The use of pointers in your C programs is not much different from this model. Each card catalog number points out the location of a book on the library shelf. In the same way, each pointer in your program will point out the location of a piece of data in computer memory.

If you wrote a program to keep track of your compact-disc collection, you might maintain a list of pointers, each one of which might point to a block of data that describes a single CD. Each block of data might contain such info as the name of the artist, the name of the album, the year of release, and a category (jazz, rock, blues). If you got more ambitious, you could create several pointer lists. One list might sort your CDs alphabetically by artist name. Another might sort them chronologically by year of release. Yet another list might sort your CDs by musical category. You get the picture.

There's a lot you can do with pointers. By mastering the techniques presented in these next few chapters, you'll be able to create programs that take full advantage of pointers.

Our goal for this chapter is to master pointer basics. We'll talk about C pointers and C pointer operations. You'll learn how to create a pointer and how to make the pointer point to a variable. You'll also learn how to use a pointer to change the value of the variable the pointer points to.

Pointer Basics

Pointers are variable addresses. Instead of an address such as:

```
1313 Mockingbird Lane
Raven Heights, California   90263
```

a variable's address refers to a memory location within your computer. As we discussed in Chapter 3, your computer's memory consists of a sequence of bytes. A 1-megabyte computer (like the Mac Plus) has exactly 2^{20} (or 1,048,576) bytes. Every one of those bytes has its own unique address. The first byte has an address of 0. The next byte has an address of 1. Computer addresses always start with 0 and continue up, one at a time, until they reach the highest address. Figure 7.2 shows the addressing scheme for a 1-megabyte computer. Notice that the addresses run from 0 (the lowest address) all the way up to 1,048,575 (the highest address).

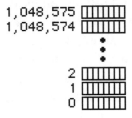

Figure 7.2   1 megabyte worth of bytes.

Variable Addresses

When you run a program, one of the first things the computer does is allocate memory for your program's variables. When you declare an int in your code, like this:

```
int myVar;
```

the compiler reserves 2 bytes of memory for the exclusive use of myVar. Each of myVar's 2 bytes has a specific address.

Figure 7.3 shows a 1-megabyte computer with 2 bytes allocated to the variable myVar. In this picture, the 2 bytes allocated to myVar have the addresses 508 and 509.

By convention, a variable's address is said to be the address of its first byte (the first byte is the byte with the lowest-numbered address). If a variable uses memory locations 508 and 509 (as myVar does), its address is 508 and its length is 2 bytes.

Important _____

When more than 1 byte is allocated to a variable, the bytes will always be consecutive (next to each other in memory). The 2 bytes allocated to an int might have such addresses as 508 and 509, or 64,000 and 64,001. You will never see an int whose byte addresses are 508 and 695. A variable's bytes are like family—they stick together!

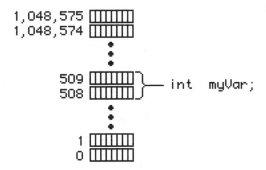

Figure 7.3   2 bytes allocated for the int named myVar.

As we showed earlier, a variable's address is a lot like the catalog number on a library catalog card. Both act as pointers, one to a book on the library shelf, and the other to a variable. From now on, when we use the term pointer with respect to a variable, we are referring to the variable's address.

Now that you understand what a pointer is, your next goal is to learn how to use pointers in your programs. The next few sections will teach you some valuable pointer-programming skills. You'll learn how to create a pointer to a variable. You'll also learn how to use that pointer to access the variable it points to.

The C language provides you with a few key tools to help you. These tools come in the form of two special operators: & and *.

The & Operator

The & operator (also called the "address of" operator) pairs with a variable name to produce the variable's address. The expression:

`&myVar`

refers to `myVar`'s address in memory. If `myVar` owned memory locations 508 and 509 (as in Figure 7.3), the expression:

`&myVar`

would have a value of 508. The expression `&myVar` is a pointer to the variable `myVar`.

As you start programming with pointers, you'll find yourself using the & operator frequently. An expression like `&myVar` is a common way to represent a pointer. Another way to represent a pointer is with a **pointer variable**. A pointer variable is a variable specifically designed to hold the address of another variable.

Declaring a Pointer Variable

C supports a special notation for declaring pointer variables. This line:

```
int *myPointer;
```

declares a variable called `myPointer`. Notice that the `*` is not part of the variable's name. Instead, it tells the compiler that the associated variable is a pointer, specifically designed to hold the address of an `int`. If there were a data type called `bluto`, you could declare a variable designed to point to a `bluto` like this:

```
bluto    *blutoPointer;
```

For now, we'll limit ourselves to pointers that point to `int`s. Look at this code:

```
int *myPointer, myVar;

myPointer = &myVar;
```

The assignment statement puts `myVar`'s address in the variable `myPointer`. If `myVar`'s address is 508, this code will leave `myPointer` with a value of 508. Note that this code has absolutely no effect on the value of `myVar`.

There will be times in your coding when you have a pointer to a variable, but not the variable itself. This happens a lot. You can actually use the pointer to manipulate the value of the variable it points to. Observe:

```
int *myPointer, myVar;

myPointer = &myVar;
*myPointer = 27;
```

As before, the first assignment statement places myVar's address in the variable myPointer. The second assignment introduces the * operator. The * operator (called the **star** operator) converts a pointer variable to the item the pointer points to.

By the Way _____

> The * that appears in the declaration statement isn't really an operator. It's only there to designate the variable myPointer as a pointer.

If myPointer points to myVar, as is the case in our example, *myPointer refers to the variable myVar. In this case, the line:

```
*myPointer = 27;
```

is the same as saying:

```
myVar = 27;
```

Confused? These memory pictures should help. Figure 7.4 joins our program in progress, just after the variables myVar and myPointer were declared:

```
int *myPointer, myVar;
```

Notice that 2 bytes were allocated for the variable myVar while 4 bytes were allocated for myPointer. Why? Because myVar is an int and myPointer is a pointer, designed to hold a 4-byte address.

Once memory is allocated for myVar and myPointer, we move on to the statement:

```
myPointer = &myVar;
```

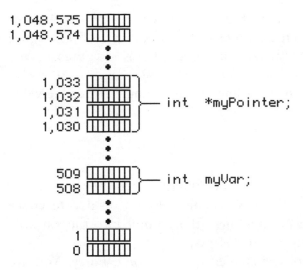

Figure 7.4   Memory allocated for `myVar` and `myPointer`.

By the Way _____

> You may have heard the phrase "32-bit addressing" associated with the Macintosh. When Apple designed the Macintosh, they decided that addresses would be 32 bits (4 bytes) in length. When you declare an `int`, the compiler allocates 2 bytes of memory for it. When you declare a pointer, such as:
>
> ```
> int    *myPointer;
> ```
>
> the compiler allocates 4 bytes of memory for it. Just remember that addresses are always 4 bytes long.

The 4-byte address of the variable myVar is written to the 4 bytes allocated to myPointer. In our example, myVar's address is 508. Figure 7.5 shows the value 508 stored in myPointer's 4 bytes. Now myPointer is said to "point-to" myVar.

OK, we're almost there. The next line of our example writes the value 27 to the location pointed to by myPointer.

```
*myPointer = 27;
```

Without the * operator, the computer would place the value 27 in the memory allocated to myPointer. The * operator **dereferences** myPointer. Dereferencing a pointer turns the pointer into the variable it points to. Figure 7.6 shows the end results.

If the concept of pointers seems alien to you, don't worry. You are not alone. Programming with pointers is one of the most difficult C concepts to master. Just keep reading, and make sure you follow each of the examples line by line. By the end of the chapter, you'll be a pointer expert!

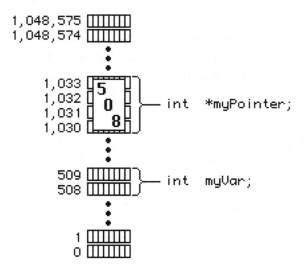

Figure 7.5   The address of myVar is assigned to myPointer.

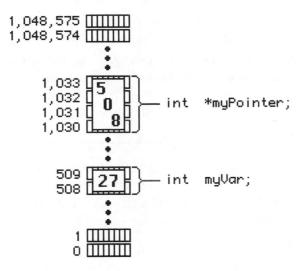

Figure 7.6   Finally, the value 27 is assigned to `*myPointer`.

Function Parameters

One of the most important uses of pointers (and perhaps the easiest to understand) lies in the implementation of **function parameters**. In this section, we'll focus on parameters and, at the same time, have a chance to see pointers in action.

What Are Function Parameters?

A function parameter is your chance to share a variable between a calling function and the called function.

Suppose you wanted to write a function called `AddTwo()` that took two numbers, added them together, and returned the sum of the two numbers. How would you get the two original numbers into `AddTwo()`? How would you get the sum of the two numbers back to the function that called `AddTwo()`?

As you might have guessed, the answer to both questions lies in the use of parameters. Before we talk about parameters, however, it's important you understand why parameters are necessary. To understand why parameters are necessary, you have to understand **variable scope**.

Variable Scope

In C, every variable is said to have a scope, or range. A variable's scope defines where in the program you have access to a variable. In other words, if a variable is declared inside one function, can another function refer to that same variable?

    C defines variable scope as follows:

A variable declared inside a function is local to that function and may only be referenced inside that function.

    This statement is important. It means you can't declare a variable inside one function, then refer to that same value inside another function. Here's an example that will never compile:

```
DrawDots()
{
    int i;

    for ( i = 0; i < numDots; i++ )
        printf( "." );
}

main()
{
    int numDots;

    numDots = 500;

    DrawDots();
}
```

The error in this code occurs when the function `DrawDots()` tries to reference the variable `numDots`. According to the rules of scope, `DrawDots()` doesn't even know about the variable `numDots`. If you tried to compile this program the compiler would complain that `DrawDots()` tried to use the variable `numDots` without declaring it.

The problem you are faced with is getting the value of `numDots` to the function `DrawDots()` so `DrawDots()` knows how many "dots" to draw. The answer to this problem is function parameters.

By the Way _____

> Why a function that draws dots? No special reason. We just wanted to show a simple example.

How Function Parameters Work

Function parameters are just like variables. Instead of being declared at the beginning of a function, function parameters are declared between the parentheses on the function's title line, like this:

```
DrawDots( int numDots )
{
    /* function's body goes here */
}
```

When you call a function, you just match up the parameters, making sure you pass the function what it expects. To call the version of `DrawDots()` we just defined, make sure you place an `int` between the parentheses. The call to `DrawDots()` inside `main()`:

```
main()
{
    DrawDots( 30 );
}
```

passes the value 30 into the function `DrawDots()`. When `DrawDots()` starts executing, it sets its parameter to the passed-in value. In this case, `DrawDots()` has one parameter, an `int` named `numDots`. When the call:

```
DrawDots( 30 );
```

executes, the function `DrawDots()` sets its parameter, `numDots`, to a value of 30. To make things a little clearer, here's a revised version of our example:

```
DrawDots( int numDots )
{
    int i;

    for ( i = 0; i < numDots; i++ )
        printf( "." );
}

main()
{
    DrawDots( 30 );
}
```

This version of `main()` calls `DrawDots()`, passing as a parameter the constant 30. `DrawDots()` receives the value 30 in its `int` parameter, `numDots`. This means that the function `DrawDots()` starts execution with a variable named `numDots` having a value of 30.

Inside `DrawDots()`, the `for` loop behaves as you might expect, drawing 30 periods in the console window. Figure 7.7 shows a picture of this program in action. You can run this example yourself. The project file, `drawDots.π`, is located in the `Projects` folder in a subfolder named `drawDots`.

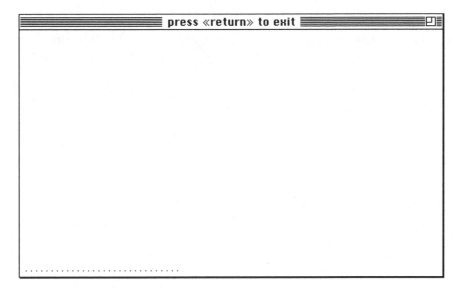

Figure 7.7   `DrawDots` in action.

Parameters are Temporary

When you pass a value from a calling function to a called function, you are creating a temporary variable inside the called function. Once the called function exits (returns to the calling function), that variable ceases to exist.

In our example, we passed a value of 30 into `DrawDots()` as a parameter. The value came to rest in the parameter variable named `numDots`. Once `DrawDots()` exited, `numDots` ceased to exist.

Remember, a variable declared inside a function can only be referenced by that function.

It is perfectly acceptable for two functions to use the same variable names for completely different purposes. It's fairly standard, for example, to use a variable name like i as a counter in a for loop. What happens when, in the middle of just such a for loop, you call a function that also uses a variable named i? Here's an example:

```
RowOfDots()
{
    int i;

    for ( i = 0; i < 50; i++ )
        printf( "." );
}

main()
{
    int i;

    for ( i = 0; i < 10; i++ )
    {
        RowOfDots();
        printf( "\n" );
    }
}
```

main() uses the variable i to keep track of the number of rows of dots printed. Once for each row, main() calls the function RowOfDots(), which also uses a variable named i. Won't RowOfDots() mess up main()'s copy of i? No! main() has its own copy of i that exists while it is the current function.

When RowOfDots() starts executing, it gets its own copy of i. It doesn't even know about main()'s variable named i. Once RowOfDots() exits, its copy of i is scrubbed from memory.

What Does All This Have to do with Pointers?

OK. Now we're getting to the crux of the whole matter. What do parameters have to do with pointers? To answer this question, you have to understand the two different methods of parameter passing.

Parameters are passed from function to function either by value or by address. Passing a parameter by value passes only the value of a variable or literal on to the called function. Take a look at this code:

```
main()
{
    int numDots;

    numDots = 30;

    DrawDots( numDots );
}
```

The call to `DrawDots()` passes the value 30 on to the receiving parameter in `DrawDots()`. No matter what `DrawDots()` does, it will have no effect on the variable `numDots`. Passing parameters by value is a one-way operation. The calling function passes a value to a called function. In this case, `main()` passes the value of 30 on to `DrawDots()`.

Since passing parameters by value is a one-way operation, there's no way to get data back from the called function. Why would you ever want to? Several reasons. You might write a function that takes an employee number as a parameter. You might want that function to return the employee's salary in another parameter. How about a function that turns yards into meters? You could pass the number of yards as a value parameter, but how would you get back the number of meters?

Passing a parameter by address (instead of by value) solves this problem. If you pass the address of a variable, the receiving function can use the * operator to change the value of the original variable. Think of it this way. Normally, one function can't see another function's variables. By passing the address of a variable as a parameter, you're telling the called function, "Hey, here's one of my variables. Use its value. Change it if you like. Just make sure you don't mess it up." Passing the address of a variable allows you to share a variable with another function.

Here's an example:

```
SquareIt( int  number, int  *squarePtr )
{
    *squarePtr = number * number;
}

main()
{
    int square;

    SquareIt( 5, &square );

    printf( "5 squared is %d.", square );
}
```

In this example, `main()` calls the function `SquareIt()`. `SquareIt()` takes two parameters. As in our last example, both parameters are declared between the parentheses on the function's title line. Notice that we used a comma to separate the parameter declarations.

The first of `SquareIt()`'s two parameters is an `int`. The second parameter is a pointer to an `int`. `SquareIt()` squares the value passed in the first parameter, using the pointer in the second parameter to return the squared value.

By the Way _____

> If it's been ten or more years since your last math class, squaring a number is the same as multiplying the number by itself. The square of 4 is 16 and the square of 5 is 25.

```
SquareIt( 5, &square );
```

In the call to `SquareIt()`, `main()` passes a value of 5 in the first parameter. `SquareIt()` receives the 5 in the first parameter, `number`. `main()` passes the address of the variable `square` as the second parameter. Remember, the & operator produces the address of a variable.

```
SquareIt( int  number, int  *squarePtr )
```

`SquareIt()` receives `square`'s address in its second parameter, the `int` pointer named `squarePtr`. At this point, `squarePtr` points to (contains) the address of `main()`'s variable named `square`. Inside the function `SquareIt()`, any reference to:

```
*squarePtr
```

is just like a reference to `square`. The assignment statement:

```
*squarePtr = number * number;
```

assigns the value 25 to the variable pointed to by `squarePtr`. This has the effect of assigning the value 25 to `square`. When `SquareIt()` returns control to `main()`, the value of `square` has been changed, as evidenced by the screen shot in Figure 7.8. If you'd like to run `SquareIt()` yourself, you'll find it in the `Projects` folder.

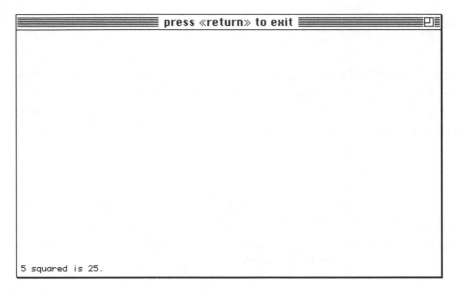

Figure 7.8   SquareIt in action.

Global Variables and Function Returns

The combination of pointers and parameters gives us one way to share variables between different functions. This section demonstrates two more techniques for doing the same.

Global variables are variables that are accessible from inside every function in your program. By declaring a global variable, two separate functions can access the same variable without passing parameters. We'll show you how to declare a global variable, a great naming convention, and we'll talk about when and when not to use global variables in your programs.

Another topic we'll discuss later in the chapter is a property common to all functions. All functions written in C **return** a value to the function that calls them. You set this return value inside the function itself. You can use a function's return value in place of a parameter, use it to pass "additional information" to the calling function, or not use it at all. We'll show you how to add a return value to your functions.

Global Variables

Earlier in the chapter, you learned how to use parameters to share variables between two functions. Passing parameters between functions is great. You can call a function, pass it some data to work on, and when the function's done, it can pass you back the results.

Global variables provide an alternative to parameters. Global variables are just like regular variables, with one exception. Global variables are immune to C's scope rules. They can be referenced inside each of your program's functions. One function might initialize the global variable, another might change its value, and another function might print the value of the global variable in the console window.

As you design your program, you'll have to make some basic decisions about data sharing between functions. If you'll be sharing a variable among a number of functions, you might want to consider making the variable a global. Globals are especially useful when you want to share a variable between two functions that are several calls apart.

Several calls apart? At times, you'll find yourself passing a parameter to a function, not because that function needs the parameter, but because the function calls another function that needs the parameter. Look at this code:

```
PrintMyVar( int myVar )
{
    printf( "myVar = %d", myVar );
}

PassAlong( int  myVar )
{
    PrintMyVar( myVar );
}
```

```
main()
{
    int myVar;

    myVar = 10;

    PassAlong( myVar );
}
```

Notice that `main()` passes `myVar` to the function `PassAlong()`. `PassAlong()` doesn't actually make use of `myVar`. Instead, it just passes `myVar` along to the function `PrintMyVar()`. `PrintMyVar()` prints `myVar`, then returns.

If `myVar` were a global, you could have avoided some parameter passing. `main()` and `PrintMyVar()` could have shared `myVar` without the use of parameters. When should you use parameters? When should you use globals? There's no easy answer. As you write more code, you'll develop your own coding style and, with it, your own sense of when to use globals versus parameters. For the moment, let's take a look at the proper way to add globals to your programs.

Adding Globals to Your Programs

Adding globals to your programs is easy. Just declare a variable at the beginning of your source code before the start of any of your functions. Here's the example we showed you earlier, using globals in place of parameters:

```
int gMyVar;

PrintMyVar()
{
    printf( "gMyVar = %d", gMyVar );
}
```

```
PassAlong()
{
    PrintMyVar();
}

main()
{
    gMyVar = 10;

    PassAlong();
}
```

This example starts with a variable declaration, right at the top of the program. Because gMyVar was declared at the top of the program, myVar becomes a global variable, accessible to each of the program's functions. Notice that none of the functions in this version use parameters. Both main() and PrintMyVar() access the same global copy of the variable gMyVar.

When to Use Globals

In general, you should try to minimize your use of globals. On one hand, global variables make programming easier, because you can access a global anywhere. With parameters, you have to pass the parameter from function to function, until it gets to where it will be used.

On the other hand, globals are expensive, memorywise. Since the memory available to your program is finite, you should try to be memory conscious whenever possible. What makes global variables expensive where memory is concerned? Whenever a function is called, memory for the function's variables is allocated on a temporary basis. When the function exits, the memory allocated to the function is freed up (put back into the pool of available memory). Global variables, on the other hand, are around for the life of your program. Memory for each global is allocated when the program first starts running and isn't freed up until the program exits.

Try to minimize your use of globals, but don't be a miser. If using a global will make your life easier, go ahead and use it.

Function Returns

Before we get to our source code examples, there's one more subject to cover. In addition to passing a parameter and using a global variable, there's one more way to share data between two functions. Every function returns a value to the function that called it. You can use this return value to pass data back from a called function.

So far, all of our examples have ignored **function return values**. The return value only comes into play when you call a function in an expression, like this:

```
AddTheseNumbers( int num1, int num2 )
{
    return( num1 + num2 );
}

main()
{
    int sum;

    sum = AddTheseNumbers( 5, 6 );

    printf( "The sum is %d.", sum );
}
```

There are a few things worth noting in this example. The first point of interest is the call of the function `AddTheseNumbers()` inside the function `main()`:

```
sum = AddTheseNumbers( 5, 6 );
```

When you use a function inside an expression, the computer makes the function call, then substitutes the function's return value for the function when it evaluates the rest of the expression. To establish a return value for a function, you use a special function called `return()`.

`return()` takes one of two forms. To immediately exit a function, without establishing a return value, use the statement:

```
return;
```

Notice that this form of return does not use any parentheses. You might use this immediate return in case of an error, like this:

```
if ( OutOfMemory() )
   return;
```

What you'll want to remember about this form of return is that it does not establish the return value of the function. You might say that this form of return leaves the function's return value in an uninitialized state. In other words, the return value is garbage!

The second form of return is the one we're interested in right now:

```
return( expression );
```

This form of return immediately returns from the function but it also sets the function's return value to the value of the expression. The function `AddTheseNumbers()` uses this form of return:

```
return( num1 + num2 );
```

The two variables used in the expression, `num1` and `num2`, were passed into `AddTheseNumbers()` as parameters. Were they passed by value or by address? You got it—both parameters were passed by value. In the expression:

```
num1 + num2
```

`num1` has a value of 5 and `num2` has a value of 6. The function `AddTheseNumbers()` will return with a value of 11. The line:

```
sum = AddTheseNumbers( 5, 6 );
```

will set the variable sum to a value of 11. Figure 7.9 shows the result when we ran this program. If you'd like to run it yourself, the source code is in the Projects folder, in the addThese subfolder.

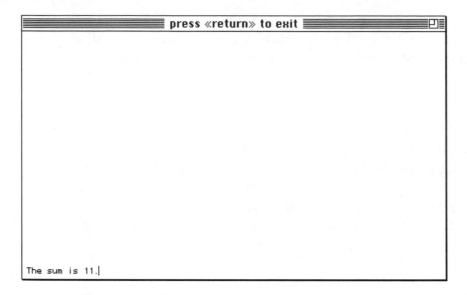

Figure 7.9   A demonstration of function return values.

Danger! Avoid Uninitialized Return Values!

Before we leave the topic of function return values, there's one pitfall worth mentioning. If you're going to use a function in an expression, make sure the function provides a return value. For example, this code will produce unpredictable results:

```
AddTheseNumbers( int num1, int num2 )
{
    return; /* Yikes! We forgot to
                set the return value */
}
```

```
main()
{
    int sum;

    sum = AddTheseNumbers( 5, 6 );

    printf( "The sum is %d.", sum );
}
```

When `AddTheseNumbers()` returns, what will its value be? No one knows! Figure 7.10 shows one possibility. As you can see, the computer used -43 as the return value for `AddTheseNumbers()`. Don't forget to set a return value if you intend to use a function in an expression.

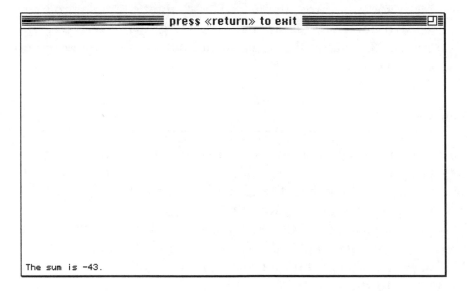

Figure 7.10   Yikes! 5 + 6 is not equal to -43. Someone forgot to set their return value!

To Return or Not to Return

Should you use a return value or a passed-by-address parameter? Which is correct? This is basically a question of style. Either solution will get the job done, so feel free to use whichever works best for you. Just remember that a function can have only one return value but an unlimited number of parameters. If you need to get more than one piece of data back to the calling function, your best bet is to use parameters.

Sample Programs

Are you ready for some programming? This chapter's sample programs make use of pointers, function parameters, global variables, and function returns. Crank up the stereo, break out the pizza, and flip on your Mac. Let's code!

listPrimes.π

Our first sample program is an updated version of Chapter 6's prime number program, `nextPrime.π`, which found the next prime number following a specified number. The example we presented reported that the next prime number after 19 was 23.

This program, called `listPrimes.π`, will list all the prime numbers between 1 and 50. Start up THIN C by double-clicking on its icon in the Finder. When prompted for a project to open, go into the `Projects` folder, then into the `listPrimes` folder and open the project called `listPrimes.π`.

Run `listPrimes.π` by selecting **Run** from the **Project** menu. `listPrimes` will step through each number from 1 to 50. If the number is a prime, it will print a line in the console window saying so. The end result should look like the console window shown in Figure 7.11. Here's how the program works.

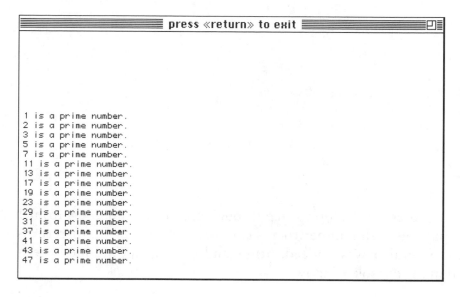

Figure 7.11   `listPrimes.π` in action.

Stepping Through the Source Code

`listPrimes.π` consists of two functions: `main()` and `IsItPrime()`.
`IsItPrime()` takes a single parameter, an `int` named `candidate`, which
is passed by value. `IsItPrime()` returns a value of `TRUE` if `candidate` is
a prime number and a value of `FALSE` otherwise.

```
#include <stdio.h>
```

Important

> `listPrimes.c` starts off with the same `#include` as
> `nextPrime.c`. The `#include` includes the file `stdio.h`,
> which contains the definitions of the constants `TRUE` and
> `FALSE`. Chapter 9 covers the `#include` in detail.

```
main()
{
    int i;

    for ( i = 1; i <= 50; i++ )
    {
        if ( IsItPrime( i ) )
            printf( "%d is a prime number.\n", i );
    }
}
```

main() uses a for loop to step through each of the numbers from 1 to 50, passing each number to IsItPrime(). If IsItPrime() returns TRUE, the number was, indeed, prime and an appropriate message is printed in the console window.

```
IsItPrime( int  candidate )
{
    int i, foundFactor;

    foundFactor = FALSE;
    for ( i = 2; i < candidate; i++ )
    {
        if ( (candidate / i) * i == candidate )
            foundFactor = TRUE;
    }

    return( foundFactor == FALSE );
}
```

IsItPrime() uses the same algorithm to search for primes as Chapter 6's nextPrime.c used. Each candidate is checked to see if it has a prime factor. (Confused? Check back to Chapter 6's nextPrime program.) If a factor is found, the number is not a prime. If a factor is not found, the number is a prime.

The key to this function is in the return statement:

```
return( foundFactor == FALSE );
```

The name of the function is `IsItPrime()`. In C, when you name a function in the form of a `TRUE` or `FALSE` question, it is good form to return a value of `TRUE` or `FALSE`. The question this function answers is, "Is the candidate prime?" It is critical that `IsItPrime()` return `TRUE` if the candidate was prime and `FALSE` otherwise. When `main()` calls `IsItPrime()`, `main()` is asking the question, "Is the candidate prime?" In the case of the `if` statement:

```
if ( IsItPrime( i ) )
    printf( ... );
```

`main()` is saying, "If the candidate is prime, do the `printf()`." Make sure your function return values make sense!

power.π

Our next program combines a global variable, a pointer parameter, and some value parameters. At the heart of the program is a function, called `DoPower()`, that takes three parameters. `DoPower()` takes a base and an exponent, raises the base to the exponent power, and returns the result in a parameter. Raising a base to an exponent power is the same as multiplying the base by itself, an exponent number of times.

For example, raising 2 to the fifth power (written as 2^5) is the same as saying $2*2*2*2*2$, which is equal to 32. In the expression 2^5, 2 is the base and 5 is the exponent. The function `DoPower()` takes a base and an exponent as parameters and raises the base to the exponent power. `DoPower()` uses a third parameter to return the result to the calling function.

The program also makes use of a global variable, an `int` named `gPrintExtraInfo`, which demonstrates one of the most important uses of a global variable. Every function in the program checks the value of the global `gPrintExtraInfo`. If `gPrintExtraInfo` is `TRUE`, each function prints a message when the function is entered, and another message when the function exits. In this way, you can follow the execution of the program. By reading the `printf()`s, you can see when a function is entered and when it leaves.

Since this program is fairly small (two functions), this may not seem particularly useful. But when you start writing programs with hundreds of functions, you'll be glad you have a way of tracking your program. If gPrintExtraInfo is set to TRUE, the extra function-tracing information will be printed in the console window. If gPrintExtraInfo is set to FALSE, the extra information will not be printed.

As you'll see in a moment, by simply changing the value of a global, you can dramatically change the way your program runs.

Important

Did you notice that funny g at the beginning of the global's name? Get used to it. In general, C programmers (especially Macintosh C programmers) start each of their global variables with the letter g (for global). Doing this will distinguish your local variables from your global variables and will make your code much easier to read.

Running power.π

Close listPrimes.π by selecting **Close Project** from the **Project** menu. When prompted for a project to open, go into the Projects folder, then into the power folder and open the project called power.π.

Run power.π by selecting **Run** from the **Project** menu. power will produce a console window similar to that found in Figure 7.12. This result was produced by three consecutive calls to the function DoPower(). The three calls calculated the result of the expressions 2^5, 3^4, and 5^3. Here's how the program works.

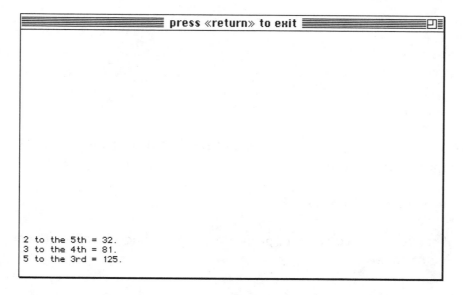

Figure 7.12 power.π running with gPrintExtraInfo set to FALSE.

Stepping Through the Source Code

```
#include <stdio.h>
```

Important _____

> power.c **starts off with the same** #include **as** nextPrime.c
> **and** listPrimes.c. **The** #include **includes the file** stdio.h,
> **which contains the definitions of the constants** TRUE **and**
> FALSE. **Chapter 9 covers the** #include **in detail.**

Next, the program declares the global variable gPrintExtraInfo:

```
int     gPrintExtraInfo;
```

The function `main()` declares an `int` to hold the results of its calls to `DoPower()`:

```
main()
{
    int power;
```

Next, `main()` initializes `gPrintExtraInfo` to `FALSE`. Later, we'll see what happens when we start `gPrintExtraInfo` with a value of `TRUE`:

```
    gPrintExtraInfo = FALSE;
```

If `gPrintExtraInfo` is `TRUE`, print a message telling us we're at the beginning of `main()`:

```
    if ( gPrintExtraInfo )
        printf( "---> Starting main()...\n" );
```

Next come three consecutive calls to `DoPower()`, paired with a `printf()` showing the value returned in the variable `power`. Notice that the & operator was used to pass `power`'s address to `DoPower()`.

```
    DoPower( &power, 2, 5 );
    printf( "2 to the 5th = %d.\n", power );

    DoPower( &power, 3, 4 );
    printf( "3 to the 4th = %d.\n", power );

    DoPower( &power, 5, 3 );
    printf( "5 to the 3rd = %d.\n", power );
```

Once again, check the value of `gPrintExtraInfo`. If it's `TRUE`, print a message telling us we're at the end of `main()`.

```
    if ( gPrintExtraInfo )
        printf( "---> Leaving main()...\n" );
}
```

The function `DoPower()` takes three parameters. `resultPtr` is a pointer to an `int`. We'll use that pointer to pass back the function results. `base` and `exponent` are value parameters that represent the—guess what?—base and exponent. When we're done, we'll pass the base raised to the exponent back to `main()`.

```
DoPower( int *resultPtr, int base, int exponent )
{
    int i, temp;
```

Once again, check the value of `gPrintExtraInfo`. If it's TRUE, print a message telling us we're at the beginning of `DoPower()`. Notice the tab character (represented by the characters \t) at the beginning of the `printf()` quoted string. You'll see what this was for when we set `gPrintExtraInfo` to TRUE.

```
    if ( gPrintExtraInfo )
        printf( "\t---> Starting DoPower()...\n" );
```

The following three lines calculate `base` raised to the `exponent` power, leaving the result in the `int` called `temp`.

```
    temp = base;
    for ( i = 1; i < exponent; i++ )
        temp *= base;
```

Once `temp` is calculated, it's copied into the variable pointed to by `resultPtr`.

```
    *resultPtr = temp;
```

Finally, if `gPrintExtraInfo` is TRUE, print a message telling us we're leaving `DoPower()`.

```
    if ( gPrintExtraInfo )
        printf( "\t---> Leaving DoPower()...\n" );
}
```

Figure 7.12 shows the console window when the program was run with `gPrintExtraInfo` set to `TRUE`. The results of three calls to `DoPower()` are displayed. No extra information is displayed. What do we mean by extra information? Take a look at the console window shown in Figure 7.13.

Notice that this run of the program gives you the same result as before, with a little information on the program's flow thrown in. As you can see, the program starts out in `main()`. Next, `DoPower()` is entered and exited. The tabs (remember those?) help show that we are in a subfunction. All the text starting on the left edge of the window was printed inside `main()`. All the text indented one tab was printed inside the function `DoPower()`.

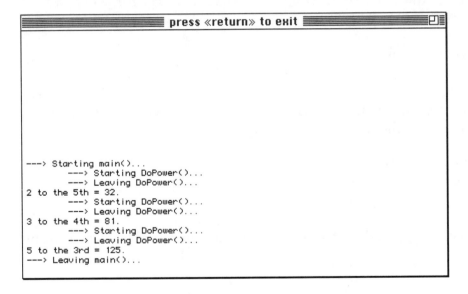

```
═══════════════ press «return» to exit ═══════════
---> Starting main()...
        ---> Starting DoPower()...
        ---> Leaving DoPower()...
2 to the 5th = 32.
        ---> Starting DoPower()...
        ---> Leaving DoPower()...
3 to the 4th = 81.
        ---> Starting DoPower()...
        ---> Leaving DoPower()...
5 to the 3rd = 125.
---> Leaving main()...
```

Figure 7.13 Running the program with `gPrintExtraInfo` set to `TRUE`.

This extra info was produced by changing the line:

```
gPrintExtraInfo = FALSE;
```

to read:

```
gPrintExtraInfo = TRUE;
```

inside the function `main()`. Try it yourself. As you start writing your own programs, you'll want to develop your own set of global variable tricks. For example, programmers who write programs that can run in color or black and white usually create a global called `gIsColor`. They set `gIsColor` to `TRUE` or `FALSE`, once they establish whether they are running in a color or black and white environment. In this way, a function buried deep inside the program doesn't have to figure out whether it's running in color or black and white. All it has to do is check the value of `gIsColor`.

What's Next?

Wow! You really are becoming a C programmer. In this chapter alone, you covered pointers, function parameters (both by-value and by-address), global variables, and function return values.

You're starting to develop a sense of just how powerful and sophisticated the C language really is. You've built an excellent foundation. Now you're ready to take off.

Our next chapter introduces the concept of data types. Throughout the book, you've been working with a single data type, the `int`. Chapter 8 will introduce the concept of arrays, strings, pointer arithmetic and typed function return values. Let's go.

Exercises

1) Predict the result of each of the following code fragments:

   a.
   ```
   AddOne( int *myVar )
   {
       (*myVar) ++;
   }

   main()
   {
       int num, i;

       num = 5;

       for ( i = 0; i < 20; i++ )
           AddOne( &num );

       printf( "Final value is %d.", num );
   }
   ```

   b.
   ```
   int gNumber;

   MultiplyIt( int *myVar )
   {
       (*myVar) *= gNumber;
   }
   ```

```
        main()
        {
            int i;
            gNumber = 1;

            for ( i = 0; i < 3; i++ )
                MultiplyIt( &gNumber );

            printf( "Final value is %d.", gNumber );
        }
```

c.
```
        int gNumber;

        MultiplyIt( int myVar )
        {
            return( myVar * gNumber );
        }

        main()
        {
            int i;
            gNumber = 1;

            for ( i = 0; i < 3; i++ )
                gNumber *= MultiplyIt( gNumber );

            printf( "Final value is %d.", gNumber );
        }
```

2) Modify power.c. Delete the first parameter of the function DoPower(), modifying the routine to return its result as a function return value instead.

3) Modify listPrimes.c. First of all, only print numbers that aren't prime. Next, print a special message next to those numbers that are multiples of 3.

Chapter 8

Variable Data Types

This Chapter
at a Glance

Other Data Types
Working With Characters
Characters and C
The ASCII Character Set
Opening ASCII.π
Running ASCII.π
Stepping Through the Source Code
Arrays
Why Use Arrays?
Opening dice.π
Running dice.π
Stepping Through the Source Code
Danger, Will Robinson!!!
Text Strings
A Text String in Memory
Opening name.π
Running name.π
Stepping Through the Source Code
The Input Buffer
On With the Program
The #define
#define Macros
Opening wordCount.π
Running wordCount.π
Stepping Through the Source Code
What's Next?
Exercises

OK, NOW WE'RE COOKING! YOU MAY NOW CONSIDER yourself a C Programmer, First Class. At this point, you've mastered all the basic elements of C programming. You know that C programs are made up of functions, one—and only one!—of which is named main(). Each of these functions uses keywords (such as if, for, and while), operators (such as =, ++, and *=), and variables to manipulate the program's data.

Sometimes you'll use a global variable to share data between several functions. At other times, you'll use a parameter to share a variable between a calling and a called function. Sometimes these parameters are passed by value, and sometimes pointers are used to pass a parameter by address.

In this chapter, we'll focus on **variable types**. Each of the variables in the previous example programs has been declared as an int. As you'll soon see, there are many other data types out there.

Other Data Types

So far, the focus has been on ints, which are extremely useful when it comes to working with numbers. You can add two ints together. You can check if an int is even, odd, or prime. There are a lot of things you can do with ints, as long as you limit yourself to whole numbers.

By the Way

> Just as a reminder, 527, 33, and -2 are all whole numbers, while 35.7, 92.1, and -1.2345 are not whole numbers.

What do you do if you want to work with nonwhole numbers, such as 3.14159 and -98.6? Check out this slice of code:

```
int myNum;

myNum = 3.5;
printf( "myNum = %d", myNum );
```

Since myNum is an int, the number 3.5 will be truncated before it is assigned to myNum. When this code ends, myNum will be left with a value of 3 and not 3.5 as intended. Do not despair. There is a special C data type, called float, which was created especially for working with nonwhole numbers.

By the Way

> In C, nonwhole numbers are also known as **floating-point** numbers, which is where the name float comes from. The name floating-point was coined by the ancient Peloponnesians, and refers to the decimal point found in all floating-point numbers.

If you want to work with floating-point numbers, use a variable of type float:

```
float myNum;

myNum = 3.5;
printf( "myNum = %f", myNum );
```

The first assignment statement leaves myNum with a value of 3.5 (pronounced three-point-five). This is important. When myNum was declared as an int (in the previous slice of code) the same assignment statement truncated the 3.5 to 3. In this case, myNum is declared as a float, and the value of 3.5 is not truncated.

Notice the use of the format specifier %f in the previous printf().
Use the %d when you are printing an int and the %f when printing a
float. Here's an interesting example:

```
main()
{
    float    myNum;

    myNum = 123.456;
    printf( "myNum = %f\n", myNum );
    printf( "myNum = %.2f\n", myNum );
    printf( "myNum = %.4f\n", myNum );
    printf( "myNum = %10.4f\n", myNum );
}
```

This example can be found on your samples disk in the folder
named float. float.π demonstrates four different examples of the %f
format specification. First, the variable myNum is declared as a float.
Next, myNum is initialized to a value of 123.456. Finally, the value of
myNum is printed using four different printf()s. The result is shown in
Figure 8.1.

The first printf() uses the format specifier %f in its default form.
Used in this way, %f prints the specified variable using an accuracy of
six decimal places. This means that six digits past the decimal point will
be printed, even if they are all zeros.

The second printf() uses the format specifier %.2f. The 2
following the decimal tells printf() that you are only interested in two
digits following the decimal point. This printf() yields the output
123.46. Notice that printf() rounded off the output to two digits past
the decimal.

The third printf() uses the format specifier %.4f. The output, as
you might expect, is 123.4560, showing four digits past the decimal
point.

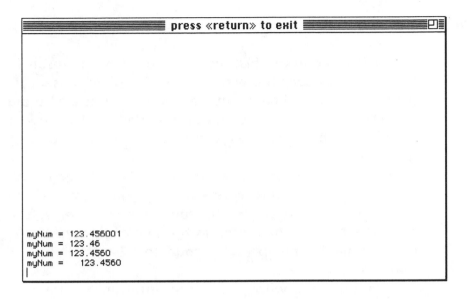

```
press «return» to exit
```

```
myNum = 123.456001
myNum = 123.46
myNum = 123.4560
myNum =    123.4560
```

Figure 8.1 float.π in action.

The final printf() uses the format specifier %10.4f. Once again, the 4 following the decimal point tells printf() that you are interested in four digits of accuracy past the decimal point. The 10 to the left of the decimal tells printf() to use a total of ten character spaces to print the result. Since the number 123.4560 would normally take up eight character spaces (don't forget a space for the decimal point), printf() will place an extra two spaces on the left side of the number to bring the total number of characters used to ten.

By the Way _____

As you can see in the first line of Figure 8.1, the result of the %f format specifier was 123.456001. As promised, six digits past the decimal point were printed. But where did the 001 come from at the end of the number? The answer has to do with the way your computer stores floating-point numbers.

The fractional part of a number (the number to the right of the decimal) is represented in binary just like any other integer. Instead of the sum of powers of 2, the fractional part is represented as the sum of powers of 1/2. For example, the number .75 is equal to 1/2 + 1/4. In binary, that's 11.

The problem with this representation is that it's impossible to represent some numbers (like 123.456) with complete accuracy. If you need a higher degree of accuracy, try using the type double instead of float. Be warned, however. doubles are slower than floats and take up twice as much room in memory. A float uses 4 bytes while a double uses 8 bytes.

The lesson here is, use floats if you want to work with floating-point numbers. Use doubles for extra accuracy, but beware the extra cost in memory usage and performance. Use ints for maximum speed, if you want to work exclusively with whole numbers, or if you want to truncate a result.

Working With Characters

The next data type on our list is called char. A char is 1 byte in length and, therefore, can hold 256 possible values.

By the Way _____

> Did you remember that a byte can hold one of 256 possible values? If not, now's the time to refer back to Chapter 3.

_____

This declaration:

```
char    c;
```

creates a signed `char`. As discussed in Chapter 3, signed variables can take on both positive and negative values. Since the variable `c` is signed, it can take on a value ranging from -128 to 127. This declaration:

```
unsigned char c;
```

creates an `unsigned char`, which can take on a value ranging from 0 to 255.

Why use a `char` instead of an `int`? Since `char`s take up only 1 byte, and `int`s take up 2 bytes, `char`s are naturally more memory efficient than `int`s. If you can live with the limited range of values available with a `char`, and you want to be as memory efficient as possible, use a `char` instead of an `int`.

Characters and C

There's an even better reason for using a `char` instead of an `int`. A `char` is the perfect size to hold a single alphabetic character. In C, an alphabetic character is a single character placed between a pair of single quotes (`'`). An alphabetic character can be used in the same way as a number, as in this example:

```
char    c;

c = 'a';
```

```
if ( c == 'a' )
    printf( "The variable c holds the character 'a'." );
```

As you can see, the character 'a' is used in both an assignment statement and an if statement, just as if it were a number or a variable.

The ASCII Character Set

In C, a char takes up a single byte and can hold a value from -128 to 127. Now, how can a char hold a numerical value, as well as a character value, such as 'a' or '+'? The answer lies with the **ASCII character set.**

By the Way

> ASCII stands for the American Standard Code for Information Interchange.

The ASCII character set is a set of 128 standard characters, featuring the 26 lower-case letters, the 26 upper-case letters, the ten numerical digits, and an assortment of other exciting characters, such as '}' and '='. Each of these characters corresponds exactly to a value between 0 and 127. The ASCII character set ignores the values between -128 and -1.

For example, the character 'a' has an ASCII value of 97. When a C compiler sees the character 'a' in a piece of source code, it substitutes the value 97. Each of the values from 0 to 127 is interchangeable with a character from the ASCII character set.

Opening ASCII.π

Here's a program that will make the ASCII character set easier to understand. First, start up THIN C. When prompted for a project to open, go into the Projects folder, then into the ASCII subfolder, and open the project ASCII.π. The ASCII.π project window should appear on your screen.

Running ASCII.π

Before we step through the project source code, let's take it for a spin. Select **Run** from the **Project** menu. A console window similar to the one in Figure 8.2 should appear. The first line of output shows the characters corresponding to the ASCII values from 32 to 47. Why start with 32? As it turns out, the ASCII characters between 0 and 31 are nonprintable characters like the backspace (ASCII 8) or the carriage return (ASCII 13). A table of the nonprintable ASCII characters is presented later on.

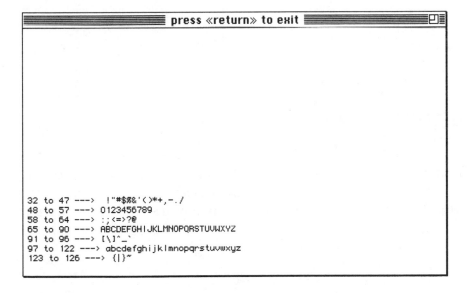

Figure 8.2 ASCII.π in action.

Notice that ASCII character 32 is a space, also known as ' '. ASCII character 33 is '!'. ASCII character 47 is '/'. This presents some interesting coding possibilities. For example, this code is perfectly legitimate:

```
int sumOfChars;

sumOfChars = '!' + '/';
```

What a strange piece of code! Though you will probably never do anything like this, try to predict the value of the variable sumOfChars after the assignment statement. And the answer is...

The character '!' has a value of 33 and the character '/' has a value of 47. Therefore, sumOfChars will be left with a value of 80 following the assignment statement. C allows you to represent any number between 0 and 127 in two different ways: as an ASCII character or as a number. Let's get back to the program ASCII.π.

The second line in Figure 8.2 shows the ASCII characters from 48 through 57. As you can see, these ten characters represent the digits 0 through 9. Here's a little piece of code that converts an ASCII digit to its numerical counterpart:

```
char    digit;
int convertedDigit;

digit = '3';

convertedDigit = digit - '0';
```

This code starts with a char named digit, initialized to hold the ASCII character '3'. The character '3' has a numerical value of 51. The next line of code subtracts the ASCII character '0' from digit. Since the character '0' has a numerical value of 48, and digit started with a numerical value of 51, convertedDigit ends up with a value of 51 - 48, also known as 3. Isn't that interesting?

Important _____

> Subtracting '0' from any ASCII digit yields that digit's numerical counterpart. Remember this rule! It will come in handy if you ever want to convert a text string representation of a number to that number's numerical value.

Let's get back to ASCII.π. The next line of the console window shown in Figure 8.2 shows the ASCII characters with values ranging from 58 to 64. The following line is pretty interesting. It shows the range of ASCII characters from 65 to 90. Notice anything familiar about these characters? They represent the complete, upper-case alphabet. Reserve a spot in the back of your brain and remember this: *The ASCII character 'A' has a numerical value of 65.*

The next line in Figure 8.2 lists ASCII characters with values from 91 through 96. The following line lists the ASCII characters with values ranging from 97 through 122. These 26 characters represent the complete lower-case alphabet.

Important _____

> Another fact worth remembering: to convert an upper-case ASCII character to its lower-case equivalent, add 32 to the upper-case value. For example, add 32 to 'E' and you get 101, which is equivalent to the ASCII character 'e'.
>
> To convert a lower-case character to its upper-case equivalent, subtract 32 from the lower-case character.

The final line in Figure 8.2 lists the ASCII characters from 123 to 126. As you'll see in the following tech block, the ASCII character with a value of 127 is another nonprintable character.

Important _____

> Figure 8.3 shows a table of "unprintables." The first column
> shows the ASCII code. The comment column shows the
> keyboard equivalent for that code along with any
> appropriate comments. The characters with comments by
> them are probably the only unprintables you'll ever make
> use of.

```
ASCII
Code                    Comment

  0    Used to terminate text strings (Explained later in chapter)
  1    Control-A
  2    Control-B
  3    Control-C
  4    Control-D  (End of file mark, Chapter 10)
  5    Control-E
  6    Control-F
  7    Control-G  (Beep character - Try it!)
  8    Control-H  (Backspace)
  9    Control-I  (Tab)
 10    Control-J  (Line feed)
 11    Control-K  (Vertical tab)
 12    Control-L  (Form-feed)
 13    Control-M  (Carriage return, no line feed)
 14    Control-N
 15    Control-O
 16    Control-P
 17    Control-Q
 18    Control-R
 19    Control-S
 20    Control-T
 21    Control-U
 22    Control-V
 23    Control-W
 24    Control-X
 25    Control-Y
 26    Control-Z
 27    Control-[  (Escape character)
 28    Control-|
 29    Control-]
 30    Control-^
 31    Control-_
127    del
```

Figure 8.3   The ASCII unprintables.

Stepping Through the Source Code

Before we move on to our next topic, let's take a look at the source code that generated the ASCII character listing in Figure 8.2. If you haven't already done so, exit the program and return to THIN C by hitting a carriage return. Once back in THIN C, the project window, labeled ASCII.π, should reappear. Double-click on the name ASCII.c to open the source code window.

The function PrintChars() takes two char parameters, low and high. PrintChars() prints a single line in the console window, containing the ASCII characters from low to high.

```
PrintChars( char low, char high )
{
    unsigned char   c;

    printf( "%d to %d ---> ", low, high );
```

First, PrintChars() uses printf() to print a label for the current line, showing the range of ASCII characters to follow.

```
    for ( c = low; c <= high; c++ )
        printf( "%c", c );
```

Next, a for loop is used to step through each of the ASCII characters, from low to high, using printf() to print each of the characters next to each other on the same line. The printf() bears closer inspection. Notice the use of %c (instead of our usual %d) to tell printf() to print a single ASCII character.

```
    printf( "\n" );
}
```

Once the line is printed, a single new line is printed, moving the cursor to the beginning of the next line in the console window. Thus ends PrintChars().

```
main()
{
    PrintChars( 32, 47 );
    PrintChars( 48, 57 );
    PrintChars( 58, 64 );
    PrintChars( 65, 90 );
    PrintChars( 91, 96 );
    PrintChars( 97, 122 );
    PrintChars( 123, 126 );
}
```

main() is pretty straightforward. It consists of seven consecutive calls to PrintChars(), printing all of the ASCII characters from 32 to 126.

The char data type is extremely useful to C programmers (such as yourself). The next two topics, arrays and text strings, will show you why. As you read through these two topics, keep the concept of ASCII characters in the back of your mind. As you reach the end of the section on text strings, you'll see an important relationship develop between all three topics.

Arrays

The next topic for discussion is **arrays**. An array turns a single variable into a list of variables. For example, this declaration:

```
int myNumber[ 3 ];
```

creates three separate int variables, referred to in your program as myNumber[0], myNumber[1], and myNumber[2]. Each of these variables is known as an **array element**. The number between the brackets ([and] are known as brackets) is called an **index**. In this declaration:

```
char    myChar[ 20 ];
```

the name of the array is `myChar`. This declaration will create an array of type `char` with a **dimension** of 20. The dimension of an array is the array's number of elements. The array elements will have **indices** (indices is the plural of index) that run from 0 to 19.

Important _____

> In C, array indices always run from 0 to one less than the array's dimension.

This slice of code first declares an array of 100 `int`s, then assigns each `int` a value of 0:

```
int myNumber[ 100 ], i;

for ( i=0; i<100; i++ )
    myNumber[ i ] = 0;
```

You could have accomplished the same thing by declaring 100 individual `int`s, then initializing each individual `int`. Here's what that code might look like:

```
int myNumber0, myNumber1, ......., myNumber99;

myNumber0 = 0;
myNumber1 = 0;
       .
       .
       .
myNumber99 = 0;
```

It would take 100 lines of code just to initialize these variables! By using an array, we've accomplished the same thing in just a few lines of code. Look at this code fragment:

```
sum = 0;
for ( i=0; i<100; i++ )
    sum += myNumber[ i ];

printf( "The sum of the 100 numbers is %d.", sum );
```

This code adds together the value of all 100 elements of the array myNumber.

Important _____

> In this example, the for loop is used to **step through** an array, performing some operation on each of the array's elements. You'll use this technique frequently in your own C programs.

Why Use Arrays?

Programmers would be lost without arrays. Arrays allow you to keep lists of things. For example, if you need to maintain a list of 50 employee numbers, declare an array of 50 ints. You can declare an array using any C type. For example, this code:

```
float    salaries[ 50 ];
```

declares an array of 50 floating-point numbers. This might be useful for maintaining a list of employee salaries.

Use an array when you want to maintain a list of related data. Here's an example.

Opening dice.π

Select **Close Project** from the **Project** menu to close ASCII.π. When prompted for a new project to open, go back up to the Projects folder, into the dice subfolder, and open the project named dice.π. dice.π simulates the rolling of a pair of dice. After each roll, the program adds the two dice together, keeping track of the total. It rolls the dice 1,000 times, then reports on the results. Give it a try!

Running dice.π

Run dice.π by selecting **Run** from the **Project** menu. A console window should appear, similar to the one in Figure 8.4. Take a look at the output—it's pretty interesting. The first column lists all the possible totals of two dice. Since the lowest possible roll of a pair of six-sided dice is 1 and 1, the first entry in the column is 2. The column counts all the way up to 12, the highest possible roll (achieved by a roll of 6 and 6).

The number in parentheses is the total number of rolls (out of 1,000 rolls) that matched that row's number. For example, the first row describes the dice rolls that total 2. In this run, the program rolled 24 2s. Finally, the program prints an x for every ten of these rolls. Since 24 2s were rolled, two x's were printed at the end of the 2s' row. Since 180 7s were rolled, 18 x's were printed at the end of the 7s' row.

By the Way

Recognize the curve depicted by the x's in Figure 8.4? The curve represents a "normal" probability distribution, also known as a **bell curve**. According to the curve, you are about 7.5 times more likely to roll a 7 as you are to roll a 2. Want to know why? Check out a book on probability and statistics.

```
┌══════════════ press «return» to exit ══════════════ ⊡ ▤
│
│
│
│
│
│
│
│
│
│  2 ( 24):   xx
│  3 ( 51):   xxxxx
│  4 ( 96):   xxxxxxxxx
│  5 ( 90):   xxxxxxxxx
│  6 (156):   xxxxxxxxxxxxxxx
│  7 (180):   xxxxxxxxxxxxxxxxxx
│  8 (130):   xxxxxxxxxxxxx
│  9 (105):   xxxxxxxxxx
│ 10 ( 83):   xxxxxxxx
│ 11 ( 63):   xxxxxx
│ 12 ( 22):   xx
│
```

Figure 8.4   dice.π in action.

Let's take a look at the source code that makes this possible.

Stepping Through the Source Code

If you haven't done so already, type a carriage return to return to THIN C. Double-click on the name dice.c in the project window to bring up the dice.c source code window. This code walk-through will start with main(), found at the bottom of the source code file.

main() declares an array of ints named rolls. rolls will keep track of the 11 possible types of dice rolls. Why 11? Count the rows in the console window in Figure 8.4. There's a row for 2, 3, 4, all the way up to 12. That's a total of 11 rows. rolls[0] will keep the total number of 2s rolled. rolls[1] will keep the total number of 3s rolled. rolls[10] will keep the total number of 12s rolled. You get the idea. The index will always be off by two from the number being tracked.

```
main()
{
    int      rolls[ 11 ], twoDice, i;

    srand( clock() );
```

The function `srand()` is part of the ANSI Standard Library. It initializes a random number generator, using a seed provided by another ANSI function, `clock()`. Once the random number is initialized, another function, `rand()`, will return an `int` with a random value.

Why random numbers? Sometimes you want to add an element of unpredictability to your program. For example, in our program, we want to roll a pair of dice again and again. The program would be pretty boring if it rolled the same numbers again and again. By using a random number generator, we can generate a random number between 1 and 6, thus simulating the roll of a single die! Let's get back to `main()`.

```
    for ( i=0; i<11; i++ )
        rolls[ i ] = 0;
```

`main()`'s next step is to initialize each of the elements of the array `rolls` to 0. This is appropriate since no rolls of any kind have taken place yet.

```
    for ( i=1; i <= 1000; i++ )
    {
        twoDice = RollOne() + RollOne();
        ++ rolls[ twoDice - 2 ];
    }
```

Now comes Miller time! This `for` loop rolls the dice 1,000 times. As you'll see, the function `RollOne()` returns a random number between 1 and 6, simulating the roll of a single die. By calling it twice, then storing the sum of the two rolls in the variable `twoDice`, we've simulated the roll of two dice.

The next line is pretty tricky, so hang on. At this point, the variable twoDice holds a value between 2 and 12, the total of two individual dice rolls. By subtracting 2 from twoDice, we get a number between 0 and 10. The numbers 0 and 10 are important, because they correspond to the range of indices of the array rolls. Take a look at the tricky line of code again:

```
++ rolls[ twoDice - 2 ];
```

This line of code increments the array element corresponding to the rolled dice. For example, if the total of the two dice was 7, we'd increment rolls[5]. If the total was 2 (the lowest possible), we'd increment rolls[0]. Get it? If not, go back and read through this again. If you still feel stymied (and it's OK if you do) find a C buddy to help you through this. It is important that you get this concept. Be patient. OK, let's get back to main().

```
    PrintRolls( rolls );
}
```

The last thing main() does before it exits is call the function PrintRolls(), passing it the array rolls as a parameter. PrintRolls() is responsible for creating the output that appears in the console window.

Important

Notice that only the array name was passed to PrintRolls(), without the use of brackets. That's the proper way to pass an array as a parameter.

```
RollOne()
{
    long    rawResult;
    int roll;

    rawResult = rand();
```

The function `RollOne()` uses the ANSI random number generator to return a number between 1 and 6 to the calling function. `Rand()` returns a random value between 0 and 32,767. This result is placed in the `long` variable `rawResult`. `long`s are 4-bytes long, and can hold much larger values than `int`s.

```
    roll = (rawResult * 6) / 32768;
```

This line of code reduces `rawResult` to a value between 0 and 5, assigning that value to the variable `roll`.

```
    return( roll + 1 );
}
```

Finally, 1 is added to `roll`, and a value between 1 and 6 is returned.

By the Way _____

> If you had trouble following the mathematics involved in the function `RollOne()`, you are not alone. This function is tricky. Unless you plan on writing some random number-generating code right off the bat, I'd ignore this function and move on to the next one. The important thing to remember is that `RollOne()` returns a random number between 1 and 6.

```
PrintRolls( int rolls[] )
{
    int      i;
```

The function `PrintRolls()` takes the name of an array of `int`s as a parameter. The pair of brackets following the array name (`rolls[]`) distinguishes `rolls` as the name of an array of `int`s, as opposed to a plain old `int`.

By the Way

> The notation:
>
> ```
> int    myArray[]
> ```
>
> is identical to the notation:
>
> ```
> int    *myArray
> ```
>
> Both of these notations describe a pointer to an `int`. C treats array names as if they were pointers. Here's how this works:
>
> When the compiler allocates the memory for an array, it allocates a single, continuous block of memory. For example, this declaration:
>
> ```
> int    myArray[ 20 ];
> ```
>
> creates a block of 40 bytes (enough memory for 20 2-byte `int`s). At the same time, the compiler also creates a separate 4-byte block, called the **parent pointer**. The compiler places the address of the first byte of the 40-byte block in this parent pointer. This arrangement is shown in Figure 8.5.

By the Way _____

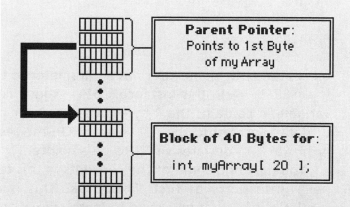

Figure 8.5   Memory diagram showing the allocation for a 20 `int` array, with its parent pointer.

Whenever the compiler wants to access the elements of an array, it starts with the address in the parent pointer, then uses the index being accessed to calculate the appropriate offset from the beginning of the array's data block. For example, the following array declaration:

```
int   myArray[ 20 ];
```

causes the compiler to allocate a 40-byte block for `myArray`'s `int`s. Now suppose your program referenced `myArray[ 5 ]`. The compiler would look in its master variable table to find the address associated with the variable `myArray`. This address is the parent pointer. Next, the compiler would use the index being referenced to calculate an offset. In this case, the compiler calculates that `myArray[ 5 ]` occupies the eleventh and twelfth bytes in the 40-byte block allocated to `myArray`. Do you see how this works?

In `main()`, the line:

```
PrintRolls( rolls );
```

passes the array name `rolls` as a parameter to the function `PrintRolls()`. In this instance, `rolls` is just like a pointer variable. It contains the 4-byte parent pointer to the block of data allocated to the `rolls` array. On the receiving end, `PrintRolls()` declares `rolls` to be a pointer (which it is).

You may find some of the concepts in this tech block to be a little fuzzy at first. That's OK. This is one of the subtleties of C that you have to learn via experimentation. As you start writing your own programs, these subtleties will become clearer.

At this point, you might want to take a short break. You've earned it! Just jam a bookmark in here and go outside and play catch or something. I'll still be here when you get back.

Let's get back to our program. Before the previous tech block, we had just started looking at `PrintRolls()`.

```
for ( i=0; i<11; i++ )
{
    printf( "%2d (%3d):  ", i+2, rolls[ i ] );
    PrintX( rolls[ i ] / 10 );
    printf( "\n" );
}
}
```

The `for` loop steps through each of `rolls`' 11 elements. For each element, `PrintRolls()` first prints the roll number and, in parentheses, the number of times (out of 1,000) that roll occurred. Next, `PrintX()` is called to print a single `x` for every ten rolls that occurred. Finally, a carriage return is printed, preparing the console window for the next roll.

```
PrintX( int howMany )
{
    int i;

    for ( i=0; i<howMany; i++ )
        printf( "x" );
}
```

`PrintX` is pretty straightforward. It uses a `for` loop to print the number of x's specified by the parameter `howMany`.

Danger, Will Robinson!!!

Before we move on to our next topic, there is one danger worth discussing at this point. See if you can spot the potential hazard in this piece of code:

```
int myInts[ 3 ];

for ( i=0; i<20; i++ )
    myInts[ i ] = 0;
```

Yikes! The array `myInts` consists of exactly three array elements, yet the `for` loop tries to initialize 20 elements. This is called **exceeding the bounds** of your array. Because C is such an informal language, it will let you "get away" with this kind of source code. To you, that means THIN C will compile this code without complaint. Your problems will start as soon as the program tries to initialize the fourth array element, which was never allocated.

What will happen? The safest thing to say is that the results will be unpredictable. The problem is, the program is trying to assign a value of 0 to a block of memory that it doesn't necessarily own. Anything could happen. The program would most likely crash, which means it stops behaving in a rational manner. I've seen some cases where the computer actually leaps off the desk, hops across the floor, and jumps face first into the trash can.

Well, OK, not really. But odd things will happen if you don't keep your array references in bounds.

Warning

> As you code, be aware of the limitations of your variables. For example, a `char` is limited to values from -128 to 127. Don't try to assign a value such as 536 to a `char`. Don't reference `myArray[ 27 ]` if you declared `myArray` with only ten elements. Be careful!

Text Strings

The first C program in this book made use of a text string:

```
printf( "Hello, world!" );
```

This section will teach you how to use text strings like `"Hello, world!"` in your own programs. It will teach you how these strings are stored in memory and how to create your own strings from scratch.

A Text String in Memory

The text string `"Hello, world!"` exists in memory as a sequence of 14 bytes (Figure 8.6). The first 13 bytes consist of the 13 ASCII characters in `"Hello, World!"`. The final byte has value of 0, not to be confused with the ASCII character `'0'`. The 0 is what makes this string a C string. Every C string ends with a byte having a value of 0. The 0 identifies the end of the string.

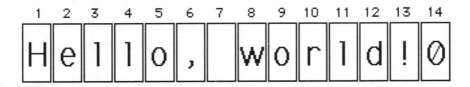

Figure 8.6   The `"Hello, world!"` text string.

When you use a quoted string like `"Hello, world!"` in your code, the compiler creates the string for you. This type of string is called a **string constant**. When you use a string constant in your code, the detail work is done for you automatically. In this example:

```
printf( "Hello, world!" );
```

the 14 bytes needed to represent the string in memory are allocated automatically. The 0 is placed in the fourteenth byte, automatically. You don't have to worry about these details when you use a string constant.

String constants are great, but they are not always appropriate. For example, suppose you want to read in somebody's name, then pass the name on to `printf()` to display in the console window. Since you won't be able to predict the name that will be typed in, you can't predefine the name as a string constant. Here's an example.

Opening name.π

If you haven't already, exit dice.π by typing a carriage return. Next, close dice.π by selecting **Close Project** from THIN C's **Project** menu. When prompted for a new project to open, go up to the Projects folder, then into the name folder and open the project named name.π.

name.π will ask you to type your first name on the keyboard. Once you've typed your first name, the program will use your name to create a custom welcome message. Then, name.π will tell you how many characters long your name is. How useful!

Running name.π

To run name.π, select **Run** from the **Project** menu. A console window will appear, prompting you for your first name, like this:

```
Type your first name, please:
```

Type your first name, then hit a carriage return. When I did, I saw the output shown in Figure 8.7. Let's take a look at the source code that generated this output.

Stepping Through the Source Code

At the heart of name.π is a new Standard Library function called scanf(). scanf() uses the same format specifiers as printf() to read text in from the keyboard. This code will read in an int:

```
int myInt;

scanf( "%d", &myInt );
```

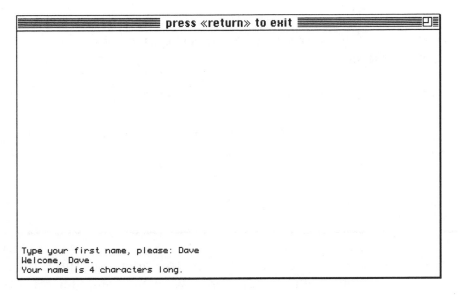

Figure 8.7   name.π in action.

The %d tells scanf() to read in an int. Notice the use of the & before the variable myInt. This passes myInt's address to scanf(), allowing scanf() to change myInt's value. To read in a float, use code like:

```
float    myFloat;

scanf( "%f", &myFloat );
```

To read in a text string, you have to first declare a variable to place the text characters in. name.π uses an array of characters for this purpose:

```
main()
{
    char    name[ 50 ];
```

The array `name` is big enough to hold a 49-byte text string. When you allocate space for a text string, remember to save 1 byte for the 0 that terminates the string.

```
printf( "Type your first name, please: " );
```

The program starts by printing a **prompt**. A prompt is a text string that lets the user know the program is waiting for input.

The Input Buffer

Before we get to the `scanf()` call, it helps to understand how the computer handles input from the keyboard. When the computer starts running your program, it automatically creates a big array of `chars` for the sole purpose of storing keyboard input to your program. This array is known as your program's **input buffer**. The input buffer is carriage-return based. Every time you hit a carriage return, all the characters typed since the last carriage return are appended to the current input buffer.

When your program starts, the input buffer is empty. If you type this line from your keyboard:

```
123 abcd
```

followed by a carriage return, the input buffer will look like Figure 8.8. The computer keeps track of the current end of the input buffer. The space character between the `'123'` and the `'abcd'` has an ASCII value of 32. Notice that the carriage return was actually placed in the input buffer. The carriage return character has an ASCII value of 10 and is equivalent to the character `'\n'`.

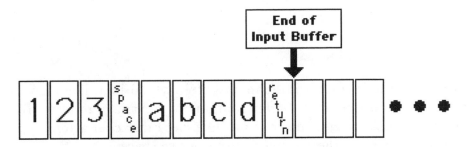

Figure 8.8   A snapshot of the input buffer.

Given the input buffer shown in Figure 8.8, suppose your program called scanf(), like this:

```
scanf( "%d", &myInt );
```

scanf() starts at the beginning of the input buffer and reads a character at a time until it hits one of the nonprintables; that is, a carriage return, tab, space, or a 0, or until it hits the end of the buffer. After the scanf(), the input buffer looks like Figure 8.9. Notice that the characters passed on to scanf() were removed from the input buffer and that the rest of the characters slid over to the beginning of the buffer. scanf() took the characters '1', '2', and '3' and converted them to the integer 123, placing 123 in the variable myInt.

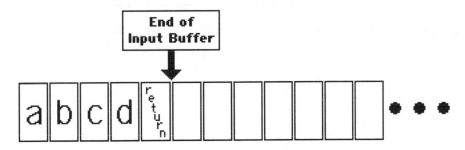

Figure 8.9   A second snapshot of the input buffer.

If you then typed the line:

`3.5 Dave`

followed by a carriage return, the input buffer would look like Figure 8.10. At this point the input buffer contains two carriage returns. To the input buffer, a carriage return is just like any other char-acter. To a function like `scanf()`, the carriage return is white space.

By the Way _____

> If you forgot what white space is, now would be a good time to turn back to Chapter 5, where white space was first described.

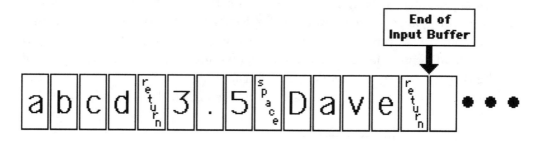

Figure 8.10   A third snapshot of the input buffer.

On With the Program

Before we started our discussion on the input buffer, main() had just called printf() to prompt the user for his or her first name:

```
printf( "Type your first name, please: " );
```

Next, we called scanf() to read the first name from the input buffer:

```
scanf( "%s", name );
```

Since the program just started, the input buffer is empty. scanf() will wait until characters appear in the input buffer, which will happen as soon as you type some characters and hit a carriage return. Type your first name and hit a carriage return.

By the Way ──

> scanf() will ignore white space characters in the input buffer. For example, if you type a few spaces and tabs, then hit a carriage return, scanf() will still sit there, waiting for some real input. Try it!

Once you type in your name, scanf() will copy the characters, a byte at a time, into the array of chars pointed to by name. Remember, because name was declared as an array, name itself refers to the array's parent pointer (Figure 8.5). name points to the first of the 50 bytes allocated for the array.

If you type in the name `Dave`, `scanf()` will place the four characters `'D'`, `'a'`, `'v'`, and `'e'` in the first four of the 50 bytes allocated for the array. Next, `scanf()` will set the fifth byte to a value of 0 to terminate the string properly (Figure 8.11). Since the string is properly terminated by the 0 in `name[ 4 ]`, we don't really care about the value of the bytes `name[ 5 ]` through `name[ 49 ]`.

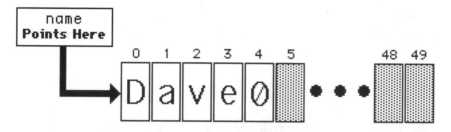

Figure 8.11   The array `name[ 50 ]` after the string `"Dave"` is copied to it. Notice that `name[ 4 ]` has a value of 0.

```
printf( "Welcome, %s.\n", name );
```

This line passes `name` on to `printf()` for use in a special welcome message. The `%s` tells `printf()` to print a 0 terminated string inside the quoted string. Since `name` is a 0 terminated string, `printf()` knows to stop printing after the fourth byte in the string.

Warning

If `name[ 4 ]` didn't contain a 0, the string wouldn't be properly terminated. Passing a nonterminated string to `printf()` is a sure way to confuse `printf()`. `printf()` will step through memory one byte at a time, printing a byte and looking for a 0. It will keep printing bytes until it happens to encounter a byte set to 0. Remember to terminate your strings!

```
    printf( "Your name is %d characters long.",
            strlen( name ) );
}
```

The next line of the program calls another Standard Library function, called `strlen()`. `strlen()` takes a pointer as a parameter and returns the length, in bytes, of the string pointed to by the parameter. `strlen()` depends on the string being 0 terminated. Notice that C allows you to call a function right in the middle of a parameter list. `printf()` will call `strlen()` and use the length returned as its parameter.

Our last program for this chapter demonstrates a few more character-handling techniques, a new Standard Library function, and an invaluable programmer's tool, the #define.

The #define

The #define (pronounced *pound-define*) tells the compiler to substitute one piece of text for another throughout your source code. For example, this statement:

```
#define MAX_PLAYERS 6
```

tells the compiler to substitute the character "6" every time it finds the text "MAX_PLAYERS" in the source code. C compilers perform two passes on your code. During the first pass, the compiler builds a list of #defines and performs all of its #define substitutions. During the second pass, the compiler compiles the #defined source code.

Important _____

> It's important to note that the #define mechanism doesn't change your original source code. The C compiler first makes a copy of your source code, performs the #defines on this copy, then compiles the #defined copy.

Here's an example of a #define in action:

```
#define MAX_ARRAY_SIZE   100

main()
{
    char    myArray[ MAX_ARRAY_SIZE ];
    int     i;

    for ( i=0; i<MAX_ARRAY_SIZE; i++ )
        myArray[ i ] = 0;
}
```

The #define at the beginning of this example substitutes "100" for "MAX_ARRAY_SIZE" for the duration of the code. In this example, the substitution will be done twice. The result of the compiler's first pass looks like this:

```
main()
{
    char    myArray[ 100 ];
    int     i;

    for ( i=0; i<100; i++ )
        myArray[ i ] = 0;
}
```

If you use #defines effectively, you'll build more flexible code. In the previous example, you can change the size of the array by modifying one line of code, the #define. If your program is designed correctly, you should be able to change the line to:

```
#define MAX_ARRAY_SIZE   200
```

then recompile your code, and your program should work properly. A good sign that you are using #defines properly is an absence of constants in your code. In the above example, the constant 100 was replaced by MAX_ARRAY_SIZE.

As you'll see in our next program, you can put practically anything, even source code, into a #define. Take a look:

```
#define PRINT_RETURN        printf( "\n" );
```

While not particularly recommended, this #define will work just fine, substituting the statement:

```
printf( "\n" );
```

for every occurrence of the text PRINT_RETURN in your source code. You can base one #define on a previous #define:

```
#define SIDE_LENGTH 5
#define AREA         SIDE_LENGTH * SIDE_LENGTH
```

Important

The substitution for a particular #define is only made from the point of the #define through the end of the file. This means that a #define won't have any effect on the source code that occurs before it in the file.

#define Macros

You can create a #define that takes one or more arguments. These #defines are known as **macros**. Here's an example:

```
#define SQUARE( a ) ((a) * (a))
```

This macro takes a single argument. The argument can be any C expression. If you called the macro like this:

```
myInt = SQUARE( myInt + 1 );
```

the compiler would use its first pass to turn the line into this:

```
myInt = (( myInt + 1 ) * ( myInt + 1 ));
```

Notice the usefulness of the parentheses in the macro. If the macro were defined like this:

```
#define SQUARE( a ) a * a
```

the compiler would have produced:

```
myInt = myInt + 1 * myInt + 1;
```

which is not what we wanted. The only multiplication that gets performed by this statement is 1 * myInt, because the * operator has a higher precedence than the + operator.

Let's move on to our final example.

Opening wordCount.π

If you haven't already, exit name.π by typing a carriage return. Close name.π by selecting **Close Project** from the **Project** menu. When prompted for a new project to open, move up to the Projects folder, down into the wordCount folder, and open the project named wordCount.π. Open the source code file wordCount.c by double-clicking on its name in the project window. Take a few minutes to look through the source code. Try to figure out what this program does.

Running wordCount.π

wordCount.π prompts you to type in a line of text, saving the line in an array of chars. The program then steps through the saved line of text, counting the number of words in the text. Run wordCount.π by selecting **Run** from the **Project** menu. When prompted, type in a line of text, followed by a carriage return. wordCount.π will then tell you how many words you typed. A sample is shown in Figure 8.12. wordCount.π will ignore any tabs and spaces in your text. Feel free to experiment.

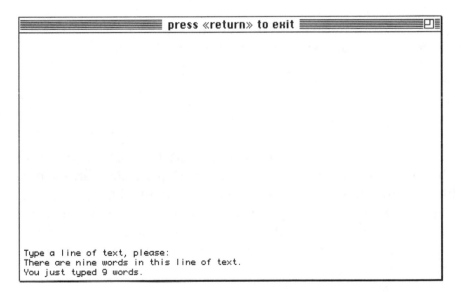

Figure 8.12 wordCount.π in action.

Stepping Through the Source Code

```
#include <stdio.h>
```

Important _____

> wordCount.c **starts off with the same** #include **as**
> nextPrime.c, listPrimes.c, **and** power.c. **The** #include
> **includes the file** stdio.h, **which contains the definitions of**
> **the constants** TRUE **and** FALSE. **Chapter 9 covers the**
> #include **in detail.**

Next, wordCount.π features a series of #defines.

```
#define MAX_LINE_LENGTH 200
```

MAX_LINE_LENGTH defines the size of the array of chars that are
used to buffer the line of text typed in response to the prompt.

```
#define C_RETURN       '\n'
#define C_TAB          '\t'
#define C_SPACE        ' '
```

C_RETURN, C_TAB, and C_SPACE represent their corresponding
ASCII characters. Their main purpose is to make the code a little more
Englishlike and, therefore, a little easier to read. The C_ at the
beginning of each of these #defines stands for character, and is used to
group these three #defines together. The C_ will have no effect on the
code, but it makes it clear to anyone reviewing the code that these three
#defines belong together.

```
main()
{
    char    line[ MAX_LINE_LENGTH ], *charPtr, inWord;
    int     numWords;
```

The array `line` is used to store the typed in text. `charPtr` is a pointer to a `char` that plays an important role in stepping through the text. You'll see how it works in a minute. `inWord` takes on a value of either `TRUE` or `FALSE`. We'll use it as we step through the line of characters to indicate whether we are currently in the middle of a word or in the middle of some white space. Finally, `numWords` keeps track of the number of words in the line of text.

```
printf( "Type a line of text, please:\n" );
```

For starters, use `printf()` to prompt for a line of text.

```
charPtr = line;
```

Next, copy the address in `line` to the pointer `charPtr`. Since `line` was declared as an array, it contains a pointer to the first of the 200 bytes allocated for the array. By copying this address into `charPtr`, `charPtr` also points to the first byte of the array.

```
numWords = 0;
inWord = FALSE;
```

`numWords` is initialized to 0 and `inWord` is set to `FALSE`.

```
while ( ( *charPtr = getchar() ) != C_RETURN )
{
```

The `while` loop is used to read in characters, one at a time, until a carriage return is typed. The function `getchar()` returns the next character from the input buffer. The character is placed into the byte pointed to by `charPtr`, which happens to be the first byte in the `line` array, also known as `line[ 0 ]`.

By the Way _____

> As was the case with `scanf()`, when a character is read from the input buffer, the character is removed and the rest of the characters in the buffer move over to take the place of the removed character.

```
if ( (*charPtr != C_TAB) && (*charPtr != C_SPACE) )
{
    if ( ! inWord )
    {
        inWord = TRUE;
        numWords++;
    }
}
```

If the character read in is not a tab and is not a space, then it must be part of a word. If we aren't already in a word, set `inWord` to `TRUE`, indicating that we are now in the middle of a word. Also, increment `numWords`, the count of words in the line so far.

```
else
    inWord = FALSE;
```

If the character was not part of a word, set `inWord` to `FALSE`.

```
    charPtr++;
}
```

Next, increment `charPtr`, making it point to the next byte in memory. If `charPtr` points to `line[ 0 ]`, incrementing it will make it point to `line[ 1 ]`.

```
printf( "You just typed %d word", numWords );
```

The loop exits when a carriage return is encountered. Once this happens, the program uses `printf()` to tell you how many words it found in the text.

```
if ( ( numWords > 1 ) || ( numWords == 0 ) )
    printf( "s." );
else
    printf( "." );
}
```

Important

This technique is known as **pointer arithmetic**. To understand why pointer arithmetic works, it's important to understand that a pointer is just a 4-byte number that represents a memory address. When you add one to a pointer, you are making the pointer point to the next byte in memory. While the compiler won't allow you to divide a pointer by 2, or multiply a pointer by itself, it will allow you to use the ++, --, +, and - operators to move a pointer forward and backward in memory.

Incrementing `charPtr` works because `line` is an array of `chars`, and a `char` takes up a single byte. Incrementing the pointer by 1 moves it from one byte to the next. If the array consisted of `ints`, you'd have to bump the pointer by 2 to get it to the next array element.

This last bit of code shows attention to detail, something very important in a good program. Notice that the previous `printf()` ended with the characters "`word`". If the program found either no words or more than one word, the printed sentence should read:

```
You just typed 0 words.
```

or

```
You just typed 2 words.
```

If the program found exactly one word, the sentence should read:

```
You just typed 1 word.
```

The last `if` statement makes sure the correct sentence ending is printed.

What's Next?

Congratulations! You've made it through one of the longest chapters in the book. You've mastered several new data types, including `floats` and `chars`. You've learned how to use arrays, especially in conjunction with `chars`. You've also learned about C's text-substitution mechanism, the `#define`.

Chapter 9 will teach you how to combine C's data types to create your own customized data types called `structs`. So go grab some lunch, lean back, prop up your legs, and turn the page.

Exercises

1) What's wrong with each of the following code fragments:

a.
```
char    c;
int i;

i=0;
for ( c=0; c<=255; c++ )
    i += c;
```

b.
```
char    c;

for ( c=0; c<=127; c++ )
    printf( "ASCII char %d is %c.\n", c, c );
```

c.
```
char    c;

c = "a";

printf( "c holds the character %c.", c );
```

d.
```
char    c[ 5 ];

c = "Hello, world!";
```

e. ```
    char   c[MAX_ARRAY_SIZE]

    #define MAX_ARRAY_SIZE   20

    int i;

    for (i=0; i<MAX_ARRAY_SIZE; i++)
        c[i] = 0;
    ```

f.  ```
    #define MAX_ARRAY_SIZE   200

    char    c[ MAX_ARRAY_SIZE ];

    c[ MAX_ARRAY_SIZE ] = 0;
    ```

g. ```
    #define MAX_ARRAY_SIZE   200

    char   c[MAX_ARRAY_SIZE], *cPtr;
    int   i;

    cPtr = c;
    for (i=0; i<MAX_ARRAY_SIZE; i++)
        cPtr++ = 0;
    ```

h.  ```
    #define MAX_ARRAY_SIZE   200

    char    c[ MAX_ARRAY_SIZE ];
    int     i;

    for ( i=0; i<MAX_ARRAY_SIZE; i++ )
    {
        *c = 0;
        c++;
    }
    ```

2) Rewrite dice.c, showing the possible rolls using three dice instead of two.

3) Rewrite wordCount.π, printing each of the words, one per line.

Chapter 9

Designing Your Own Data Structures

This Chapter
at a Glance

Structures
Model A: Three Ways
    Multi-Dimensional Arrays
    Back to Model A
Model B: The Data Structure
Approach
    Opening structSize.π
    Running structSize.π
        Stepping Through the Source Code
    struct Arrays
    Using Pointers With structs
Allocating Your Own Memory
    malloc()
    free()
Keep Track of That Address!
Working With Linked Lists
    Why Linked Lists?
    Creating a Linked List
    Opening cdTracker.π
    Running cdTracker.π
        Stepping Through the Source Code
Order in the Code
What's Next?
Exercises

IN CHAPTER 8, WE INTRODUCED SEVERAL NEW DATA types, namely `float` and `char`. We discussed the range of each type and introduced the format specification characters necessary to print each type using `printf()`. Next, we introduced the concept of arrays, focusing on the relationship between `char` arrays and text strings. Along the way, we discovered the `#define`, C's text substitution mechanism.

This chapter will show you how to use existing C types as building blocks to design your own customized data structures.

Structures

There will be times when your programs will want to bundle certain data together. For example, suppose you were writing a program to organize your compact disc collection. Imagine the type of information you'd like to access for each CD. At the least, you'd want to keep track of the artist's name and the name of the CD. You might also want to rate each CD's listenability on a scale of 1 to 10.

In the next few sections, we'll look at two separate approaches to a basic CD-tracking program. Each approach will revolve around a different set of data structures. One will make use of arrays and the other a set of custom designed data structures.

Model A: Three Arrays

One way to model your CD collection is with a separate array for each CD's attributes:

```
#define MAX_CDS              300
#define MAX_ARTIST_CHARS      50
#define MAX_TITLE_CHARS       50

char    rating[ MAX_CDS ],
        artist[ MAX_CDS ][ MAX_ARTIST_CHARS ],
        title[ MAX_CDS ][ MAX_TITLE_CHARS ];
```

This code fragment uses three #defines. MAX_CDS defines the maximum number of CDs this program will track. MAX_ARTIST_CHARS defines the maximum length of a CD artist's name. MAX_TITLE_CHARS defines the maximum length of a CD's title.

rating will hold a rating, from 1 to 10, for each CD in the collection. artist and title will each store a text string representing the artist and title of each CD in the collection. Notice the extra pair of brackets in the declaration of the arrays artist and title. Both are examples of **multi-dimensional arrays**.

Multi-Dimensional Arrays

When an array is declared, the **dimensions** of the array are used to calculate the number of bytes of memory to allocate for that array's use. In this declaration:

```
char    name[ 40 ];
```

the dimension of the array name is 40. A block of 40 consecutive bytes of memory will be allocated for name. name is known as a **one-dimensional array**.

C allows you to declare multi-dimensional arrays as well. Here's the declaration of a two-dimensional array:

```
char    severalNames[ 5 ][ 40 ];
```

severalNames is a two-dimensional array because of the two sets of brackets following the array name. severalName's dimension is 5 times 40, or 200. A block of 200 consecutive bytes will be allocated for severalNames. The main difference between name and severalNames is that severalNames is an array of arrays.

```
severalNames[ 0 ]
```

is an array of 40 chars. Your program can access those 40 chars by referring to severalNames[0][0] on up to severalNames[0][39]. severalNames[1] is also an array of 40 chars. So are severalNames[2], severalNames[3], and severalNames[4].

An array reference that includes both dimensions, such as severalNames[0][0], refers to a single char. Try to predict the results of this code fragment:

```
char severalNames[ 5 ][ 40 ];

severalNames[ 3 ][ 0 ] = 'H';
severalNames[ 3 ][ 1 ] = 'i';
severalNames[ 3 ][ 2 ] = '!';
severalNames[ 3 ][ 3 ] = 0;

printf( "Here's the message: %s", severalNames[ 3 ] );
```

This example treats severalNames[3] as an individual array of chars. It copies the string "Hi!" one byte at a time into the array, then passes severalNames[3] on to printf(). Notice that printf() uses the %s format specification to print the 0-terminated string severalNames[3].

By the Way _____

C allows you to create arrays of any dimension. Some computers limit you to a maximum of six dimensions. As you'll see later in the chapter, you'll rarely have a need for more than one dimension.

Back to Model A

When programmers assess the efficiency of a program design, they look at many factors. One of the most important factors is **memory usage**. As a general rule, the less memory a program uses, the more efficiently it runs. Let's take a look at Model A's memory usage. As a reminder, here's another look at Model A's array declarations:

```
#define MAX_CDS                300
#define MAX_ARTIST_CHARS       50
#define MAX_TITLE_CHARS        50

char    rating[ MAX_CDS ],
        artist[ MAX_CDS ][ MAX_ARTIST_CHARS ],
        title[ MAX_CDS ][ MAX_TITLE_CHARS ];
```

- The array ratings requires a total of MAX_CDS (#defined as 300) bytes.
- artist requires MAX_CDS * MAX_ARTIST_CHARS (300 * 50 = 15,000) bytes.
- title requires MAX_CDS * MAX_TITLE_CHARS (300 * 50 = 15,000) bytes.

As long as the total number of CDs stays under 300, Model A will use 300 + 15,000 + 15,000 = 30,300 bytes for its CD information.

By the Way

> Model A uses 30,300 bytes to represent 0 CDs or 300 CDs. As soon as the program starts up, 30,300 bytes of memory are used up, even if you haven't entered the data for a single CD!

Let's look at this data another way:

- The array `rating` uses 1 byte per CD (enough for a 1-byte rating from 1 to 10).
- The array `artist` uses 50 bytes per CD (enough for a text string holding the artist's name, up to 50 bytes in length).
- The array `title` also uses 50 bytes per CD (enough for a text string holding the CD's title, up to 50 bytes in length).

Add those three together and you find that Model A allocates 101 bytes per CD. Since Model A allocates space for 300 CDs when it declares its three key arrays, it uses 300 * 101 = 30,300 bytes, as we discovered earlier.

Since the program really only needs 101 bytes per CD, wouldn't it be nice if you could allocate the memory for a CD when you need it? With this type of approach, if your collection only consisted of 50 CDs, you'd only have to use 50 * 101 = 5,050 bytes of memory instead of 30,300.

As you'll see by the end of the chapter, C provides a mechanism for allocating memory as you need it. Model B takes a first step toward memory efficiency by creating a single data structure that contains all the information relevant to a single CD. Later in the chapter you'll learn how to allocate enough memory for a single structure.

Model B: The Data Structure Approach

As stated earlier, our CD program must keep track of a rating (from 1 to 10), the CD artist's name, and the CD's title. For each CD, we need three variables:

```
#define MAX_ARTIST_CHARS    50
#define MAX_TITLE_CHARS     50
```

```
char     rating,
         artist[ MAX_ARTIST_CHARS ],
         title[ MAX_TITLE_CHARS ];
```

C provides the perfect mechanism for wrapping all three of these variables in one tidy bundle. A `struct` allows you to associate any number of variables together under another name. Here's an example of a `struct` declaration:

```
#define MAX_ARTIST_CHARS     50
#define MAX_TITLE_CHARS      50

struct CDInfo
{
    char     rating;
    char     artist[ MAX_ARTIST_CHARS ];
    char     title[ MAX_TITLE_CHARS ];
}
```

This code declares a `struct` **type** named `CDInfo`. A `struct` type is similar to a type like `int` or `char`, but not quite the same. A `struct` type is used to create individual `struct`s. Here's an example:

```
struct CDInfo   myInfo;
```

This declaration creates a `struct`, of type `CDInfo`, named `myInfo`. `myInfo` contains three fields, named `rating`, `artist`, and `title`. Here's how you refer to `myInfo`'s `rating` field:

```
myInfo.rating = 7;
```

Notice the `.` between the `struct` name (`myInfo`) and the field name (`rating`). The `.` following a `struct` name tells the compiler that a field name is to follow.

Important

> It's important to understand the difference between a struct **type** and a struct. You declare a struct **type** for convenience. You can use a struct **type** later in your program to declare an individual struct.
>
> A struct **is declared to be of a specific** struct **type. Once you declare a** struct, **you can use the fields of the** struct **to hold your program's data.**

Opening structSize.π

Here's a program that demonstrates the declaration of a struct type, as well as an individual struct. First, start up THIN C. When prompted for a project to open, go into the Projects folder, then into the structSize subfolder, and open the project structSize.π. The structSize.π project window should appear on your screen.

Running structSize.π

structSize.π declares the CDInfo struct type. Then, structSize.π declares an individual CDInfo struct. Finally, structSize.π prints out the amount of memory allocated to each of the struct's fields and to the struct as a whole. Ready? Let's run it!

Select **Run** from the **Project** menu. Compare your output with the console window shown in Figure 9.1. They should be the same. The first three lines of output show the rating, artist, and title fields. To the right of each field name, you'll find printed the number of bytes of memory allocated to that field. The last line of output shows the memory allocated to the entire struct. Notice that the sum of the three individual fields is not equal to the memory allocated to the entire struct. What gives? You'll find out in the next section, when we walk through the source code... .

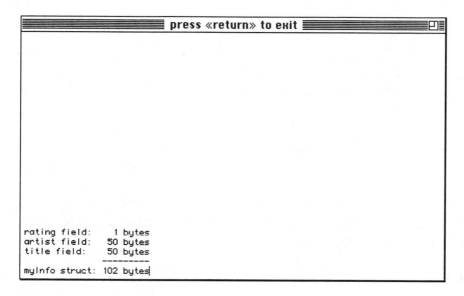

```
════════════════ press «return» to exit ════════════════ ⊡▤



















 rating field:    1 bytes
 artist field:   50 bytes
 title field:    50 bytes
               ─────────
 myInfo struct: 102 bytes|
```

Figure 9.1 structSize.π in action.

Stepping Through the Source Code

If you haven't done so already, type a carriage return to exit structSize.π. Open the source code file structSize.c by double-clicking on its name in the project window. Take a minute to look over the source code in structSize.c. Once you feel comfortable with it, read on.

```
#define MAX_ARTIST_CHARS    50
#define MAX_TITLE_CHARS     50
```

structSize.c starts with the familiar #defines for MAX_ARTIST_CHARS and MAX_TITLE_CHARS.

```
struct CDInfo
{
    char      rating;
    char      artist[ MAX_ARTIST_CHARS ];
    char      title[ MAX_TITLE_CHARS ];
}
```

Next comes the declaration of the struct type CDInfo. Notice that the struct type declaration came before main(), in the spot where you would declare your program's global variables, if any. This declaration doesn't declare a variable. It only declares a type. Since we want this type to be available throughout the program, we declared it before any of the program's functions.

Important

> The struct type CDInfo could have been declared inside of main(). Declaring it inside main() would have limited its scope to inside of main(). That means that no other function would know about the struct type CDInfo.
>
> In this example, either method would have worked. In general, you'll want to declare your struct types just before your global variables. That will allow you to declare a global struct using your global struct type.

```
main()
{
    struct CDInfo    myInfo;
```

main() starts by declaring a struct named myInfo. myInfo is declared to be of type CDInfo. The compiler allocates enough memory to hold a struct the size of CDInfo. How does the compiler know how much memory to allocate? First, it calculates the size of each of the fields declared within CDInfo. It then adds those values together to determine the size of the struct.

By the Way _____

> Most computers refuse to allocate memory in odd-size chunks. If you ask for 53 bytes, most computers will give you 54. Since the computer always gives you enough memory, you usually don't care if you get a little extra. As you'll see, however, knowing about your computer's little idiosyncrasies can sometimes explain somewhat odd (oops!) behavior.

```
printf( "rating field:    %d bytes\n",
        sizeof( myInfo.rating ) );
```

This `printf()` calls a function named `sizeof()`. `sizeof()` is not part of the Standard Library. Instead, like `while` and `switch`, `sizeof()` is built into the C language. `sizeof()` takes any variable as a parameter and returns the number of bytes allocated for that variable. As you can see in Figure 9.1, 1 byte was allocated for `myInfo.rating`.

```
printf( "artist field:   %d bytes\n",
        sizeof( myInfo.artist ) );
```

This `printf()` uses `sizeof()` to print the fact that 50 bytes were allocated for `myInfo.artist`.

```
printf( "title field:    %d bytes\n",
        sizeof( myInfo.title ) );
```

This `printf()` tells us that 50 bytes were also allocated for the field `myInfo.title`.

```
printf( "                        ---------\n" );
```

This `printf()` was purely for aesthetics. Notice the way everything lines up in Figure 9.1?

```
printf( "myInfo struct: %d bytes",
        sizeof( myInfo ) );
    }
```

Now for the *pièce de résistance*. `printf()` uses `sizeof()` to print the size of the variable `myInfo`.

By the Way _____

> Notice that `myInfo` weighs in at 102 bytes, while its three fields sum up to only 101 bytes. When the computer allocated space for `myInfo`, it recognized 101 as an odd number and threw in the extra byte to keep things even.

The previous few sections demonstrated the basics of working with `struct`s. Next, we'll explore the creation of an array of `struct`s.

struct Arrays

Just as you can declare an array of `char`s or `int`s, you can also declare an array of `struct`s:

```
struct CDInfo   myCDs[ 50 ];
```

This declaration creates an array of 50 `struct`s of type `CDInfo`. The array is named `myCDs`. Each of the 50 `struct`s will have the three fields `rating`, `artist`, and `title`. You access the fields of the `struct`s as you would expect. Here's an example:

```
myCDs[ 10 ].rating = 9;
```

Note the use of the all-important . in the example.

Using Pointers With structs

Just as you can declare a pointer to a char or an int, you can also declare a pointer to a struct. Here's an example:

```
struct CDInfo myInfo, *myInfoPtr;

myInfoPtr = &myInfo;
```

The first line declares two variables. myInfo is a struct of type CDInfo. myInfoPtr is a pointer to a struct of type CDInfo. The second line makes the pointer myInfoPtr point to the struct myInfo. Now myInfoPtr can be used to access the fields of myInfo:

```
(*myInfoPtr).rating = 7;
```

This line sets the rating field of myInfo to 7. This only works because myInfoPtr currently points to myInfo. Notice the use of parentheses in the example. The parentheses tell the compiler to first dereference myInfoPtr, turning it from a pointer to a CDInfo struct into a CDInfo struct. Next, the . is applied, telling the compiler you want to access one of the struct's fields.

C provides a shorthand notation for turning a pointer to a struct into one of the struct's fields:

```
myInfoPtr->rating = 7;
```

This line is *exactly* equivalent to the previous example. The operator between myInfoPtr and rating consists of a - immediately followed by a >. Feel free to use either notation, though you'll probably find the second notation a bit easier to read.

Allocating Your Own Memory

One of the most important skills you'll use as a programmer is the ability to allocate memory for your program's variables. One of the limitations of Model A, our first CD-tracking model, was its use of arrays. The problem with arrays is that the memory for the array is allocated as soon as the array is declared. If you know in advance exactly how many elements your array requires, arrays are just fine.

In many situations, however, you can't predict how many array elements you'll need. In Model A of our CD example, we solved the problem by #defining a maximum number of CDs the program can handle:

```
#define MAX_CDS 300
```

As discussed previously, this approach will work as long as we limit ourselves to a maximum of 300 CDs. If we track less than 300 CDs, we'll waste memory.

By the Way

Wasting memory isn't the same as wasting paper or gasoline. It's more like wasting closet space. If your closet is arranged inefficiently, you can't fit as much into it as you could with a little careful planning and rearrangement.

Memory is the same way. You have a limited amount of space to store all of your program's data. If you waste memory, you might run out before you accomplish your task. Techniques that conserve memory are especially valuable. You'll learn a few in this book. You'll learn many more from experience.

malloc()

C provides a mechanism for allocating a block of memory of a specified size. The Standard Library function `malloc()` takes a single parameter, the size of the requested block in bytes. `malloc()` attempts to allocate a block of that size and, if successful, returns a pointer to the first byte of the newly allocated block. If `malloc()` fails, it returns a pointer with a value of 0.

For example, here's a code fragment that allocates a single `CDInfo` struct:

```
struct CDInfo    *myInfoPtr;

myInfoPtr = malloc( sizeof( struct CDInfo ) );
```

First, `myInfoPtr` is declared as a pointer to a struct of type `CDInfo`. Next, `sizeof()` is called to calculate the size of the `CDInfo` struct type.

Once `sizeof()` calculates the size of a `CDInfo` struct, it passes the size on to `malloc()`. `malloc()` attempts to allocate a chunk of memory that size. If it succeeds, it returns a pointer to the first byte of that block. This address is then assigned to `myInfoPtr`.

If `malloc()` succeeded, `myInfoPtr` points to a struct of type `CDInfo`. For the duration of the program, we can use `myInfoPtr` to access the fields of this newly allocated struct:

```
myInfoPtr->ratings = 7;
```

By the Way

In an earlier example, we passed a variable to `sizeof()`. In this example, we passed a type. `sizeof()` is not particular. It will tell you the size of both variables and types.

free()

The memory we just allocated will stick around for the duration of the program unless we de-allocate it ourselves. The Standard Library provides a function, called `free()`, which returns a previously allocated block of memory back to the pool of available memory. `free()` takes a single argument, a pointer to the first byte of a previously allocated block. This line:

```
free( myInfoPtr );
```

returns the block allocated earlier to the free memory pool. Use `malloc()` to allocate a block of memory. Use `free()` to free up a block of memory allocated via `malloc()`. When a program exits, the operating system automatically frees up all allocated memory.

Warning

> Caution: Never put a fork in an electrical outlet. Never pass an address to `free()` that didn't come from `malloc()`. Both will make you extremely unhappy!

Keep Track of That Address!

The address returned by `malloc()` is critical. If you lose it, you've lost access to the block of memory you just allocated. Even worse, you can never `free()` the block, and it will just sit there, wasting valuable memory, for the duration of your program.

By the Way _____

> One great way to lose a block's address is to call `malloc()` inside a function, saving the address returned by `malloc()` in a local variable. When the function exits, your local variable goes away, taking the address of your new block with it!

One way to keep track of a newly allocated block of memory is to place the address in a global variable. Another way is to place a pointer to a `struct` inside another `struct`. This last technique creates something called a **linked list**.

Working With Linked Lists

The linked list is one of the most widely used data structures in C. A linked list is a series of `structs`, each of which contains, as a field, a pointer. Each `struct` in the series uses its pointer to point to the next `struct` in the series. Figure 9.2 shows a linked list containing three elements.

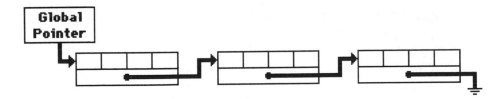

Figure 9.2   A linked list containing three elements.

A linked list starts with a **master pointer**. The master pointer is a pointer variable, typically a global, that points to the first `struct`. This first `struct` contains a field, also a pointer, which points to the second `struct` in the linked list. The second `struct` contains a pointer field that points to the third element. The linked list in Figure 9.2 ends with the third element. The pointer field in the last element of a linked list is typically set to 0.

Why Linked Lists?

Linked lists are extremely memory efficient. A linked list starts out as a single master pointer. When you want to add an element to the list, call `malloc()` to allocate a block of memory for the new element. Next, make the master pointer point to the new block. Finally, set the new block's next element pointer to 0.

If your program needs exactly 50 elements, you can allocate and add 50 elements to your linked list. Linked lists are memory efficient. They provide exactly the right solution for Model B of our CD-tracking program.

Creating a Linked List

The first step in creating a linked list is the design of the main link, the linked list `struct`. Here's a sample:

```
#define MAX_ARTIST_CHARS    50
#define MAX_TITLE_CHARS     50

struct CDInfo
{
    char            rating;
    char            artist[ MAX_ARTIST_CHARS ];
    char            title[ MAX_TITLE_CHARS ];
    struct CDInfo   *next;
}
```

The change here is the addition of a fourth field, a pointer to a `struct` of type `CDInfo`. The `next` field is the key to connecting two different `CDInfo` structs together. If `myFirstPtr` is a pointer to one `CDInfo` struct and `mySecondPtr` is a pointer to a second `struct`, this line:

```
myFirstPtr->next = mySecondPtr;
```

connects the two `struct`s together. Once they are connected, you can use a pointer to the first `struct` to access the second `struct`'s fields! For example:

```
myFirstPtr->next->ratings = 7;
```

This line sets the `ratings` field of the second `struct` to 7. Using the `next` field to get from one `struct` to the next is also known as **traversing** a linked list.

Our next (and final) program for this chapter will incorporate the new version of the `CDInfo` struct to demonstrate a memory-efficient CD-tracking program. This program is pretty long, so you may want to take a few moments to let the dog out and answer your mail.

By the Way _____

> There are many variants of the linked list. If you connect the last element of a linked list to the first element, you create a never ending circular list. You can add a `prev` field to the `struct` and use it to point to the previous element in the list (as opposed to the next one). This technique allows you to traverse the linked list in two directions and creates a doubly-linked list.

Opening cdTracker.π

`cdTracker.π` implements Model B of our CD-tracking system. It uses a text-based menu, allowing you to quit, add a new CD to the collection, or list all of the currently tracked CDs.

Close `structSize.π` by selecting **Close Project** from the **Project** menu. When prompted for a project to open, go into the `Projects` folder, then into the `cdTracker` subfolder, and open the project `cdTracker.π`. The `cdTracker.π` project window should appear on your screen.

Running cdTracker.π

Select **Run** from the **Project** menu. The console window will appear, showing the prompt:

```
Enter command (q=quit, n=new, l=list):
```

At this point you have three choices. You can type a q, followed by a carriage return, to quit the program. You can type an n, followed by a carriage return, to enter a new CD to your collection. Finally, you can type an l, followed by a carriage return, to list all the CDs in your collection.

Start by typing an l, followed by a carriage return. You should see the message:

```
No CDs have been entered yet...
```

Next, the original command prompt should reappear:

```
Enter command (q=quit, n=new, l=list):
```

This time type an n, followed by a carriage return. You will be prompted for the artist's name and the title of a CD you'd like added to your collection:

```
Enter Artist's Name:  Shawn Colvin
Enter CD Title:  Steady On
```

Next, you'll be prompted for a rating for the new CD. The program expects a number between 1 and 10. Try typing something unexpected, such as the letter x, followed by a carriage return:

```
Enter CD Rating (1-10):  x
Enter CD Rating (1-10):  10
```

The program checks your input, discovers it isn't in the proper range, and repeats the prompt. This time, type a number between 1 and 10, followed by a carriage return. The program returns you to the main command prompt:

```
Enter command (q=quit, n=new, l=list):
```

Type the letter l, followed by a carriage return. The single CD you just entered will be listed and the command prompt will again be displayed:

```
Artist:  Shawn Colvin
Title:   Steady On
Rating:  10

- - - - - - - - - -
Enter command (q=quit, n=new, l=list):
```

Type an n, followed by a carriage return and enter another CD. Repeat the process one more time, adding a third CD to the collection. Now enter the letter l, followed by a carriage return to list all three CDs. Here's my list:

```
Enter command (q=quit, n=new, l=list):  l


- - - - - - - - - -
Artist:  Shawn Colvin
Title:   Steady On
Rating:  10


- - - - - - - - - -
Artist:  XTC
Title:   The Big Express
Rating:  8


- - - - - - - - - -
Artist:  Jane Siberry
Title:   Bound by the Beauty
Rating:  9


- - - - - - - - - -
Enter command (q=quit, n=new, l=list):
```

Finally, enter a q, followed by a carriage return to quit the program. Let's hit the source code.

Stepping Through the Source Code

If you haven't already, hit a carriage return to return to THIN C. Next, open the file cdTracker.c by double-clicking its name in the project window. We'll start at the top of the file.

```
#include <stdlib.h>
#include <stdio.h>
```

These lines introduce an important part of C. The `#include` is similar to the `#define`, in that it gets performed during the first pass of the compiler. The compiler will replace the `#include` line with the entire contents of the file whose name appears between either angle brackets (< and >) or double quotes ("). Just as source code files always end with `.c`, `#include` files always end with `.h`.

The included files fall into two categories. If the file name is placed between angle brackets, the file belongs to the Standard Library. THIN C keeps all of the Standard Library `#include` files inside the THIN C folder. The file referenced above, `<stdlib.h>`, contains predefined constants, variable declarations, and other information needed by the Standard Library function `malloc()`.

By the Way _____

> In Chapter 6, the constants TRUE and FALSE were introduced. Some C development environments `#define` values for TRUE and FALSE in one of their `#include` files. Some development environments don't. THIN C provides built-in values for TRUE and FALSE in the `#include` file `<stdio.h>`.
>
> If you find yourself in a development environment that doesn't predefine TRUE and FALSE, just create the `#defines` yourself.

Appendix D lists each of the Standard Library functions used in the book, as well as the `#include` file that goes with that function. If you call a Standard Library function, make sure you `#include` the file that goes with that function. If you call the function twice, or if you call two different functions that make use of the same `#include` file, you should only `#include` the file once.

As an example, `malloc()` makes use of the file `<stdlib.h>`. `printf()` makes use of the file `<stdio.h>`. So far, we've scraped by without the proper `#includes`. From now on, each example will get it right.

By the Way _____

> The second category of #include places its file name in double quotes. This tells the compiler to look in the same folder as the project file for the #included file. The double quote #include is provided for your own benefit. You might want to create a separate file for your global variables and call it "global.h". How about a separate file for all your #defines? As you start writing your own programs, you'll develop your own #include style.

```
#define MAX_ARTIST_CHARS      50
#define MAX_TITLE_CHARS       50

struct CDInfo
{
    char            rating;
    char            artist[ MAX_ARTIST_CHARS ];
    char            title[ MAX_TITLE_CHARS ];
    struct CDInfo   *next;
} *gFirstPtr, *gLastPtr;
```

The #defines and the declaration of CDInfo should look familiar. Notice the addition of the next field. We'll use next as a pointer to the next element in the linked list of CDs.

You should also notice the two variables hanging off the end of the struct declaration. Placing a variable (or list of variables) at the end of a struct type declaration declares those variables to be of the specified type.

gFirstPtr and gLastPtr have been declared as pointers to a struct of type CDInfo. Since they were declared outside of any function, both variables were also declared as globals. gFirstPtr will always point to the first struct in the linked list. gLastPtr will always point to the last `struct` in the linked list. We'll use `gFirstPtr` when we want to step through the linked list, starting at the beginning. We'll use `gLastPtr` when we want to add an element to the end of the list.

```
/******************************  main  ***/

main()
{
    char            command;
```

We'll start our function tour at the bottom of the file, with the function `main()`. The variable `command` holds the command character typed in by the user.

```
    qFirstPtr = NULL;
    gLastPtr = NULL;
```

Next, the variables `gFirstPtr` and `gLastPtr` are set to a value of NULL. NULL is #`defined` in the file `<stdio.h>` to be a pointer with a value of 0. If `gFirstPtr` is NULL, the linked list is empty.

```
    while ( (command = GetCommand() ) != 'q' )
    {
```

Next, `main()` enters a `while` loop, calling the function `GetCommand()`. `GetCommand()` prompts you for a one-character command, either a 'q', 'n', or 'l'. Once `GetCommand()` returns a 'q', we drop out of the `while` loop and exit the program.

```
        switch( command )
        {
            case 'n':
                AddToList( ReadStruct() );
                break;
```

If `GetCommand()` returns an 'n', the user wants to enter information on a new CD. First we call `ReadStruct()`, which allocates space for a `CDInfo` struct, then prompts the user for the information to place in the new struct's fields. Once the struct is filled out, `ReadStruct()` returns a pointer to the newly allocated struct.

The pointer returned by `ReadStruct()` is passed on to `AddToList()`, which adds the new struct to the linked list.

```
        case 'l':
            ListCDs();
            break;
    }
}
```

If `GetCommand()` returns an 'l', the user wants to list all the CDs in his or her collection. That's what the function `ListCDs()` does.

```
    printf( "Goodbye..." );
}
```

Before the program exits, it says "Goodbye...".

```
/******************************  GetCommand  ***/

char    GetCommand()
{
    char    command = 0;
```

Next up on the panel is `GetCommand()`. `GetCommand()` declares a `char` named `command`, used to hold the user's command. Notice that `command` was initialized to 0 on the same line as it was declared. This is known as **explicit initialization**. Although you can place any expression on the right side of the assignment statement, most programs limit explicit initialization to simple assignment statements, such as the one above.

```
    while ( (command != 'q') && (command != 'n')
                && (command != 'l') )
    {
```

By the Way _____

> You can explicitly initialize global variables. You can also explicitly initialize arrays. Here's an example:
>
> ```
> char  s[ 20 ] = "Hello";
> ```
>
> What a convenient way to initialize an array of `chars`! Here's another way to accomplish the same thing:
>
> ```
> char  s[ 20 ] = { 'H', 'e', 'l', 'l', 'o', 0 };
> ```
>
> To explicitly initialize an array, one element at a time, place the list of elements inside a pair of curlies. In this example, notice that the last element was a zero, used to terminate the string.

The `while` loop won't exit until `command` is equal to a `'q'`, `'n'`, or `'l'`. Since `command` was initialized to 0, this `while` loop will run at least one time.

```
        printf( "Enter command (q=quit, n=new, l=list):   "
                );
        scanf( "%c", &command );
        Flush();
    }
```

First, prompt the user for a command. Next, use `scanf()` to retrieve the next character typed by the user. Finally, call `Flush()` to get rid of any extra characters typed after the command. At the very least, `Flush()` will remove the carriage return from the input buffer.

```
        printf( "\n----------\n" );
        return( command );
}
```

Once we get a `'q'`, `'n'`, or `'l'`, print a line (for aesthetics) and return the `command`.

```
/******************************  ReadStruct  ***/

struct CDInfo    *ReadStruct()
{
```

Next up is `ReadStruct()`. Notice the unusual declaration of the function name. The line:

```
struct CDInfo    *ReadStruct()
```

says that `ReadStruct()` returns a pointer to a `CDInfo` struct.

By the Way _____

By default, a function is assumed to return a value of type `int`. By placing a type specification in front of the function name, you can create functions that return any type you want. If you check back, you'll see that the function `GetCommand()` returns a `char`. As you read on, you'll notice that some of the functions return a type called `void`. Declaring a function to be of type `void` is a nice way to let the compiler (and anyone who's trying to read your source code) know that the function doesn't return a value at all.

Remember, if you don't declare the function to be of a specific type, the compiler assumes it's of type `int`. Since functions don't have to return a value, this will rarely cause you problems. However, it's good practice to always declare your functions to be of one type or another. The one exception to this rule is the most important function, `main()`. Declare `main()` just the way you see it in this program, with no return type.

```
struct CDInfo    *infoPtr;
int              num;
```

ReadStruct() uses malloc() to allocate a block of memory the size of a CDInfo struct. The variable infoPtr will act as a pointer to the new block. The variable num serves as a temporary int.

```
infoPtr = malloc( sizeof( struct CDInfo ) );
```

ReadStruct() calls malloc() to allocate a CDInfo struct, assigning the address of the block returned to infoPtr.

```
if ( infoPtr == NULL )
{
    printf( "Out of memory!!!  Goodbye!\n" );
    exit( 0 );
}
```

If malloc() cannot allocate a block of the requested size, it will return a value of NULL. If this happens, we'll print an appropriate message and call the Standard Library function exit(). As its name implies, exit() causes the program to immediately exit.

By the Way _____

> On a Macintosh, the parameter passed to exit() is ignored. On some computers, however, the parameter is passed back to the operating system. For now, we'll pass a value of 0 to exit().

```
printf( "Enter Artist's Name:   " );
ReadLine( infoPtr->artist );

printf( "Enter CD Title:   " );
ReadLine( infoPtr->title );
```

If we're still here, `malloc()` must have succeeded. Next, we'll print a prompt for the CD artist's name, then call `ReadLine()` to read a line from the input buffer. `ReadLine()` will place the line in the `artist` field of the newly allocated `struct`.

We then repeat the process to prompt for and read in the CD title.

```
num = 0;
while ( ( num < 1 ) || ( num > 10 ) )
{
```

Next, we'll enter a `while` loop that continues until the value of `num` is between 1 and 10.

```
    printf( "Enter CD Rating (1-10):  " );
    scanf( "%d", &num );
    Flush();
}
```

First, the loop prompts for a number. Next, `scanf()` is called to read in the number. `Flush()` gets rid of any characters remaining in the input buffer, once `scanf()` has its number.

```
infoPtr->rating = num;
```

Once a number is read in that's between 1 and 10, the number is assigned to the `rating` field of the newly allocated `struct`.

```
    printf( "\n----------\n" );

    return( infoPtr );
}
```

Finally, a separating line is printed and the pointer to the new `struct` is returned.

```
/****************************   ReadLine   ***/

void    ReadLine( char *line )
{
```

ReadLine() takes a pointer to a char as a parameter. Remember, a pointer to a char is the same as the name of an array of chars.

```
    char c;

    while ( (c = getchar()) != '\n' )
    {
```

The while loop uses getchar() to read a char at a time from the input buffer. It keeps reading characters until it hits a carriage return.

```
        *line = c;
        line++;
    }
```

Each char is read into c using getchar(), then assigned to the char pointed to by line. At the beginning, line points to line[0]. The statement line++ makes line point to the next char. If line pointed to line[0], line++ makes line point to line[1].

```
    *line = 0;
}
```

Finally, the value 0 is placed at the end of the last character read to 0-terminate the string. We need a 0-terminated string if we are going to pass the string to printf(), which we do in the function ListCDs().

```
/****************************   Flush   ***/

void    Flush()
{
    while ( getchar() != '\n' )
        ;
}
```

Flush() uses getchar() to read characters from the input buffer until it reads in a carriage return. Flush() is a good utility routine to have around.

```
/******************************  AddToList  ***/

void    AddToList( struct CDInfo *curPtr )
{
```

AddToList() takes a pointer to a CDInfo struct as a parameter. It uses the pointer to add the struct to the linked list.

```
    if ( gFirstPtr == NULL )
        gFirstPtr = curPtr;
```

If gFirstPtr is NULL, the list must be empty. If so, make gFirstPtr point to the new struct.

```
    else
        gLastPtr->next = curPtr;
```

If gFirstPtr is not NULL, there's at least one element in the linked list. In that case, make the next field of the very last element on the list point to the new struct.

```
    gLastPtr = curPtr;
    curPtr->next = NULL;
}
```

In either case, set gLastPtr to point to the new "last element in the list." Finally, make sure the next field of the last element in the list is NULL. You'll see why we did this in the next function, ListCDs().

```
/******************************  ListCDs  ***/

void    ListCDs()
{
    struct CDInfo    *curPtr;
```

ListCDs() lists all the CDs in the linked list. The variable curPtr is used to point to the link element currently being looked at.

```
if ( gFirstPtr == NULL )
{
    printf( "No CDs have been entered yet...\n" );
    printf( "\n----------\n" );
}
```

If no CDs have been entered yet, we'll print an appropriate message.

```
else
{
    curPtr = gFirstPtr;
```

Now that we know there's at least one CD in the linked list, we'll start with the first one.

```
while ( curPtr != NULL )
{
```

The while loop continues until curPtr has a value of NULL. curPtr starts off pointing to the first struct in the list. Once that element has been printed out, curPtr gets whatever value is in the next field of the current struct. That value will make curPtr point to the next element in the list. This continues until we eventually hit the last element on the list, the only element whose next field is set to NULL. Once curPtr gets assigned a value of NULL, we drop out of the while loop.

```
printf( "Artist:  %s\n", curPtr->artist );
printf( "Title:   %s\n", curPtr->title );
```

The first two printf()s use the "%s" format specifier to print the strings in the fields artist and title.

```
printf( "Rating:  %d\n", curPtr->rating );

printf( "\n----------\n" );
```

Next, the `rating` field and a separating line are printed.

```
        curPtr = curPtr->next;
    }
  }
}
```

Finally, the `next` field is used to point `curPtr` to the next `struct`.

Order in the Code

One final note: Have you ever wondered why `main()` is at the bottom of the file? This is interesting. The compiler compiles your source code from top to bottom. As it reads your code, it periodically encounters function calls. If the compiler hasn't seen the function yet (because the function itself is lower down in the file) the compiler assumes the function returns an `int`. If the line of code being compiled assumes that the function returns a different type, the compiler will report an error. For example, in this piece of code:

```
main()
{
    char    *line;

    line = ReadALine();
}
```

the function `ReadALine()` returns a pointer to a `char`. If `main()` is at the top of the file, the compiler will hit the call of `ReadALine()` before it actually sees the declaration of `ReadALine()`. When the compiler tries to compile this line, it assumes that `ReadALine()` returns an `int`. It then sees this supposed `int`-returning function trying to assign an `int` to a pointer variable. The compiler scratches its head, and finally returns an error.

There are two solutions to this problem. The solution used in this book is to place `main()` at the bottom of the file, then place the functions called by `main()` above it in the file, placing the functions called by these functions next, and so on, building up toward the top of the file. In this way, the compiler will never hit a call of a function before it hits the function itself.

Another solution is to include a one-line declaration for each of your functions at the top of the file, in the same area you would declare your global variables. For example, a function that returns a pointer to a `char` might have a declaration line like:

```
char    *ReadALine();
```

The function itself is written in its normal form somewhere down below. The declaration line at the top of the file alerts the compiler that the function returns a type other than `int`. If you do decide to go this route, consider gathering all of your function declarations in a separate `#include` file. You might call it `"routines.h"`, or something similar.

What's Next?

This chapter covered a wide range of topics, from `#include`s to linked lists. The intent of the chapter, however, was to attack a real-world programming problem; in this case, a program to catalog CDs. The chapter showed several design approaches, discussing the pros and cons of each. Finally, the chapter presented a prototype for a CD-tracking program. The program allows you to enter information about a series of CDs and, on request, will present a list of all the CDs tracked.

One problem with this program is that once you exit, all of the data you entered is lost. The next time you run the program, you have to start all over again.

Chapter 10 offers a solution to this problem. The chapter introduces the concept of files and file management, showing you how to save your data from memory out to your hard-disk drive and how to read your data back in again. The chapter updates cdTracker.π, storing the CD information collected in a file on your disk drive.

Exercises

1) What's wrong with each of the following code fragments:

a. `char line[ 5 ] = "Hello";`

b. `char line[ 5 ] = { 'H', 'e', 'l', 'l', 'o', 0 };`

c.
```
struct Employee
{
    char    name[ 20 ];
    int employeeNumber
};
```

d. `while ( getchar() == '\n' ) ;`

e. `#include "stdio.h"`

f.
```
struct Link
{
    name[ 50 ];
    Link    *next;
};
```

g.
```
struct Link
{
    struct Link next;
    struct Link prev;
}
```

h.
```
char    line[ 10 ] = "Hello";
int     i;

while ( *line != 0 )
    line++;

printf( "%s", line );
```

2) Update cdTracker.c so it maintains its linked list in alphabetical order.

3) Update cdTracker.c, adding a prev field to the CDInfo struct so it maintains a doubly-linked list. As before, the next field will point to the next link in the list. Now, however, the prev field should point to the previous link in the list. Add an option to the menu that prints the list backward, from the last struct in the list to the first.

Chapter 10

Working With Files

This Chapter at a Glance

What is a File?
Working with Files, Part One
Opening a File
Reading a File
Opening printFile.π
Running printFile.π
Stepping Through the Source Code
stdin and stdout
Working with Files, Part Two
Writing to a File
The Output Buffer
Opening cdFiler.π
Exploring cdData
Running cdFiler.π
Stepping Through the Source Code
What's Next?
Exercises

CHAPTER 9 INTRODUCED cdTracker, A PROGRAM DESIGNED to keep track of your compact disc collection. cdTracker allowed you to enter a new CD, as well as list all of the existing CDs. cdTracker's biggest shortcoming was that it didn't save the CD information when it exited. If you ran cdTracker, entered information on ten CDs, and then quit, your information would be gone. The next time you ran cdTracker, you'd have to start from scratch.

The solution to this problem is to somehow save all of the CD information before you quit the program. This chapter will show you how. Chapter 10 introduces the concept of **files**, the long-term storage for your program's data.

What is a File?

A file is a series of bytes residing on a magnetic storage media. In the Macintosh world, most files are stored on floppy disks and hard-disk drives. The copy of MacPaint you keep on your hard drive resides in a file. The floppy disk that came with this book contains many different files. Some of the files make up the THIN C development environment. Others contain projects and source code that THIN C will open.

All of the files on your computer share a common set of traits. For example, each file has a size. The file `LaserWriter` in my `System Folder` has a size of 64,595 bytes. The file `Microsoft Word` in my `Applications` folder has a size of 683,274 bytes. Each of these files resides on a hard-disk drive attached to my computer.

Working With Files, Part One

In the C world, each file consists of a stream of consecutive bytes. When you want to access the data in a file, you **open** the file using a Standard Library function called `fopen()`, pronounced *eff-open*. Later in the chapter, we'll explore a program called `cdFiler`. `cdFiler` adds two important features to `cdTracker`. `cdFiler` knows how to save your CD information in a file and can also read the information back in again. `cdFiler` makes extensive use of `fopen()`.

Opening a File

`fopen()` takes two parameters, a file **name** and a **mode**. The file name defines the file you want to open. Examples of file names are `LaserWriter` and `Microsoft Word`. `cdFiler` will use `fopen()` to open a file named `cdData`.

The mode parameter defines the way you'll be accessing the file and is one of "r", "w", or "a". "r" stands for **read** and is used when you want to open the file for reading. "w" stands for **write** and is used when you want to open the file for writing. Finally, "a" stands for **append** and is used when you want to add data to the end of a file.

Warning

> Beware! If you open a file for writing, all of the existing data from the file is replaced with whatever new data you write into it! Use *append* mode if you just want to add more data to the file. If you want to change the data in the file, *read* in the data, change it in memory, then *write* it back out. cdFiler will show you how.

Here's what happens when you call fopen():

- If you call fopen() to open a file for reading, and the file doesn't exist, fopen() returns the value NULL.
- If you call fopen() to open a file for writing or appending, and the file doesn't exist, fopen() will attempt to create a new file with the given name. If this fails, fopen() returns NULL.
- If fopen() was able to open the file, it returns a pointer to a data structure of type FILE.

fopen() is declared as follows:

```
FILE    *fopen( char *filename, char *mode );
```

You'll want to declare a variable of the same type to handle the value returned by fopen():

```
FILE    *fp;
```

Here's a sample call of `fopen()`:

```
fp = fopen( "cdData", "r" );
```

This line looks into the same folder as the project file for a file named `"cdData"`, and opens the file for reading. If the file `cdData` doesn't exist, `fp` will have a value of `NULL`. If the file does exist, `fp` will point to a `struct` of type `FILE`. As you'll see, you won't be accessing the fields of the `FILE` struct. Instead, you'll pass `fp` to various Standard Library functions that allow you to read, write, and close your file.

Reading a File

If you open a file for reading, the next step is to **read** data from the file. When you read from the keyboard, you used such functions as `getchar()` and `scanf()` to fetch data from the input buffer associated with the keyboard. When you read from a file, you use a similar set of file functions to fetch data from the file's input buffer.

The function `fgetc()` reads a single character from a file's input buffer and returns either the character or the value `EOF`. `EOF` stands for end-of-file and is `#defined` in the file `<stdio.h>`. `fgetc()` returns a value of `EOF` when the last character in the file has already been read—in other words, when the end of the file is reached. `fgetc()` takes a single parameter, a pointer to a `FILE`. `fgetc()` is declared as follows:

```
int fgetc( FILE *fp );
```

The function `fscanf()` is similar to `scanf()`. Instead of scanning the keyboard's input buffer for input, `fscanf()` scans the input buffer associated with the specified file. `fscanf()` is declared as follows:

```
int fscanf( FILE *fp, char*format, ... );
```

The first parameter specifies the file whose input buffer is to be scanned. The second is the format specification text string. Any further parameters depend on the contents of the format specification string.

Chapter 10's first program, `printFile.π`, demonstrates the use of the functions `fopen()` and `fgetc()` in opening and reading a file.

Opening printFile.π

`printFile.π` opens a file named `"My Data File"`, reads in all the data from the file one character at a time and prints each character in the console window. First, start up THIN C. When prompted for a project to open, go into the `Projects` folder, then into the `printFile` subfolder, and open the project `printFile.π`. The `printFile.π` project window should appear on your screen.

Running printFile.π

Select **Run** from the **Project** menu. Compare your output with the console window shown in Figure 10.1. They should be the same. Type a carriage return to return to THIN C. Let's take a look at the data file read in by `printFile.π`. Select **Open...** from the **File** menu. THIN C will prompt you for a text file to open. Select the file named `My Data File`. A window will open allowing you to edit the contents of the file named `My Data File`. Feel free to make some changes to the file and run the program again. Make sure you don't change the name of the file.

Let's take a look at the source code.

Stepping Through the Source Code

Open the source code file `printFile.c` by double-clicking on its name in the project window. Take a minute to look over the source code. Once you feel comfortable with it, read on.

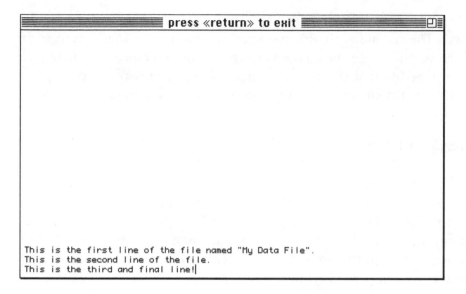

Figure 10.1   printFile.π in action.

```
#include <stdio.h>
```

Each of the Standard Library functions in this program requires the inclusion of <stdio.h>.

```
main()
{
    FILE    *fp;
    int     c;
```

The file pointer fp will be used whenever we want to reference the file we are working with. The variable c is used to receive the characters returned by fgetc().

```
    fp = fopen( "My Data File", "r" );
```

By the Way _____

> Notice that c is declared as an int instead of a char. This is because fgetc() is declared to return an int and not a char. fgetc() will return values ranging from 0 to 255 (the range of an unsigned char) when it reads a byte from the file's input buffer. fgetc() needs one more value, however, to return when it hits the end of the file. The constant EOF is #defined to a value of -1. This puts it outside the range of an unsigned char, and that's why fgetc() is declared as an int function.
>
> If you forget which function returns which data type, look up the function in Appendix C.

This call of the function fopen() opens the file named My Data File for reading, returning the file pointer to the variable fp.

```
if ( fp != NULL )
{
```

If fp is not NULL, the file was opened successfully.

```
while ( (c = fgetc( fp )) != EOF )
    putchar( c );
```

The while loop continuously calls fgetc(), passing it the file pointer fp. fgetc() returns the next character in fp's input buffer. The returned character is assigned to c. If c is not equal to EOF, putchar() is called, taking c as a parameter. putchar() prints the specified character to the console window. We could have accomplished the same thing by using printf():

```
printf( "%c", c );
```

By the Way

> As you program, you'll often find two different solutions to the same problem. Should you use `putchar()` or `printf()`? If performance is critical, pick the option that is more specific to your particular need. In this case, `printf()` is designed to handle many different data types. `putchar()` is designed to handle one data type, an `int`. Chances are the source code for `putchar()` is simpler and more efficient than the source code for `printf()` *when it comes to printing an* `int`. If performance is critical, you might want to use `putchar()` instead of `printf()`. If performance isn't critical, go with your own preference.

```
        fclose( fp );
    }
}
```

Once all the characters in `My Data File` have been displayed in the console window, use `fclose()` to close the file.

stdin and stdout

C provides you with two file pointers that are always available and always open. `stdin` represents the keyboard and `stdout` represents the console window. In `printFile.π`, we used the function `fgetc()` to read a character from a previously opened file. This line:

```
c = fgetc( stdin );
```

will read the next character from the keyboard's input buffer.

```
fgetc( stdin )
```

is equivalent to calling

```
getchar()
```

As you'll see in the next few sections, whenever C provides a mechanism for reading or writing to a file, C will also provide a similar mechanism for reading from stdin or writing to stdout. Though you probably won't use stdin and stdout in your code, it's good to know what they are and what they do.

Working With Files, Part Two

So far, you've learned how to open a file using fopen() and how to read from a file using fgetc(). You've seen that you can often use two different functions to solve the same problem. Now let's look at the functions that allow you to write data out to a file.

Writing to a File

The Standard Library offers several functions that write data out to a previously opened file. This section will introduce three of them: fputc(), fputs(), and fprintf().

fputc() takes an int holding a character value, and writes the character out to the specified file. fputc() is declared as follows:

```
int fputc( int c, FILE *fp );
```

If fputc() successfully writes the character out to the file, it returns the value passed to it in the parameter c. If the write fails for some reason, fputc() returns the value EOF.

fputs() is similar to fputc(), but writes out a 0-terminated string instead of a single character. fputs() is declared as follows:

```
int fputs( char *s, FILE *fp );
```

fputs() writes out all the characters in the string, but does not write out the terminating 0. If the write succeeds, fputs() returns a 0. If the write fails, fputs() returns EOF.

fprintf() works just like printf(). Instead of sending its output to the console window, fprintf() writes its output to the specified file. fprintf() is declared as follows:

```
int fprintf( FILE *fp, char *format, ... );
```

The first parameter specifies the file to be written to. The second is the format specification text string. Any further parameters depend on the contents of the format specification string.

The Output Buffer

Just as data read from a file or the keyboard first passes through an input buffer, data written to a file must first pass through an output buffer. When you use functions such as fprintf() and fputc() to write data to a file, the data is first written to the output buffer. When the buffer fills up, its contents are written out to the file.

For the most part, you will never work directly with a file's output buffer. There may be times, however, when you need direct access to the output buffer. Unfortunately, the details of the output buffer are beyond the scope of this book. When you feel ready to tackle file input and output at a more detailed level, find the documentation for the operating system of the computer you are working on. Are you programming a Macintosh? Is your computer running an operating system called Unix?

Find out as much as you can about the environment in which you'll be programming. Since you're programming in C, most things won't change as you move from computer to computer. Get a copy of the Standard Libraries reference guide for the computer you'll be working with. The Standard Libraries guide will tell you everything you need to know to make use of the Standard Library functions. In addition to listing each of the functions, the reference guide tells you which file you'll need to #include to use the function, which parameters the function expects, and what values the function can return.

Your best bet is to hook up with someone with programming experience on the computer you want to work with. They'll help you through the technical tough spots. In the meantime, let's get back to the subject at hand.

Opening cdFiler.π

In Chapter 9, we ran cdTracker.π, a program designed to help you track your compact disc collection. The big shortcoming of cdTracker.π is its inability to save your carefully entered CD data. As you quit the program, the CD information you entered gets discarded, forcing you to start over the next time you run cdTracker.π.

Our next program, cdFiler.π, solves this problem by adding two special functions to cdTracker.π. ReadFile() opens a file named "cdData", reads in the CD data in the file, and uses the data to build a linked list of cdInfo structs. WriteFile() writes the linked list back out to the file.

In THIN C, select **Close Project** from the **Project** menu to close printFile.π. When prompted for a project to open, go into the Projects folder, then into the cdFiler subfolder, and open the project cdFiler.π. The cdFiler.π project window should appear on your screen (Figure 10.2).

Look at the project window. Notice anything unusual? In addition to the file ANSI.lib, there are two source code files in this project. The file cdMain.c is almost identical to the file cdTracker.c from Chapter 9. The file cdFiles.c contains the functions that allow cdFiler.π to read and write the file cdData.

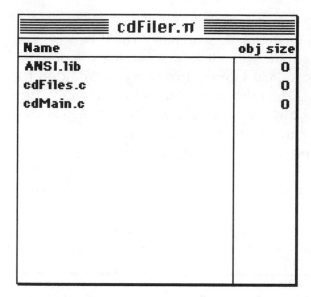

Figure 10.2 The cdFiler.π project window.

Exploring cdData

Before you run the program, take a quick look at the file cdData. Select **Open...** from the **File** menu. When prompted for a text file to open, select the file cdData. A text-editing window for cdData will appear on the screen. At first glance, the contents of the file may not make much sense, but the text does follow a well-defined pattern:

```
3
Shawn Colvin
Steady On
10
XTC
The Big Express
8
Jane Siberry
Bound by the Beauty
9
```

The first line of the file tells you how many CD descriptions follow. In this case, the file describes three CDs. From this point on, the file is organized in clusters of three lines each. Each cluster contains a one-line CD artist, a one-line CD title, and a one-line numerical CD rating.

Important

> The layout of your data files is as important a part of the software design process as the layout of your program's functions. The file described above follows a well-defined pattern. As you lay out a file for your next program, think about the future. Can you live with one-line CD titles? Do you want the ability to add a new CD field, perhaps the date of the CD's release?
>
> The time to think about these types of questions is at the beginning of your program's life, during the design phase.

Running cdFiler.π

Before you run the program, you must close cdData's text-editing window.

Warning

> To create this window, THIN C had to open the file cdData. If you don't close the window before you run the program, the file will remain open. When you run cdFiler.π, it will also open the file. You'll have the same file open in two places. This is not a good idea. Although C allows you to do this, your results can be somewhat unpredictable.

Once the window is closed, run cdFiler.π by selecting **Run** from the **Project** menu. The console window will appear, prompting you for a 'q', 'n', or 'l':

```
Enter command (q=quit, n=new, l=list): l
```

Type an l, followed by a carriage return. This will list the CDs currently in the program's linked list. If you need a refresher on linked lists, now would be a perfect time to turn back to Chapter 9:

```
Enter command (q=quit, n=new, l=list): l

- - - - - - - - - -
Artist: Shawn Colvin
Title:  Steady On
Rating: 10

- - - - - - - - - -
Artist: XTC
Title:  The Big Express
Rating: 8

- - - - - - - - - -
Artist: Jane Siberry
Title:  Bound by the Beauty
Rating: 9

- - - - - - - - - -
Enter command (q=quit, n=new, l=list):
```

Chapter 9's cdTracker.π started with an empty linked list. cdFiler.π, on the other hand, first reads in the CDs described in cdData, placing these descriptions into the linked list. Now, type an 'n', followed by a carriage return and add a new CD to your list:

```
Enter command (q=quit, n=new, l=list): n

- - - - - - - - - -
Enter Artist's Name: Adrian Belew
Enter CD Title: Mr. Music Head
Enter CD Rating (1-10): 8

- - - - - - - - - -
Enter command (q=quit, n=new, l=list):
```

Next, type an 'l' to make sure your new CD made it into the list:

```
Enter command (q=quit, n=new, l=list): l

- - - - - - - - - -
Artist: Shawn Colvin
Title:  Steady On
Rating: 10

- - - - - - - - - -
Artist: XTC
Title:  The Big Express
Rating: 8

- - - - - - - - - -
Artist: Jane Siberry
Title:  Bound by the Beauty
Rating: 9

- - - - - - - - - -
Artist: Adrian Belew
Title:  Mr. Music Head
Rating: 8

- - - - - - - - - -
Enter command (q=quit, n=new, l=list):
```

Finally, type a 'q' followed by a carriage return. This causes the program to write the current linked list back out to the file cdData. To prove this worked, run cdFiler.π one more time. When prompted for a command, type an 'l' to list your current CDs. You should find your new CD nestled at the bottom of the list. Let's see how this works.

Stepping Through the Source Code

The file cdMain.c is almost exactly the same as the file cdTracker.c from Chapter 9. There are two differences:

```
/******************************* main ***/

main()
{
    char              command;

    gFirstPtr = NULL;
    gLastPtr = NULL;

    ReadFile();
```

As the program starts, it calls the function ReadFile(). ReadFile() reads in the contents of cdData, and is contained in the file cdFiles.c.

```
    while ( (command = GetCommand() ) != 'q' )
    {
        switch( command )
        {
            case 'n':
                AddToList( ReadStruct() );
                break;
            case 'l':
                ListCDs();
                break;
        }
```

```
    }

    WriteFile();

    printf( "Goodbye..." );
}
```

The second change occurs just before `main()` exits when the function `WriteFile()` is called. `WriteFile()` writes the current linked list back out to the file `cdData`.

Important _____

> As your programs get larger and larger, you'll want to divide your source code into two or more files. In general, I name the file containing the function `main()` something like `xxxMain.c`, where `xxx` ties in with the name of the project. I give the other files names that indicate the nature of the functions contained within. A name like `xxxFiles.c` is appropriate for file handling functions. Again, the `xxx` matches the `xxx` in the file `xxxMain.c`.
>
> Once your projects reach the five-file level, you'll start to reap the benefits of carefully thought-out file names.

```
#include <stdio.h>
#include <stdlib.h>
```

The file `cdFiles.c` starts with a pair of `#include`s. Between `<stdio.h>` and `<stdlib.h>`, all of the Standard Library functions called in this file are covered.

```
#define CD_FILE_NAME    "cdData"
```

The `#define CD_FILE_NAME` refers to the file containing all of the CD information.

```
#define MAX_ARTIST_CHARS    50
#define MAX_TITLE_CHARS     50

struct CDInfo
{
    char            rating;
    char            artist[ MAX_ARTIST_CHARS ];
    char            title[ MAX_TITLE_CHARS ];
    struct CDInfo   *next;
};
```

The #defines MAX_ARTIST_CHARS and MAX_TITLE_CHARS and the declaration of the CDInfo struct type should be familiar from cdTracker.c. Notice that the globals gFirstPtr and gLastPtr have been left out of this declaration. You'll see why next.

```
extern  struct CDInfo *gFirstPtr;
```

The extern type modifier tells the compiler that this variable has been declared in another file. This declaration gives us access to the gFirstPtr declared in the file cdMain.c.

Important

> In general, your globals should be declared in the same file as main(). Any other file that needs access to a particular global should declare that global using extern.
>
> Another strategy you might want to consider calls for the creation of a file called xxxVars.h, which contains an extern declaration of all of your global variables. You #include xxxVars.h in each of your source code files except xxxMain.c. In xxxMain.c, declare the globals normally (without extern) toward the top of the file. This strategy gives each of your source code files access to all of your globals.

```
/****************************** ReadFile ***/

char    ReadFile()
{
    FILE            *fp;
    struct CDInfo   *infoPtr;
    int             numCDs, num, i;

    if ( ( fp = fopen( CD_FILE_NAME, "r" ) ) == NULL )
        return( FALSE );
```

The function ReadFile() tries to open the file cdData for reading. If the file could not be opened, the function returns FALSE. If you flip back up to the function main(), you'll notice that the return value from ReadFile() is ignored. That's OK.

By the Way

> For the moment, main() doesn't care whether the file was opened. If you wanted to, you could put the call of ReadFile() inside an if statement. If ReadFile() returns FALSE, print a message that says the file could not be opened. If ReadFile() returns TRUE, print a message that says the file was opened successfully.
>
> Whether you take advantage of ReadFile()'s return value or not, the feature is there waiting.

```
    fscanf( fp, "%d", &numCDs );
    FlushFile( fp );
```

Once the file is opened, fscanf() is called to read in the number of CDs described in the file. Since fscanf() doesn't read in the carriage return that follows the number, the function FlushFile() was created. FlushFile() will read in characters until it gets a carriage return or an EOF. FlushFile() discards any characters it reads in.

```
for ( i=1; i<=numCDs; i++ )
{
    infoPtr = malloc( sizeof( struct CDInfo ) );
```

This `for` loop runs from 1 to the number of CDs described in the file. For each CD, `malloc()` is called to allocate a block of memory the size of a `CDInfo` struct. For the moment, `infoPtr` is set to point to this newly allocated block of memory.

```
if ( infoPtr == NULL )
{
    printf( "Out of memory!!! Goodbye!\n" );
    exit( 0 );
}
```

If `infoPtr` is `NULL`, the call to `malloc()` failed to allocate the necessary amount of memory. In this case, an appropriate message is printed and the program exits.

```
ReadFileLine( fp, infoPtr->artist );
ReadFileLine( fp, infoPtr->title );
```

If `malloc()` succeeded, `ReadFileLine()` is called to read in a line of text for the artist's name and a line of text for the CD's title. `ReadFileLine()` does read in the carriage return at the end of the line, so a call of `FlushFile()` is not necessary.

```
fscanf( fp, "%d", &num );
infoPtr->rating = num;
FlushFile( fp );
```

Next, `fscanf()` is called to read in an `int`, representing the CD's rating. Since the `rating` field was declared as a `char`, and the `"%d"` format specifier reads in an `int`, we'll use a temporary variable to receive the `int` from `fscanf()`, then use an assignment statement to copy the `int` into the `char` represented by `infoPtr->rating`.

By the Way

> If we passed the address of the `rating` field directly to
> `fscanf()`, `fscanf()` would try to write a 2-byte value in a
> block of memory the size of a `char` (1 byte). The results of
> this operation would be unpredictable at best.

```
        AddToList( infoPtr );
    }
```

Once the fields of the `struct` are filled, `AddToList()` is called to
add the `struct` to the linked list. `AddToList()` is found in the file
`cdMain.c`.

```
    fclose( fp );

    return( TRUE );
}
```

Finally, the file is closed and a value of `TRUE` is returned by
`ReadFile()`.

```
/******************************* FlushFile ***/

void    FlushFile( FILE *fp )
{
    int c;

    while ( ( (c = fgetc( fp )) != '\n') && (c != EOF ) )
        ;
}
```

The function `FlushFile()` uses `fgetc()` inside a `while` loop to read
a character at a time. The `while` loop exits as soon as either a carriage
return or an `EOF` is read.

```
/***************************** ReadFileLine ***/

void    ReadFileLine( FILE *fp, char *line )
{
    char c;
```

ReadFileLine() takes a file pointer and a pointer to an array of chars as parameters.

```
    while ( (c = fgetc( fp )) != '\n' )
    {
        *line = c;
        line++;
    }
```

fgetc() is called inside a while loop to read characters one at a time. The loop places the characters inside the line array, incrementing the pointer line each time through the loop. The loop exits when a carriage return is read.

```
    *line = 0;
}
```

Once the entire line is read in, a 0 is copied to the end of the line, creating a 0-terminated string.

```
/***************************** WriteFile ***/

void    WriteFile()
{
    FILE            *fp;
    struct CDInfo   *infoPtr;
    int             numCDs, i, num;
```

WriteFile() writes the contents of the linked list out to the file cdData.

```
if ( ( fp = fopen( CD_FILE_NAME, "w" ) ) == NULL )
{
    printf( "***ERROR: Could not write CD file!" );
}
```

First, fopen() is used to open the file for writing. If the file couldn't be opened, an error message is printed.

```
else
{
    numCDs = CountCDs();
```

If the file was opened successfully, CountCDs() is called to find out how many CDs will be written out to the file.

```
fprintf( fp, "%d\n", numCDs );
```

fprintf() is used to write the number of CDs, followed by a carriage return, out to the file.

```
infoPtr = gFirstPtr;

for ( i=1; i<=numCDs; i++ )
{
    fprintf( fp, "%s\n", infoPtr->artist );
    fprintf( fp, "%s\n", infoPtr->title );

    num = infoPtr->rating;
    fprintf( fp, "%d\n", num );
    infoPtr = infoPtr->next;
}
```

Next, a for loop is used to step through the linked list, one element at a time. The artist, title, and rating fields are written to the file, each followed by a carriage return. Once again, a temporary int is used to hold the value of the char infoPtr->rating. The int is used because fprintf() expects a 2-byte value to go along with the "%d" format specifier.

```
        fclose( fp );
    }
}
```

Once the contents of the file are written out, the file is closed.

```
/****************************** CountCDs ***/

int CountCDs()
{
    struct CDInfo    *infoPtr;
    int              numCDs;

    infoPtr = gFirstPtr;
    numCDs = 0;

    while ( infoPtr != NULL )
    {
        infoPtr = infoPtr->next;
        numCDs++;
    }

    return( numCDs );
}
```

CountCDs() steps through the linked list an element at a time. It uses the variable numCDs to count the number of elements in the list, returning numCDs at the end.

What's Next?

Chapter 11 tackles a wide assortment of programming topics. We'll look at typecasting, the technique used to translate from one type to another. We'll cover recursion, the ability of a function to call itself. We'll also examine function pointers, variables that can be used to pass a function as a parameter.

Exercises

1) What's wrong with each of the following code fragments:

    a.
    ```
    FILE     *fp;

    fp = fopen( "w", "My Data File" );
    if ( fp != NULL )
        printf( "The file is open." );
    ```

    b.
    ```
    char myData = 7;
    FILE     *fp;

    fp = fopen( "r", "My Data File" );
    fscanf( "Here's a number: %d", &myData );
    ```

    c.
    ```
    FILE     *fp;
    char     *line;

    fp = fopen( "My Data File", "w" );
    fscanf( fp, "%s", &line );
    ```

    d.
    ```
    FILE     *fp;
    char     *line;

    fp = fopen( "My Data File", "r" );
    fscanf( fp, "%s", &line );
    ```

e.
```
FILE    *fp;
char    *line;

fp = fopen( "My Data File", "r" );
fscanf( fp, "%s", line );
```

2) Write a function that reads in a file with the following format:
   a) The first line is the number of lines to be read in.
   b) Each of the lines that follow this first line consists of a series of three numbers separated by tabs.

3) Write a function that reads in a file with the following format:
   a) The first line contains two numbers separated by tabs.
   b) The first number specifies the number of lines to be read in.
   c) The second number specifies the number of numbers on each line. In this example:

```
2   3
4   5   6
5   6   7
```

   the first line specifies that two lines are to follow, each line containing three numbers.

4) Modify cdFiler.π so memory for the artist and title lines is allocated as the lines are read in. First, you'll need to change the CDInfo struct declaration as follows:

```
struct CDInfo
{
    char            rating;
    char            *artist;
    char            *title;
    struct CDInfo   *next;
};
```

Not only will you call `malloc()` to allocate a `CDInfo` struct, you'll also call `malloc()` to allocate space for the `artist` and `title` strings. Don't forget to leave enough space for the terminating 0 at the end of each string.

Chapter 11

Filling in the Gaps

This Chapter
at a Glance

What is Typecasting?
Cast With Care
Casting With Pointers
Unions
Why Use Unions?
Function Recursion
A Recursive Approach
Binary Trees
Searching Binary Trees
Recursion and Binary Trees
Function Pointers
More on Strings
strcpy
strcat
strcmp
strlen
What's Next?
Exercises

CONGRATULATIONS! BY NOW YOU'VE MASTERED MOST
of the fundamental C programming concepts. This chapter will fill you
in on some useful C programming tips, tricks, and techniques that will
enhance your programming skills. We'll start with a look at typecasting,
C's mechanism for translating one data type to another.

What is Typecasting?

There often will be times when you find yourself trying to convert a variable of one type to a variable of another type. For example, this code fragment:

```
float    f;
int      i;

f = 3.5;
i = f;

printf( "i is equal to %d", i );
```

causes this line:

```
i is equal to 3
```

to appear in the console window. Notice that the original value assigned to f was truncated from 3.5 to 3 when the value in f was assigned to i. This truncation was caused when the compiler saw an int on the left side and a float on the right side of this assignment statement:

```
i = f;
```

The compiler automatically translated the float to an int. In general, the right side of an assignment statement is always translated to the type on the left side when the assignment occurs. In this case, the compiler handled the type conversion for you.

Typecasting is a mechanism you can use to translate the value of an expression from one type to another. A **typecast**, or just plain **cast**, always takes this form:

```
(type) expression
```

where `type` is any legal C type. In this code fragment:

```
float f;

f = 1.5;
```

the variable `f` gets assigned a value of 1.5. In this code fragment:

```
float f;

f = (int)1.5;
```

the value of 1.5 is cast as an `int` before being assigned to `f`. Just as you might imagine, casting a `float` as an `int` truncates the `float`, turning the value 1.5 into 1. In this example, two casts were performed. First, the `float` value 1.5 was cast to the `int` value 1. When this `int` value was assigned to the `float` `f`, the value was cast to the `float` value 1.0.

Cast With Care

Use caution when you cast from one type to another. Problems can arise when casting between types of a different size. Consider this example:

```
int     i;
char    c;

i = 500;
c = i;
```

Here, the value 500 is assigned to the `int` `i`. So far, so good. Next, the value in `i` is cast to a `char` as it is assigned to the `char` `c`. See the problem? Since a `char` can only hold values between -128 and 127, assigning a value of 500 to `c` doesn't make sense.

Casting With Pointers

Typecasting can also be used when working with pointers. This notation:

```
(int *) myPtr
```

casts the variable `myPtr` as a pointer to an `int`. Casting with pointers allows you to link together `struct`s of different types. For example, suppose you declared two `struct` types, as follows:

```
struct Dog
{
    struct Dog  *next;
} ;

struct Cat
{
    struct Cat *next;
} ;
```

By using typecasting, you could create a linked list that contains both `Cat`s and `Dog`s. You can make a `Dog` point to a `Cat` (Figure 11.1):

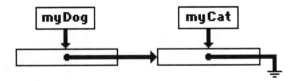

Figure 11.1   `myDog.next` points to `myCat.next`, which points to `NULL`.

```
struct Dog   myDog;
struct Cat   myCat;

myDog.next = &myCat;     /*  <-- Compiler complains  */
myCat.next = NULL;
```

In the first assignment statement, a pointer of one type is assigned to a pointer of another type. &myCat is a pointer to a struct of type Cat. myDog.next is declared to be a pointer to a struct of type Dog. Unfortunately, while the compiler is good about automatically typecasting C's built-in types, it doesn't automatically perform the typecast for types you design yourself. If you tried to compile the code above, THIN C would report an error, complaining that the pointer types don't match. Here's the corrected version:

```
struct Dog   myDog;
struct Cat   myCat;

myDog.next = (struct Dog *)(&myCat);
myCat.next = NULL;
```

Notice the extensive use of parentheses in the first assignment statement. Whenever you perform a typecast, make sure you are casting what you want to cast. For example:

```
struct Dog   *dogPtr;

dogPtr = &myDog;

(struct Cat *)dogPtr->next = &myCat;   /*  <-- Not what you
                                                think  */
```

This code attempts to cast a Dog's next field to a Cat pointer. That's not what happens, however. Instead of next being cast, dogPtr is cast. This is a common error. Here's the corrected version:

```
struct Dog   *dogPtr;

dogPtr = &myDog;

(struct Cat *)(dogPtr->next) = &myCat;
```

As you can see, the parentheses make a big difference.

Unions

Before we leave the topic of structs and typecasting, there's one more area worth discussing. C offers a special data type, known as a **union**, which allows a single variable to disguise itself as several different data types. unions are declared just like structs. Here's an example:

```
union Number
{
    int     i;
    float   f;
    char    *s;
}   myUnion;
```

This declaration creates a union type named Number. It also creates an individual Number named myUnion. If this were a struct declaration, you'd be able to store three different values in the three fields of the struct. unions don't work this way.

When a union is declared, the compiler allocates the space required by the largest of the union's fields, sharing that space with all of the union's fields. Since an int requires 2 bytes, a float 4 bytes, and a pointer 4 bytes, myUnion is allocated exactly 4 bytes. You can store an int, a float, or a char pointer in myUnion. The compiler allows you to treat myUnion as any of these types. To refer to myUnion as an int, refer to:

```
myUnion.i
```

To refer to myUnion as a float, refer to:

```
myUnion.f
```

To refer to myUnion as a char pointer, refer to:

```
myUnion.s
```

You are responsible for remembering which form the union is currently occupying.

Warning ───

> If you store an int in myUnion by assigning a value to myUnion.i, you'd best remember that fact. If you proceed to store a float in myUnion.f, you've just trashed your int. Remember, there are only 4 bytes allocated to the entire union.

───

One way to keep track of the current state of the union is to declare an int to go along with the union, as well as a #define for each of the unions fields:

```
#define INT        1
#define FLOAT      2
#define POINTER    3

union Number
{
    int     i;
    float   f;
    char    *s;
} myUnion;

int myUnionTag;
```

If you are currently using myUnion as a float, assign the value FLOAT to myUnionTag. Later in your code you can use myUnionTag when deciding which form of the union you are dealing with:

```
if ( myUnionTag == INT )
    DoIntStuff( myUnion.i );
```

```
else if ( myUnionTag == FLOAT )
    DoFloatStuff( myUnion.f );
else
    DoPointerStuff( myUnion.s );
```

Why Use Unions?

In general, unions are most useful when dealing with two data structures that share a set of common fields, but differ in some small way. For example, consider these two struct declarations:

```
struct Pitcher
{
    char    name[ 40 ];
    int     team;
    int     strikeouts;
    int     runsAllowed;
} ;

struct Batter
{
    char    name[ 40 ];
    int     team;
    int     runsScored;
    int     homeRuns;
} ;
```

These structs might be useful if you were tracking the pitchers and batters on your favorite baseball team. Both structs share a set of common fields, the array of chars named name and the int named team. Both structs have their own unique fields as well. The Pitcher struct contains a pair of fields appropriate for a pitcher, strikeouts and runsAllowed. The Batter struct contains a pair of fields appropriate for a batter, runsScored and homeRuns.

One solution to your baseball-tracking program would be to maintain two types of structs, a Pitcher and a Batter. There is nothing wrong with this approach. There is an alternative, however. You can declare a single struct that contains the fields common to Pitcher and Batter, with a union for the unique fields:

```
#define METS      1
#define REDS      2

#define PITCHER 1
#define BATTER  2

struct Pitcher
{
    int     strikeouts;
    int     runsAllowed;
} ;

struct Batter
{
    int     runsScored;
    int     homeRuns;
} ;

struct Player
{
    int     type;
    char    name[ 40 ];
    int     team;
    union
    {
        struct Pitcher  pStats;
        struct Batter   bStats;
    } u;
}
```

Here's an example of a Player declaration:

```
struct Player    myPlayer;
```

Once you created the `Player` struct, you would initialize the `type` field with one of either `PITCHER` or `BATTER`:

```
myPlayer.type = BATTER;
```

You would access the `name` and `team` fields like this:

```
myPlayer.team = METS;
printf( "Stepping up to the plate:  %s", myPlayer.name );
```

Finally, you'd access the `union` fields like this:

```
if ( myPlayer.type == PITCHER )
  myPlayer.u.pStats.strikeouts = 20;
```

The `u` was the name given to the union in the declaration of the `Player` type. Every `Player` you declare will automatically have a `union` named `u` built into it. The `union` gives you access to either a `Pitcher` struct named `pStats` or a `Batter` struct named `bStats`. The example above references the `strikeouts` field of the `pStats` field.

`union`s provide an interesting alternative to maintaining multiple data structures. Try them. Write your next program using a `union` or two. If you don't like them, you can return them for a full refund.

Function Recursion

Some programming problems are best solved by repeating a mathematical process. For example, to learn whether a number is prime (see Chapter 6) you might step through each of the integers between 1 and the number itself, one at a time, searching for a factor. If no factor is found, you have a prime. The process of stepping through the numbers between 1 and the possible prime is called **iteration**.

In programming, iterative solutions are fairly common. Almost every time you use a `for` loop, you are applying an iterative approach to a problem. An alternative to the iterative approach is known as **recursion**. In a recursive approach, instead of repeating a process in a loop, you embed the process in a function and have the function call itself until the process is complete. The key to recursion is a function calling itself.

Suppose you wanted to calculate 5 factorial (also known as 5!). The factorial of a number is the product of each integer from 1 up to the number. For example, 5 factorial is:

$$5! = 5 * 4 * 3 * 2 * 1 = 120$$

Using an iterative approach, you might write some code like this:

```
main()
{
    int i, num, fac;

    num = 5;
    fac = 1;

    for ( i=1; i<=num; i++ )
        fac *= i;

    printf( "%d factorial is %d.", num, fac );
}
```

By the Way

> If you are interested in trying this code, it is provided on disk in the `Projects` folder, under the subfolder named `iterate`.

If you ran this program, you'd see this line printed in the console window:

```
5 factorial is 120.
```

As you can see from the source code, the algorithm steps through (iterates) the numbers 1 through 5, building the factorial with each successive multiplication.

A Recursive Approach

You can use a recursive approach to solve the same problem. For starters, you'll need a function to act as a base for the recursion, a function that will call itself. There are two things you'll need to build into your recursive function. First, you'll need a mechanism to keep track of the depth of the recursion. In other words, you'll need a variable or parameter that changes, depending on the number of times the recursive function calls itself.

Second, you'll need a terminating condition, something that tells the recursive function when it's gone deep enough. Here's one version of a recursive function that calculates a factorial:

```
int factorial( int num )
{
    if ( num > 1 )
        num *= factorial( num - 1 );

    return( num );
}
```

factorial() takes a single parameter, the number whose factorial you are trying to calculate. factorial() first checks to see whether the number passed to it is greater than 1. If so, factorial() calls itself, passing 1 less than the number passed into it. This strategy guarantees that, eventually, factorial() will get called with a value of 1.

Figure 11.2 shows this process in action. The process starts with a call to `factorial()`:

```
result = factorial( 3 );
```

Take a look at the leftmost `factorial()` source code in Figure 11.2. `factorial()` is called with a parameter of 3. The `if` statement checks to see if the parameter is greater than 1. Since 3 is greater than 1, the statement:

```
num *= factorial( num - 1 );
```

is executed. This statement calls `factorial()` again, passing a value of n-1, or 2, as the parameter. This second call of `factorial()` is pictured in the center of Figure 11.2.

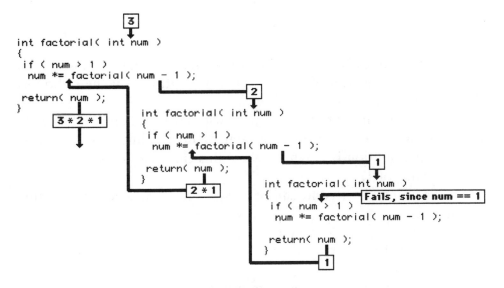

Figure 11.2 The recursion process caused by the call `factorial( 3 )`.

Important

> It's important to understand that this second call to `factorial()` is treated just like any other function call that occurs in the middle of a function. The calling function's variables are preserved while the called function runs. In this case, the called function is just another copy of `factorial()`.

This second call of `factorial()` takes a value of 2 as a parameter. The `if` statement compares this value to 1 and, since 2 is greater than 1, executes the statement:

```
num *= factorial( num - 1 );
```

This statement calls `factorial()` yet again, passing `num-1`, or 1, as a parameter. The third call of `factorial()` is portrayed on the rightmost side of Figure 11.2.

The third call of `factorial()` starts with an `if` statement. Since the input parameter was 1, the `if` statement fails. Thus, the recursion termination condition is reached. Now, this third call of `factorial()` returns a value of 1.

At this point, the second call of `factorial()` resumes, completing the statement:

```
num *= factorial( num - 1 );
```

Since the call of `factorial()` returned a value of 1, this statement is equivalent to:

```
num *= 1;
```

leaving num with the same value it came in with, namely 2. This second call of factorial() returns a value of 2.

At this point, the first call of factorial() resumes, completing the statement:

```
num *= factorial( num - 1 );
```

Since the second call of factorial() returned a value of 2, this statement is equivalent to:

```
num *= 2;
```

Since the first call of factorial() started with the parameter num taking a value of 3, this statement sets num to a value of 6. Finally, the original call of factorial() returns a value of 6. This is as it should be, since 3 factorial = 3 * 2 * 1 = 6.

Important

> The recursive version of the factorial program is also provided on disk. You'll find it in the Projects folder, under the subfolder named recurse. Open the project and follow the program through, line by line.

Binary Trees

As you learn more about data structures, you'll discover new applications for recursion. For example, one of the most-used data structures in computer programming is the binary tree (Figure 11.3). As you'll see later, binary trees were just made for recursion. The binary tree is similar to the linked list. Both consist of structs connected by pointers embedded in each struct.

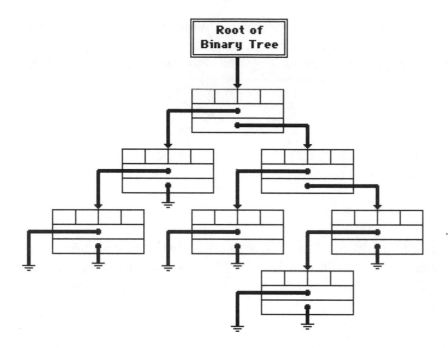

Figure 11.3   A binary tree.

Linked lists are linear. Each `struct` in the list is linked by pointers to the `struct` behind it and in front of it in the list. Binary trees always start with a single `struct`, known as the root `struct` or **root node**. Where the linked-list `struct`s we've been working with contain a single pointer, called `next`, binary-tree `struct`s each have two pointers, usually known as `left` and `right`.

Check out the binary tree in Figure 11.3. Notice that the root node has a left **child** and a right child. The left child has its own left child but its `right` pointer is set to `NULL`. The left child's left child has two `NULL` pointers. A node with two `NULL` pointers is known as a **leaf node** or **terminal node**.

Binary trees are extremely useful. They work especially well when the data you are trying to sort has a **comparative relationship**. This means that if you compare one piece of data to another, you'll be able to judge the first piece as greater than, equal to, or less than the second piece. For example, numbers are comparative. Words in a dictionary can be comparative, if you consider their alphabetical order. The word *iguana* is greater than *aardvark*, but less than *xenophobe*.

Here's how you might store a sequence of words, one at a time, in a binary tree. We'll start with this list of words:

```
opulent
entropy
salubrious
ratchet
coulomb
yokel
tortuous
```

Figure 11.4 shows the word opulent added to the root node of the binary tree. Since it is the only word in the tree so far, both the left and right pointers are set to NULL. Figure 11.5 shows the word entropy added to the binary tree. Since entropy is less than opulent (i.e., comes before it alphabetically), entropy is stored as opulent's left child.

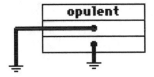

Figure 11.4   The word opulent is entered into the binary tree.

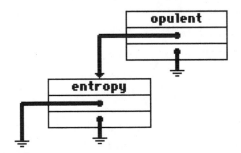

Figure 11.5   The word entropy is less than the word opulent and is added to its left in the tree.

Next, Figure 11.6 shows the word salubrious added to the tree. Since salubrious is greater than opulent, it becomes opulent's right child. Figure 11.7 shows the word ratchet added to the tree. First, ratchet is compared to opulent. Since ratchet is greater than opulent we follow the right pointer. Since there's a word there already, we'll have to compare ratchet to this word. Since ratchet is less than salubrious, we'll store it as salubrious's left child.

Figure 11.8 shows the binary tree after the remainder of the word list has been added. Do you understand how this scheme works? What would the binary tree look like if coulomb was the first word on the list? The tree would have no left children and would lean heavily to the right.

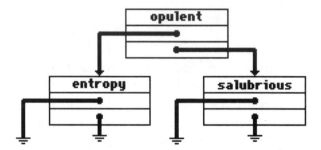

Figure 11.6 The word salubrious is greater than the word opulent and is added to its right in the tree.

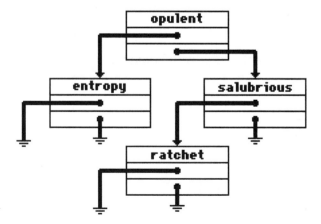

Figure 11.7 The word ratchet is greater than opulent but less than salubrious and is placed in the tree accordingly.

What if yokel was the first word entered? As you can see, this particular use of binary trees depends on the order of the data. Randomized data that starts with a value close to the average produces a **balanced tree**. If the words had been entered in alphabetical order, you would have ended up with a binary tree that looked like a linked list.

By the Way _____

> Data structure theory is one of my favorite topics in all of computer science. Though I'd like to rattle on and on about variant tree structures and binary tree balancing algorithms, my editors would like me to get this book out sometime this year. This shouldn't stop you, though. Go to your library and check out a book on data structures and another on sorting and searching algorithms (which we'll get to in a minute). Or, if you can wait, get Volume II of this series, which I guarantee will have more on my favorite subject.

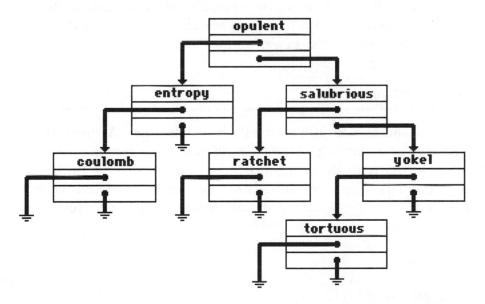

Figure 11.8   The words coulomb, yokel, and tortuous are added to the tree.

Searching Binary Trees

Now that your word list is stored in the binary tree, the next step is to look up a word in the tree. This is known as **searching** the tree. Suppose you wanted to look up the word `tortuous` in your tree. You'd start with the root node, comparing `tortuous` with `opulent`. Since `tortuous` is greater than `opulent`, you'd follow the right pointer to `salubrious`.

You'd follow this algorithm down to `yokel` and finally `tortuous`. A binary tree that contained just words may not be that interesting, but imagine that these words were names of great political leaders. Each `struct` might contain a leader's name, biographical information, perhaps a pointer to another data structure containing great speeches. The value, name, or word that determines the order of the tree is said to be the **key**.

You don't always search a tree based on the key. Sometimes, you'll want to step through every node in the tree. For example, suppose your tree contained the name and birth date of each of the presidents of the United States. Suppose also that the tree was built using each president's last name as a key. Now suppose you wanted to compose a list of all presidents born in July. In this case, searching the tree alphabetically won't do you any good. You'll have to search every node in the tree. This is where recursion comes in.

Recursion and Binary Trees

Binary trees and recursion were made for each other. As mentioned earlier, recursion requires a changing condition and a terminating condition. For binary trees, the changing condition is the traversal of the left and right pointers. The terminating condition occurs when you reach a terminal node. Here's an example of a tree traversing, recursive function:

```
struct Tree
{
    int         value;
    struct Tree *left;
```

```
    struct Tree *right;
} myTree;


Searcher( struct Tree *treePtr )
{
    if ( treePtr != NULL )
    {
        VisitNode( treePtr );
        Searcher( treePtr->left );
        Searcher( treePtr->right );
    }
}
```

The function Searcher() takes a pointer to a tree node as its parameter. If the pointer is NULL, we must be at a terminal node and there's no need to recurse any deeper. If the pointer points to a Tree node, the function VisitNode() is called. VisitNode() performs whatever function you want performed for each node in the binary tree. In our current example, VisitNode() could check to see if the president associated with this node was born in July. If so, VisitNode() might print the president's name in the console window.

Once the node is visited, Searcher() calls itself twice, once passing a pointer to its left child and once passing a pointer to its right child. If this version of Searcher() were used to search the tree in Figure 11.8, the tree would be searched in the order described in Figure 11.9. This type of search is known as a **preorder search,** because the node is visited before the two recursive calls take place.

Here's a slightly revised version of Searcher(). Without looking at Figure 11.10, can you predict the order that the tree will be searched? This version of Searcher() performs an **in-order search** of the tree:

```
Searcher( struct Tree *treePtr )
{
    if ( treePtr != NULL )
    {
        Searcher( treePtr->left );
```

```
        VisitNode( treePtr );
        Searcher( treePtr->right );
    }
}
```

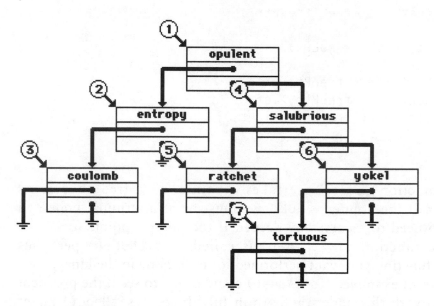

Figure 11.9   The search order produced by the first version of
`Searcher()`.

Here's a final look at `Searcher()`. This version performs a
postorder search of the tree:

```
Searcher( struct Tree *treePtr )
{
    if ( treePtr != NULL )
    {
        Searcher( treePtr->left );
        Searcher( treePtr->right );
        VisitNode( treePtr );
    }
}
```

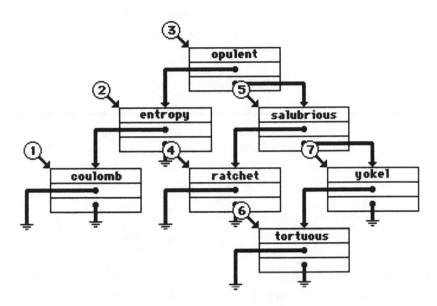

Figure 11.10   An in-order search of a binary tree.

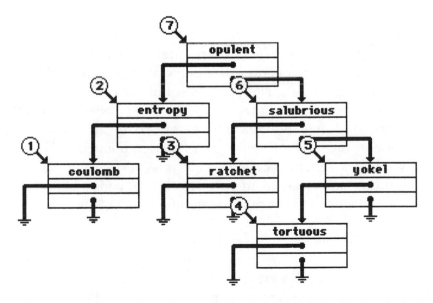

Figure 11.11   A postorder search of a binary tree.

Recursion and binary trees are two extremely powerful programming tools. Learn how to use them—they'll pay big dividends.

Function Pointers

Next on the list is the subject of **function pointers**. Function pointers are exactly what they sound like: pointers that point to functions. Up to now, the only way to call a function was to place its name in the source code:

```
MyFunction();
```

Function pointers give you a new way to call a function. Function pointers allow you to say, "Execute the function pointed to by this variable." Here's an example:

```
int (*myFuncPtr)( float );
```

This line of code declares a function pointer named `myFuncPtr`. `myFuncPtr` is a pointer to a function that takes a single parameter, a `float`, and that returns an `int`. The parentheses in the declaration are all necessary. The first pair tie the * to `myFuncPtr`, ensuring that `myFuncPtr` is declared as a pointer. The second pair surround the parameter list and distinguish `myFuncPtr` as a function pointer.

Suppose we had a function called `DealTheCards()` that took a `float` as a parameter and returned an `int`. This line of code assigns the address of `DealTheCards()` to the function pointer `myFuncPtr`:

```
myFuncPtr = DealTheCards;
```

Notice that the parentheses were left off the end of `DealTheCards()`. This is critical. If the parentheses were there, the code would have called `DealTheCards()`, returning a value to `myFuncPtr`. You may also have noticed that the & operator wasn't used. When you refer to a function without using the parentheses at the end, the compiler knows you are referring to the address of the function.

Now that you have the function's address in the function pointer, there's only one thing left to do—call the function. Here's how it's done:

```
int result;

result = (*myFuncPtr)( 3.5 );
```

This line calls the function `DealTheCards()`, passing it the parameter 3.5, and returning the function value to the `int result`. Once again, both sets of parentheses are necessary.

By the Way _____

There's a lot you can do with function pointers. You can create an array of function pointers. How about a binary tree of function pointers? You can pass a function pointer as a parameter to another function. Taking this one step further, you can create a function that does nothing but call other functions. Cool!

By the Way _____

For your enjoyment, there's a function-calling example on the source code disk. You'll find the project in the `Projects` folder, inside the `funcPtr` subfolder. The program is pretty simple, but it should serve as a useful reference when you start using function pointers in your own programs.

More on Strings

The last topic we'll tackle in this chapter is **string manipulation**. Although we've done some work with strings in previous chapters, there are a number of Standard Library functions that haven't been covered. Each of these functions requires that you include the file <string.h>. Here are a few examples...

strcpy

strcpy() is declared as follows:

```
char    *strcpy( char *dest, char *source );
```

strcpy() copies the string pointed to by source into the string pointed to by dest. strcpy() copies each of the characters in source, including the terminating 0 byte. That leaves dest as a properly terminated string. strcpy() returns the pointer dest.

An important thing to remember about strcpy() is that you are responsible for ensuring that source is properly terminated, and that enough memory is allocated for the string returned in dest. Here's an example of strcpy() in action:

```
char    name[ 20 ];

strcpy( name, "Dave Mark" );
```

This example uses a string literal as the source string. The string is copied into the array name. The return value was ignored.

strcat

`strcat()` is declared as follows:

```
char *strcat( char *dest, *source );
```

   `strcat()` appends a copy of the string pointed to by `source` onto the end of the string pointed to by `dest`. As was the case with `strcpy()`, `strcat()` returns the pointer `dest`. Here's an example of `strcat()` in action:

```
char    name[ 20 ];

strcpy( name, "Dave " );
strcat( name, "Mark" );
```

   The call of `strcpy()` copies the string `"Dave "` into the array `name`. The call of `strcat()` copies the string `"Mark"` onto the end of `dest`, leaving `dest` with the properly terminated string `"Dave Mark"`. Again, the return value was ignored.

strcmp

`strcmp()` is declared as follows:

```
int strcmp( char *s1, char *s2 );
```

   `strcmp()` compares the strings `s1` and `s2`. `strcmp()` returns 0 if the strings are identical, a positive number if `s1` is greater than `s2`, and a negative number if `s2` is greater than `s1`. The strings are compared one byte at a time. If the strings are not equal, the first byte that is not identical determines the return value.
   Here's a sample:

```
if ( strcmp( "Hello", "Goodbye" ) )
    printf( "The strings are not equal!" );
```

   Notice that the `if` succeeds when the strings are not equal.

strlen

`strlen()` is declared as follows:

```
typedef size_t  unsigned long;

size_t  strlen( char *s );
```

By the Way

> The `typedef` statement is used to create a custom type. `typedef` follows this pattern:
>
> ```
> typedef newTypeName    existingType;
> ```
>
>   This statement:
>
> ```
> typedef size_t  unsigned long;
> ```
>
> creates a new type called `size_t` which is equivalent to the type `unsigned long`. Once you've created a type using `typedef`, you can use the new type name in your variable declarations.

`strlen()` returns the length of the string pointed to by s. As an example, this call:

```
length = strlen( "Aardvark" );
```

returns a value of 8, the number of characters in the string, not counting the terminating zero.

What's Next?

Chapter 12 answers the question, "Where do you go from here?" Do you want to learn to create programs with that special Macintosh look and feel? Would you like more information on data structures and C programming techniques? Chapter 12 offers some suggestions to help you find your programming direction.

Exercises

1) What's wrong with each of the following code fragments:

a.
```
struct Dog
{
    struct Dog  *next;
} ;

struct Cat
{
    struct Cat *next;
} ;

struct Dog  myDog;
struct Cat  myCat;

myDog.next = &myCat;
myCat.next = NULL;
```

b.
```
struct Dog
{
    struct Dog  *next;
} myDog, *dogPtr;

struct Cat
{
    struct Cat *next;
} myCat;
```

```
dogPtr = &myDog;

(struct Cat *)dogPtr->next = &myCat;
```

c.   union Number

```
{
    int     i;
    float   f;
    char    *s;
} ;

Number  myUnion;

myUnion.f = 3.5;
```

d.   struct Player

```
{
    int         type;
    char        name[ 40 ];
    int         team;
    union
    {
        int     myInt;
        float   myFloat;
    } u;
} myPlayer;

myPlayer.team = 27;
myPlayer.myInt = -42;
myPlayer.myFloat = 5.7;
```

e.   int   *myFuncPtr(int);

```
myFuncPtr = main;
*myFuncPtr();
```

f. ```
    char   s[20];

    strcpy(s, "Hello ");

    if (strcmp(s, "Hello"))
        printf("The strings are the same!");
    ```

g.  ```
    char *s;

    s = malloc( 20 );
    strcpy( "Heeeers Johnny!", s );
    ```

h. ```
    char *s;

    strcpy(s, "Aardvark");
    ```

2)  Write a program similar to `cdFiler` that uses a binary tree instead of a linked list. The tree should order the information using the alphabetizing approach demonstrated in this chapter, using the `artist` field as the key. The list function should use a recursive algorithm to search the entire tree.

3)  Add a function to the program in Exercise 9 that randomizes the tree when the user types `'r'` in response to the command prompt. One way to randomize the tree is to:

   a. Pull all the nodes out, creating a single linked list comprising all the nodes in the tree.
   b. Use `rand()` to generate a random number from 1 to the number of elements remaining in the linked list. Use the random number to select the appropriate element from the linked list.
   c. Add the element to the tree, deleting it from the linked list.
   d. Go back to step b, repeating the process until all the elements in the linked list have been placed back in the tree.
    ```

Chapter 12

Adding the Macintosh Interface

This Chapter at a Glance

The Macintosh User Interface
The Graphical User Interface
The Macintosh Toolbox
  Opening windowMaker.π
  Running windowMaker.π
Getting Started With the Mac Toolbox
Inside Macintosh
The Macintosh C Programming Primer
Macintosh Programming Secrets
Go Get 'Em

NOW THAT YOU'VE MASTERED THE FUNDAMENTALS OF C, you're ready to dig into the specifics of Macintosh programming. As you've run the example programs in the previous chapters, you've probably noticed that none of the programs sport the look and feel that make a Mac program a Mac program.

For one thing, all of the interaction between you and your program focuses on the keyboard and the console window. None of the programs take advantage of the mouse. None offer color, pull-down menus, or a selection of different fonts. These are all part of the Macintosh user interface.

341

The Macintosh User Interface

User interface is the part of your program that interacts with the user. So far, your user interface skills have focused on writing to and reading from the console window, using functions such as `printf()`, `scanf()`, and `getchar()`. The advantage of this type of user interface is that each of the aforementioned functions is available on every machine that supports the C language. Programs written with a console-based user interface are extremely portable.

On the down side, console-based user interfaces tend to be limited. With a console-based interface, you can't use an elegant graphic to make a point. Text-based interfaces can't provide animation or digital sound. In a nutshell, the console-based interface is simple and, at the same time, simple to program. The Macintosh's graphical user interface (GUI) offers an elegant, more sophisticated method of working with a computer.

The Graphical User Interface

A Macintosh just wouldn't be the same without windows, pull-down and pop-up menus, icons, push buttons, and scroll bars. You can and should add these user interface elements to your C programs. The hard part is deciding which features to use where.

Once you've identified the pieces of the Mac interface you want in your program, you're ready to take advantage of the Mac's version of the Standard Library: the Macintosh Toolbox.

The Macintosh Toolbox

Every Mac that rolls off the assembly line comes with a slew of user interface functions built in. Each Mac comes with a **read-only memory (ROM)** chip that contains the more than 700 functions that make up the **Macintosh Toolbox**. The Mac Toolbox contains functions that create windows on the screen and others that draw text in these windows.

There are functions for drawing shapes, lines, and dots in color and in black and white. There's a set of functions that allows you to implement your own pull-down menus. The Mac Toolbox is huge.

Every program that supports the standard Macintosh interface relies on the Mac Toolbox. That's why Macintosh programs have such a consistent look and feel. Take a look at the pull-down menu in Figure 12.1. Notice the close resemblance to every other Mac pull-down menu. That's because the Toolbox provides a set of functions that implements a standard Macintosh pull-down menu bar. When a Mac programmer wants to implement a pull-down menu, he or she always turns to this set of functions, collectively known as the **Menu Manager**. The Menu Manager has a set of rules it follows when pulling down a menu. For example, a standard Macintosh menu is always drawn using the **Chicago** font. The **Chicago** font is built into the Mac's ROM.

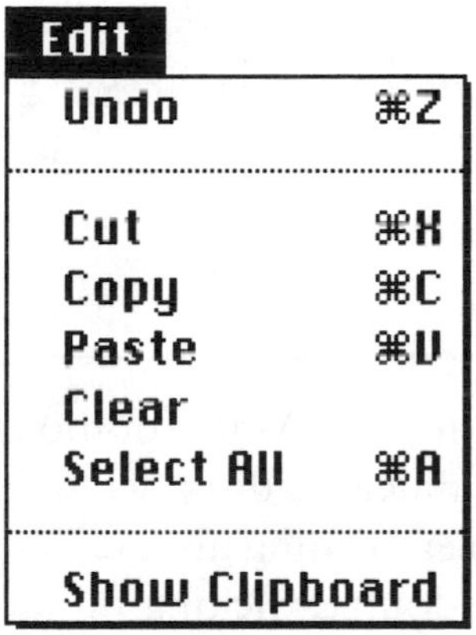

Figure 12.1   An **Edit** menu. Do you know where it came from?

By the Way

This particular menu comes from the **Finder**, the application that runs when your Macintosh first starts up. The Finder is the application containing all of the windows and icons you use to launch other applications.

The Toolbox is divided into a series of managers. As you learn to implement a standard Mac interface, you'll learn about the functions that make up each manager. For example, you'll learn how to use the functions that make up the **Window Manager** to create and maintain your program's windows. You'll use the **Control Manager** to manage scroll bars, push buttons, and other standard Macintosh controls, like the ones shown in Figure 12.2.

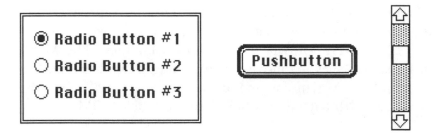

Figure 12.2   A set of radio buttons, a push button, and a scroll bar. Each of these is created and maintained via the Control Manager.

Opening windowMaker.π

Our final project, windowMaker.π, presents a complete Mac Toolbox application. Although windowMaker.π doesn't do much, it does demonstrate some of the user interface concepts you've been reading about.

If you're not already in it, launch THIN C by double-clicking on its icon in the Finder. When prompted for a project to open, go into the Projects folder, then into the windowMaker subfolder, and open the project named windowMaker.π.

Running windowMaker.π

Run the project by selecting **Run** from the **Project** menu. Once THIN C recompiles your source code, the menu bar in Figure 12.3 will appear on the top of your screen. If you have a color system with the color turned on, the ⌘ should appear in color.

Figure 12.3 windowMaker's menu bar.

For starters, select the first item from the menu, **About WindowMaker....** You should hear a short beep, then the window shown in Figure 12.4 should appear on the screen. I'll tell you about the *Macintosh C Programming Primer* a little later. For the moment, click your mouse in the **OK** button to dismiss the window.

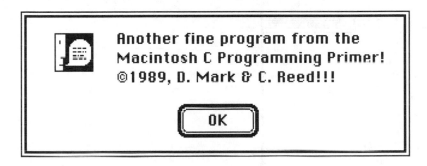

Figure 12.4 This window appears when you select **About WindowMaker...** from the menu.

Next, click your mouse on the File menu. The menu shown in Figure 12.5 should appear. Note the Command-key equivalents located to the right of each menu item. A Command-key equivalent equates a keyboard sequence to a menu item. For example, if you hold down the Command key (the key with the ⌘ on it) and type an *N*, the **New** item will be selected.

Select the first item, **New**. A window will appear, bearing the title **Window** (Figure 12.6). A celebratory picture will appear, centered in the window. Select **New** several more times. Several more windows will appear. Try clicking your mouse in a window's close box. The window should close. Open a few more windows. Select **Close** to close a window. Click on a back window to bring it to the front. Notice that as a window is uncovered, its picture is automatically redrawn. When you are done, select **Quit** from the **File** menu to exit the program.

Figure 12.5   `windowMaker`'s **File** menu.

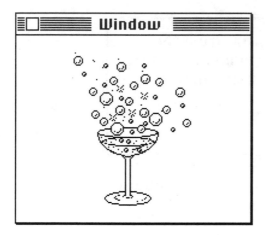

Figure 12.6   A `windowMaker` window.

Getting Started With the Mac Toolbox

The next step in your programming education is to learn how to use the Mac Toolbox in your own programs. The first thing you should do is buy a copy of the THINK C development environment from Symantec.

THINK C comes with everything you'll need to interface with the Toolbox, and then some. If you'd like to learn more about THINK C, turn to Appendix E.

By the Way

When you order THINK C, make sure you take advantage of the money-saving coupon in the back of the book.

Once you've purchased your copy of THINK C, you're ready to start using the Toolbox. Fortunately, there's a lot of literature available to help ease you through the Toolbox learning curve.

Inside Macintosh

If there is one item found on every Macintosh programmer's bookshelf, it's a well-worn copy of *Inside Macintosh*, Apple's official Macintosh programmer's reference guide. It covers the Toolbox in depth, listing every Toolbox function, along with the function's parameters, and that function's place in the Mac universe.

Inside Macintosh is broken out as a series, Volumes I through VI, and a cross reference that covers the first five volumes is also available. Get a copy of Volume I, which introduces the Macintosh graphical user interface and describes most of the Toolbox functions you'll need to get started.

Once you get comfortable with the Toolbox, you'll probably want to pick up the rest of the *Inside Macintosh* series. If you only get one more book after Volume I, make sure it's Volume V, which covers, in detail, the parts of the Toolbox that deal with color. If you're going to program using color, Volume V is essential. Next on the priority list is Volume VI, which covers the changes Apple made to the Toolbox when they introduced System 7.0. Once you have Volume VI, pick up Volume IV, which covers changes made to the Toolbox when the Mac Plus was introduced. Volume IV contains a complete revision of the File Manager information presented in Volume I. If you want to work with files, you'll want to check out Volume IV. Last on the list are Volumes II and III.

By the Way

There is also a hardcover edition of *Inside Macintosh*, which contains Volumes I, II, and III. For my money, however, the softcover editions are a better buy. The hardcover combination of I-III is both heavy and unwieldy.

The Macintosh C Programming Primer

When *Inside Macintosh* was written, Pascal was the primary Macintosh programming language. Because of this, all of the function descriptions and examples presented in *Inside Macintosh* were written in Pascal. In addition, the books were written as a reference and not a tutorial. Basically, *Inside Macintosh* is critical once you understand the basics of programming with the Toolbox.

There is a book that helps bridge the gap for first-time Macintosh programmers. The *Macintosh C Programming Primer*, by Dave Mark and Cartwright Reed, offers a step-by-step tour through the mysteries of the Toolbox. The *Mac Primer* walks you through each of the Toolbox Managers, punctuating each chapter with a variety of sample programs. The *Mac Primer* takes the sting out of learning to program using the Mac Toolbox.

The *Mac Primer* also offers a lot of advice for programmers looking to get involved with the Macintosh development community. Whether you are interested in developing your own best-selling Macintosh application, or just want to hook up with other Mac developers, the *Mac Primer* can help. Inside, you'll find descriptions of Apple's developer relations programs, designed to help you get your products out the door. You can read about AppleLink, Apple's internal electronic mail system that you can be a part of. There are descriptions of technical reference material available from Apple, as well as from third parties.

In general, Cartwright and I tried to put everything into the Primer that we were looking for when we were first learning to program the Macintosh. We hope you enjoy it.

Macintosh Programming Secrets

A book that I frequently turn to is Scott Knaster's excellent *Macintosh Programming Secrets*. This book is full of Macintosh programming tips, tricks, and techniques. Scott takes his years of experience as an Apple employee and puts them to good use, revealing some of the deep, dark secrets that only a Mac aficionado could know. Once you've mastered the basics of Macintosh Toolbox programming, give this book a try.

Go Get 'Em

Well, that's about it. I hope you enjoyed reading this book as much as I enjoyed writing it. Above all, I hope you are excited about C. Now that you have C under your belt, go out there and write some source code.

If you get a chance, stop by the *Learn Programming* forum and say hello. Log in to CompuServe, type GO MACDEV, and check out section 11. I'd love to hear from you . . .

Glossary

algorithm: The technical approach used to solve a problem.

ANSI C: The standard version of the C programming language established by the American National Standards Institute.

append: A mode used when opening a file for writing. Append mode specifies that any data written to the file is written after any existing data.

argument: Another word for **parameter**.

array: A variable containing a sequence of data of a particular type. For example, you can declare an array of 50 ints.

array element: The smallest addressable unit of an array. In an array of 50 ints, each int represents an element of the array.

ASCII character set: A set of 128 standard characters defined by the American Standard Code for Information Interchange.

backslash sequence: A single character represented by the combination of the backslash (\\) and another character. For example, the sequence '\\n' represents a new line character.

balanced tree: A binary tree that maintains a uniform depth. The more unbalanced a tree becomes, the less efficient some tree-searching algorithms become.

bell curve: A bell-shaped statistical curve that represents a normal probability distribution. Plotting the possible rolls of a pair of six-sided dice yields a bell curve.

binary: A system of mathematics based on the two digits 0 and 1. Computers use binary to represent the value stored in memory.

bit: The smallest unit of computer memory, a bit has a value of either 0 or 1.

case-sensitive: Sensitive to the difference between upper- and lower-case letters. C is a case-sensitive language and therefore distinguishes between names such as `MyFunction()` and `MYFUNCTION()`.

cast: See **typecast**.

Central Processing Unit (CPU): The integrated circuit that controls the processing of a computer. The Macintosh family of computers is driven by a 68000 series CPU.

child: A node in a tree pointed to by another node. The node that points to a child node is known as the child's parent.

Command-key equivalent: A key sequence tied to a specific pull-down menu item. Command-key equivalents always consist of a keyboard key combined with the Command (⌘) key.

comparative operator: An operator that compares its left side with its right side, producing a value of either `TRUE` or `FALSE`.

comparative relationship: The relationship between the two sides of a comparative operator that determines whether the operator returns a value of `TRUE` or `FALSE`.

compiler: A program that translates source code into the machine code understood by a computer.

complex statements: Statements made up of several parts, and possibly including other statements.

console: A terminal or window that receives the output from Standard Library functions, such as `printf()` and echoes the input from the keyboard.

Control Manager: The functions in the Macintosh Toolbox that deal with controls, such as radio buttons, push buttons, and scroll bars.

counter: A variable whose sole purpose is to keep a running count of an event. The variable that changes each time through a `for` loop is a counter.

declaration: A statement used to define a new variable, function, or type. A variable declaration establishes both the name and type of the variable.

decrement: Decrease in value. Typically, decrementing a variable decreases its value by 1.

dereference: Use a pointer to retrieve the contents of the memory location that the pointer points to.

dimension: The number of array elements associated with an array.

doping: The process of using a laser beam to create impurities in the silicon of an integrated circuit.

exceeding the bounds: Exceeding the bounds of an array means trying to access an inappropriate element of the array, such as the 51st `int` in an array of 50 `int`s.

explicit initialization: Initialization that occurs in a variable's declaration statement.

file: A series of bytes residing on a magnetic storage media. Files are used as long-term storage for program data.

file mode: The type of access used when opening a file. Examples of file modes are read, write, and append.

file name: The name associated with a disk file.

Finder: The application that runs when your Macintosh first starts up. The Finder is the application with all of the windows and icons you use to launch other applications.

floating-point numbers: Numbers that contain a decimal point. For example, 3.5, -27.6874, and 3.14159 are all floating-point numbers.

flow control: The ability to control the order in which your program's statements are executed.

fractional part: The part of a floating point to the right of the decimal point.

function: A sequence of source code that accomplishes a specific task. C functions have a title and a body. The title contains the function's name and parameters. The body contains the function's code.

function body: The portion of the function that contains the function's code. The body of a function starts with a left curly bracket and ends with a right curly bracket.

function parameter: A class of variable that allows data sharing between a calling function and a called function.

function pointer: A variable containing a pointer to a function. Function pointers can be used to call the function they point to.

function return value: The value returned by a function. Functions of type void are the only types of functions that do not return a value.

function title: The portion of a function that contains the function's name and parameters.

global variable: A variable that is accessible from inside every function in your program.

graphical user interface (GUI): A user interface that features graphical elements, such as pictures, icons, and windows. The Mac is a great example of a graphical user interface.

increment: Increase in value. Typically, incrementing a variable increases its value by 1.

index: The number used to refer to an individual array element. An array index usually appears between the brackets following the array name.

initialization: The process of assigning a value to a variable for the first time. Initializing a variable in its declaration statement is known as **explicit initialization.**

initialized: Containing a known value.

in-order search: A binary tree search that recursively searches a node's left child, visits the node itself, then recursively searches the node's right child.

input buffer: A block of memory designed to accumulate input from the keyboard for later retrieval by your program.

input device: A device that allows a user to provide input to your program. The mouse and the keyboard are both input devices.

integer: A whole number, such as 1, -26, or 3,876,560.

integer part: The part of a floating-point number to the left of the decimal point.

Integrated Circuit (IC): An electronic device with a body, constructed of many fine layers of silicon, and legs, made of a conductive material. Integrated circuits produce a predetermined effect on voltages applied to their legs. They can be used to control a wide variety of electronic devices, from the fuel injector in a car to the Macintosh on your desk.

iteration: The process of stepping through a list or array. `for` loops that step from 1 to an upper limit are typical signs of iteration.

key: The field in a tree `struct` that determines the search order of the tree.

leaf node: A terminal node of a tree. In a binary tree, a leaf node has two `NULL` pointers.

linked list: A data structure consisting of two or more `struct`s, linked together by pointers.

literal: A constant of any type. The number 123 is an example of an `int` literal. `"Hello"` is an example of a literal text string.

loop: Any repeating source code sequence. `do`, `while`, and `for` are examples of C loop statements.

machine code: A machine readable translation of your source code. Machine code is made up of the binary digits 1 and 0.

macro: A `#define` that takes a parameter.

master pointer: The pointer to the first element in a linked list.

memory: A portion of a computer, composed of specially designed integrated circuits, used for the temporary storage of programs and data.

Menu Manager: The functions in the Macintosh Toolbox that deal with the menu bar and pull-down and pop-up menus.

motherboard: Part of a computer that acts as a docking station for all of the other elements of the computer. The hard drive, floppy disk drive, and computer memory all connect to the motherboard.

multi-dimensional array: An array declared with more than one index.

object code: Another name for **machine code**. THIN C stores its object code in a project file.

one-dimensional array: An array declared with a single index.

open a file: Perform the necessary work prior to accessing a file's data. Files can be opened using several different modes, among them read, write, and append.

operator: A special character (or set of characters) that represents a specific computer operation. =, ++, and / are examples of operators.

output device: A device that your program uses to provide output to the user. Most of the programs in this book use the console window as an output device.

parameter: See **function parameter**.

parent pointer: A special 4-byte block of memory, associated with the name of an **array**, that points to the first element of the array.

passing: The technique of including a parameter in a function call.

pointer: A special variable, designed specifically to hold the address of another variable.

pointer arithmetic: The process of incrementing or decrementing a pointer to point to the next or previous memory location.

pointer variable: See **pointer**.

postfix notation: The use of the ++ or -- operator following a variable. In postfix notation, the value of the variable is returned before the variable is incremented or decremented.

postorder search: A binary tree search that recursively searches a node's left child, recursively searches the node's right child, then visits the node itself.

prefix notation: The use of the ++ or -- operator preceding a variable. In prefix notation, the variable is incremented or decremented before the value of the variable is returned.

preorder search: A binary tree search that visits a node, then recursively searches the node's left and right children.

project file: A special file THIN C uses to gather information about your project. The project object code is stored in the project file.

project window: A window listing each of the source code files associated with the project. The project window also lists the current size of the object code associated with each source code file.

prompt: A text string that tells the user what your program expects him or her to do. For example, a prompt might ask the user to type in a number between 1 and 10.

random access memory (RAM): See memory.

read a file: The process of transferring the data stored in a file into your program.

read-only memory (ROM): A memory chip that can be read but not written to. The Macintosh Toolbox is found on a set of ROM chips mounted on the Mac's motherboard.

recursion: The process that occurs when a function calls itself. Recursive functions normally feature a parameter that keeps track of the depth of the recursion (the number of times the function has called itself). The recursive function will exit once a terminating condition has been met.

root node: The first node in a tree. A root node has no parents.

root struct: Another name for a root node.

run: The process of stepping through the compiled version of your program. THIN C will run your program when you select **Run** from the **Project** menu.

searching: The process of traversing a tree or list, looking for a particular feature or value.

signed: A variable capable of storing both positive and negative values.

simple statement: An assignment statement or function call. Simple statements never have substatements.

source code: A sequence of statements that tells the computer what to do. Source code is written in a specific programming language, such as C or Pascal.

source code editor: A program that allows you to review and modify your source code. THIN C has a source code editor built in.

Standard Library: A set of built-in functions that comes with every ANSI standard compiler.

statement: A combination of function calls, operators, and variables that performs a set of computer operations. Statements are usually followed by a semicolon.

stepping through: Usually associated with an array or a linked list. Stepping through an array or linked list means performing an operation on each element of the array or linked list.

string constant: A string literal, such as `"Hello"`.

string manipulation: The process of copying or altering a string variable. String manipulation is normally performed on a 0-terminated string embedded in an array of `chars`.

syntax error: An error in your source code that prevents the compiler from compiling your code. THIN C reports syntax errors by printing an error message in a separate window.

tech block: A block of text set off in its own little box, intended to add a bit of technical detail to the subject currently being discussed. Tech blocks fit in one of three categories: "By the Way," "Important," and "Warning."

terminal node: Another name for a **leaf node**.

text editor: A program that allows you to review and modify text files. Text editors are usually able to edit source code and source code editors are usually able to edit text files.

text string: A sequence of consecutive bytes containing ASCII characters, usually terminated by a byte with a value of 0. Text strings are frequently implemented via an array of `chars`.

Toolbox: The Macintosh Toolbox contains the Mac's version of the Standard Library. The Toolbox contains over 700 functions that make the Mac a Mac. These functions include the Menu Manager, the Control Manager, the Window Manager, and more.

traversal: The process of stepping through a linked list, binary tree, or similar data structure. Traversals usually follow a specific pattern, such as preorder, in-order, or postorder.

type: The class a variable belongs to. A variable's type determines the type of data that can be stored in the variable. `char`, `int`, and `float` are examples of variable types.

typecast: A C mechanism for converting a variable from one type to another.

typecasting: The process of applying a typecast to a variable.

typo: Slang for a typographical error.

unsigned: A variable capable of storing only positive values.

user interface: The part of your program that interacts with the user.

variable: A container for your program's data. Variables have a name and a type.

variable scope: Within a program, a variable's scope determines where in the program the variable can be accessed. Local variables are only accessible within the function they are declared in. Global variables are accessible throughout the file they are declared in.

variable type: See **type.**

white space: An invisible character, such as a space, tab, or carriage return. White space is ignored by the compiler.

Window Manager: The functions in the Macintosh Toolbox that deal with the display and management of windows on the Mac's screen.

write a file: The process of transferring data stored in your program's variables out to a disk file.

Complete Program Listings

---

addThese.c

```
AddTheseNumbers( int num1, int num2 )
{
    return( num1 + num2 );
}

main()
{
    int sum;

    sum = AddTheseNumbers( 5, 6 );

    printf( "The sum is %d.", sum );
}
```

ASCII.c

```
PrintChars( char low, char high )
{
    unsigned char   c;

    printf( "%d to %d ---> ", low, high );
    for ( c = low; c <= high; c++ )
        printf( "%c", c );

    printf( "\n" );
}


main()
{
    PrintChars( 32, 47 );
    PrintChars( 48, 57 );
    PrintChars( 58, 64 );
    PrintChars( 65, 90 );
    PrintChars( 91, 96 );
    PrintChars( 97, 122 );
    PrintChars( 123, 126 );
}
```

cdFiles.c

```
#include <stdio.h>
#include <stdlib.h>

#define CD_FILE_NAME     "cdData"

#define MAX_ARTIST_CHARS     50
#define MAX_TITLE_CHARS      50
```

```
struct CDInfo
{
    char        rating;
    char        artist[ MAX_ARTIST_CHARS ];
    char        title[ MAX_TITLE_CHARS ];
    struct CDInfo   *next;
};

extern  struct CDInfo *gFirstPtr;


/******************************  CountCDs  ***/

int     CountCDs()
{
    struct CDInfo    *infoPtr;
    int             numCDs;

    infoPtr = gFirstPtr;
    numCDs = 0;

    while ( infoPtr != NULL )
    {
        infoPtr = infoPtr->next;
        numCDs++;
    }

    return( numCDs );
}


/******************************  FlushFile  ***/

void    FlushFile( FILE *fp )
{
    int c;
```

```
    while ( ( (c = fgetc( fp )) != '\n') && (c != EOF ) )
        ;
}


/****************************  ReadFileLine  ***/

void    ReadFileLine( FILE *fp, char *line )
{
    char c;

    while ( (c = fgetc( fp )) != '\n' )
    {
        *line = c;
        line++;
    }

    *line = 0;
}


/******************************  ReadFile  ***/

char    ReadFile()
{
    FILE          *fp;
    struct CDInfo   *infoPtr;
    int           numCDs, num, i;

    if ( ( fp = fopen( CD_FILE_NAME, "r" ) ) == NULL )
        return( FALSE );

    fscanf( fp, "%d", &numCDs );
    FlushFile( fp );

    for ( i=1; i<=numCDs; i++ )
    {
        infoPtr = malloc( sizeof( struct CDInfo ) );
```

```
        if ( infoPtr == NULL )
        {
            printf( "Out of memory!!!  Goodbye!\n" );
            exit( 0 );
        }

        ReadFileLine( fp, infoPtr->artist );
        ReadFileLine( fp, infoPtr->title );
        fscanf( fp, "%d", &num );
        infoPtr->rating = num;
        FlushFile( fp );

        AddToList( infoPtr );
    }

    fclose( fp );

    return( TRUE );
}


/*********************************  WriteFile  ***/

void    WriteFile()
{
    FILE            *fp;
    struct CDInfo   *infoPtr;
    int             numCDs, i, num;

    if ( ( fp = fopen( CD_FILE_NAME, "w" ) ) == NULL )
    {
        printf( "***ERROR: Could not write CD file!" );
    }
    else
    {
        numCDs = CountCDs();

        fprintf( fp, "%d\n", numCDs );
```

```
        infoPtr = gFirstPtr;

        for ( i=1; i<=numCDs; i++ )
        {
            fprintf( fp, "%s\n", infoPtr->artist );
            fprintf( fp, "%s\n", infoPtr->title );

            num = infoPtr->rating;
            fprintf( fp, "%d\n", num );
            infoPtr = infoPtr->next;
        }

        fclose( fp );
    }
}
```

cdMain.c

```
#include <stdlib.h>
#include <stdio.h>

#define MAX_ARTIST_CHARS    50
#define MAX_TITLE_CHARS     50

struct CDInfo
{
    char        rating;
    char        artist[ MAX_ARTIST_CHARS ];
    char        title[ MAX_TITLE_CHARS ];
    struct CDInfo   *next;
} *gFirstPtr, *gLastPtr;

/****************************** Flush ***/

void    Flush()
{
    while ( getchar() != '\n' )
        ;
}
```

```c
/****************************** ReadLine ***/

void    ReadLine( char *line )
{
    char c;

    while ( (c = getchar()) != '\n' )
    {
        *line = c;
        line++;
    }

    *line = 0;
}


/****************************** ListCDs ***/

void    ListCDs()
{
    struct CDInfo   *curPtr;

    if ( gFirstPtr -- NULL )
    {
        printf( "No CDs have been entered yet...\n" );
        printf( "\n----------\n" );
    }
    else
    {
        curPtr = gFirstPtr;

        while ( curPtr != NULL )
        {
            printf( "Artist:  %s\n", curPtr->artist );
            printf( "Title:   %s\n", curPtr->title );
            printf( "Rating:  %d\n", curPtr->rating );

            printf( "\n----------\n" );
```

```
                    curPtr = curPtr->next;
            }
        }
}


/*******************************  AddToList  ***/

void    AddToList( struct CDInfo *curPtr )
{
    if ( gFirstPtr == NULL )
        gFirstPtr = curPtr;
    else
        gLastPtr->next = curPtr;

    gLastPtr = curPtr;
    curPtr->next = NULL;
}


/********************************  ReadStruct  ***/

struct CDInfo   *ReadStruct()
{
    struct CDInfo    *infoPtr;
    int              num;

    infoPtr = malloc( sizeof( struct CDInfo ) );

    if ( infoPtr == NULL )
    {
        printf( "Out of memory!!!  Goodbye!\n" );
        exit( 0 );
    }

    printf( "Enter Artist's Name:  " );
    ReadLine( infoPtr->artist );
```

```c
    printf( "Enter CD Title:  " );
    ReadLine( infoPtr->title );

    num = 0;
    while ( ( num < 1 ) || ( num > 10 ) )
    {
        printf( "Enter CD Rating (1-10):  " );
        scanf( "%d", &num );
        Flush();
    }

    infoPtr->rating = num;

    printf( "\n----------\n" );

    return( infoPtr );
}


/******************************  GetCommand   ***/

char    GetCommand()
{
    char    command = 0;

    while ( (command != 'q') && (command != 'n')
            && (command != 'l') )
    {
        printf( "Enter command (q=quit, n=new, l=list):  " );
        scanf( "%c", &command );
        Flush();
    }

    printf( "\n----------\n" );
    return( command );
}
```

```
/******************************  main  ***/

main()
{
    char            command;

    gFirstPtr = NULL;
    gLastPtr = NULL;

    ReadFile();

    while ( (command = GetCommand() ) != 'q' )
    {
        switch( command )
        {
            case 'n':
                AddToList( ReadStruct() );
                break;
            case 'l':
                ListCDs();
                break;
        }
    }

    WriteFile();

    printf( "Goodbye..." );
}
```

cdTracker.c

```
#include <stdlib.h>
#include <stdio.h>

#define MAX_ARTIST_CHARS    50
#define MAX_TITLE_CHARS     50
```

```
struct CDInfo
{
    char        rating;
    char        artist[ MAX_ARTIST_CHARS ];
    char        title[ MAX_TITLE_CHARS ];
    struct CDInfo    *next;
} *gFirstPtr, *gLastPtr;


/*******************************  Flush  ***/

void    Flush()
{
    while ( getchar() != '\n' )
        ;
}


/*******************************  ReadLine  ***/

void    ReadLine( char *line )
{
    char c;

    while ( (c = getchar()) != '\n' )
    {
        *line = c;
        line++;
    }

    *line = 0;
}


/*******************************  ListCDs  ***/

void    ListCDs()
{
    struct CDInfo    *curPtr;
```

```
        if ( gFirstPtr == NULL )
        {
            printf( "No CDs have been entered yet...\n" );
            printf( "\n----------\n" );
        }
        else
        {
            curPtr = gFirstPtr;

            while ( curPtr != NULL )
            {
                printf( "Artist:  %s\n", curPtr->artist );
                printf( "Title:   %s\n", curPtr->title );
                printf( "Rating:  %d\n", curPtr->rating );

                printf( "\n----------\n" );

                curPtr = curPtr->next;
            }
        }
}


/********************************  AddToList   ***/

void    AddToList( struct CDInfo *curPtr )
{
    if ( gFirstPtr == NULL )
        gFirstPtr = curPtr;
    else
        gLastPtr->next = curPtr;

    gLastPtr = curPtr;
    curPtr->next = NULL;
}
```

```
/******************************  ReadStruct  ***/

struct CDInfo   *ReadStruct()
{
    struct CDInfo    *infoPtr;
    int              num;

    infoPtr = malloc( sizeof( struct CDInfo ) );

    if ( infoPtr == NULL )
    {
        printf( "Out of memory!!!  Goodbye!\n" );
        exit( 0 );
    }

    printf( "Enter Artist's Name:  " );
    ReadLine( infoPtr->artist );

    printf( "Enter CD Title:  " );
    ReadLine( infoPtr->title );

    num = 0;
    while ( ( num < 1 ) || ( num > 10 ) )
    {
        printf( "Enter CD Rating (1-10):  " );
        scanf( "%d", &num );
        Flush();
    }

    infoPtr->rating = num;

    printf( "\n----------\n" );

    return( infoPtr );
}
```

```c
/******************************   GetCommand   ***/

char    GetCommand()
{
    char    command = 0;

    while ( (command != 'q') && (command != 'n')
                && (command != 'l') )
    {
        printf( "Enter command (q=quit, n=new, l=list):  " );
        scanf( "%c", &command );
        Flush();
    }

    printf( "\n----------\n" );
    return( command );
}


/******************************   main   ***/

main()
{
    char            command;

    gFirstPtr = NULL;
    gLastPtr = NULL;

    while ( (command = GetCommand() ) != 'q' )
    {
        switch( command )
        {
            case 'n':
                AddToList( ReadStruct() );
                break;
            case 'l':
                ListCDs();
                break;
        }
```

```
    }

    printf( "Goodbye..." );
}
```

dice.c

```
RollOne()
{
    long    rawResult;
    int     roll;

    rawResult = rand();

    roll = (rawResult * 6) / 32768;

    return( roll + 1 );
}

PrintX( int howMany )
{
    int i;

    for ( i=0; i<howMany; i++ )
        printf( "x" );
}

PrintRolls( int rolls[] )
{
    int     i;

    for ( i=0; i<11; i++ )
    {
        printf( "%2d (%3d):  ", i+2, rolls[ i ] );
        PrintX( rolls[ i ] / 10 );
        printf( "\n" );
    }
}
```

```
main()
{
    int     rolls[ 11 ], twoDice, i;

    srand( clock() );

    for ( i=0; i<11; i++ )
        rolls[ i ] = 0;

    for ( i=1; i <= 1000; i++ )
    {
        twoDice = RollOne() + RollOne();
        ++ rolls[ twoDice - 2 ];
    }

    PrintRolls( rolls );
}
```

drawDots.c

```
DrawDots( int numDots )
{
    int i;

    for ( i = 0; i < numDots; i++ )
        printf( "." );
}

main()
{
    DrawDots( 30 );
}
```

float.c

```
main()
{
    float    myNum;

    myNum = 123.456;
    printf( "myNum = %f\n", myNum );
    printf( "myNum = %.2f\n", myNum );
    printf( "myNum = %.4f\n", myNum );
    printf( "myNum = %10.4f\n", myNum );
}
```

funcPtr.c

```
#include <stdio.h>


/******************************  SquareIt   ***/

int SquareIt( int num )
{
    return( num * num );
}


/******************************  main   ***/

main()
{
    int     (*myFuncPtr)( int );
    int     num = 5;

    myFuncPtr = SquareIt;
    printf( "%d squared is %d.", num, (*myFuncPtr)( num ) );
}
```

hello.c

```
main()
{
    printf( "Hello, world!" );
}
```

hello2.c

```
SayHello()
{
    printf( "Hello, world!" );
}

main()
{
    SayHello();
}
```

isOdd.c

```
main()
{
    int i;

    for ( i = 1; i <= 20; i++ )
    {
        printf( "The number %d is ", i );

        if ( (i / 2) * 2 == i )
            printf( "even" );
        else
            printf( "odd" );

        if ( (i / 3) * 3 == i )
            printf( " and is a multiple of 3" );
```

```
        printf( ".\n" );
    }
}
```

iterate.c

```c
#include <stdio.h>


/******************************* main ***/

main()
{
    int i, num, fac;

    num = 5;
    fac = 1;

    for ( i=1; i<=num; i++ )
        fac *= i;

    printf( "%d factorial is %d.", num, fac );
}
```

listPrimes.c

```c
IsItPrime( int  candidate )
{
    int i, foundFactor;

    foundFactor = FALSE;
    for ( i = 2; i < candidate; i++ )
    {
        if ( (candidate / i) * i == candidate )
            foundFactor = TRUE;
    }
```

```
        return( foundFactor == FALSE );
}

main()
{
    int i;

    for ( i = 1; i <= 50; i++ )
    {
        if ( IsItPrime( i ) )
            printf( "%d is a prime number.\n", i );
    }
}
```

name.c

```
main()
{
    char    name[ 50 ];

    printf( "Type your first name, please: " );

    scanf( "%s", name );

    printf( "Welcome, %s.\n", name );
    printf( "Your name is %d characters long.",
                                    strlen( name ) );
}
```

nextPrime.c

```
main()
{
    int    startingPoint, candidate, i;
    int    done, foundFactor;
```

```
        done = FALSE;
        startingPoint = 19;
        candidate = startingPoint;

        while ( ! done )
        {
            candidate++;

            foundFactor = FALSE;
            for ( i = 2; i < candidate; i++ )
            {
                if ( (candidate / i) * i == candidate )
                    foundFactor = TRUE;
            }

            done = (foundFactor == FALSE);
        }

        printf( "The next prime after %d is %d.  Happy?",
                    startingPoint, candidate );
}
```

operator.c

```
main()
{
    int     myInt;

    myInt = 3 * 2;
    printf( "myInt ---> %d\n", myInt );

    myInt += 1;
    printf( "myInt ---> %d\n", myInt );

    myInt -= 5;
    printf( "myInt ---> %d\n", myInt );
```

```
    myInt *= 10;
    printf( "myInt ---> %d\n", myInt );

    myInt /= 4;
    printf( "myInt ---> %d\n", myInt );

    myInt /= 2;
    printf( "myInt ---> %d", myInt );
}
```

postfix.c

```
main()
{
    int     myInt;

    myInt = 5;
    printf( "myInt ---> %d\n", myInt++ );
    printf( "myInt ---> %d", ++myInt );
}
```

power.c

```
int     printExtraInfo;

DoPower( int *resultPtr, int base, int exponent )
{
    int i, temp;

    if ( printExtraInfo )
        printf( "\t---> Starting DoPower()...\n" );

    temp = base;
    for ( i = 1; i < exponent; i++ )
        temp *= base;
```

```c
    *resultPtr = temp;

    if ( printExtraInfo )
        printf( "\t---> Leaving DoPower()...\n" );
}

main()
{
    int power;

    printExtraInfo = FALSE;

    if ( printExtraInfo )
        printf( "---> Starting main()...\n" );

    DoPower( &power, 2, 5 );
    printf( "2 to the 5th = %d.\n", power );

    DoPower( &power, 3, 4 );
    printf( "3 to the 4th = %d.\n", power );

    DoPower( &power, 5, 3 );
    printf( "5 to the 3rd = %d.\n", power );

    if ( printExtraInfo )
        printf( "---> Leaving main()...\n" );
}
```

printFile.c

```c
#include <stdio.h>

main()
{
    FILE    *fp;
    int c;
```

```
        fp = fopen( "My Data File", "r" );

        if ( fp != NULL )
        {
            while ( (c = fgetc( fp )) != EOF )
                putchar( c );

            fclose( fp );
        }
}
```

recurse.c

```
#include <stdio.h>


/****************************** main ***/

main()
{
    int     result, num;

    num = 5;
    result = factorial( num );

    printf( "%d factorial is %d.", num, result );
}


int factorial( int num )
{
    if ( num > 1 )
        num *= factorial( num - 1 );

    return( num );
}
```

slasher.c

```
main()
{
    printf( "0000000000\r" );
    printf( "11111\n" );

    printf( "0000\b\b11\n" );

    printf( "Here's a backslash...\\...for you.\n" );
    printf( "Here's a double quote...\"...for you.\n" );

    printf( "Here's a few tabs...\t\t\t\t...for you.\n" );

    printf( "Here's some beeps...\a\a\a\a...for you." );
}
```

squareIt.c

```
SquareIt( int   number, int *squarePtr )
{
    *squarePtr = number * number;
}

main()
{
    int square;

    SquareIt( 5, &square );

    printf( "5 squared is %d.", square );
}
```

structSize.c

```
#define MAX_ARTIST_CHARS     50
#define MAX_TITLE_CHARS      50
struct CDInfo
{
    char    rating;
    char    artist[ MAX_ARTIST_CHARS ];
    char    title[ MAX_TITLE_CHARS ];
};

main()
{
    struct CDInfo    myInfo;

    printf( "rating field:    %d bytes\n",
            sizeof( myInfo.rating ) );

    printf( "artist field:    %d bytes\n",
            sizeof( myInfo.artist ) );

    printf( "title field:    %d bytes\n",
            sizeof( myInfo.title ) );

    printf( "                 ---------\n" );

    printf( "myInfo struct: %d bytes",
            sizeof( myInfo ) );
}
```

sumFive.c

```
main()
{
    int i, num, sum;
```

```
    sum = 0;

    for ( i=1; i<=5; i++ )
    {
        printf( "Enter number %d --->", i );
        scanf( "%d", &num );
        sum = sum + num;
    }

    printf( "The sum of these numbers is %d.", sum );
}
```

windowMaker.c

```
/**********************************************************/
/*                                                        */
/*    WindowMaker Code from Chapter Seven of              */
/*                                                        */
/*        *** The Macintosh Programming Primer ***        */
/*                                                        */
/*    Copyright 1989, Dave Mark and Cartwright Reed       */
/*                                                        */
/*    WindowMaker handles desk accessories, as well       */
/*    as error checking and a few other things.  Since    */
/*    we went to press, we've made a few minor changes    */
/*    to WindowMaker.  The changes are commented and are   */
/*    found in the HandleEvent routine.                   */
/*                                                        */
/*    The WindowMaker project is a good place to start    */
/*    with your own standalone application code.          */
/*                                                        */
/**********************************************************/

#define BASE_RES_ID          400
#define NIL_POINTER          0L
#define MOVE_TO_FRONT        -1L
#define REMOVE_ALL_EVENTS    0
```

```
#define APPLE_MENU_ID           400
#define FILE_MENU_ID            401
#define EDIT_MENU_ID            402

#define ABOUT_ITEM              1
#define ABOUT_ALERT             400
#define ERROR_ALERT_ID          401

#define NO_MBAR                 BASE_RES_ID
#define NO_MENU                 BASE_RES_ID+1
#define NO_PICTURE              BASE_RES_ID+2
#define NO_WIND                 BASE_RES_ID+3

#define NEW_ITEM        1
#define CLOSE_ITEM      2
#define QUIT_ITEM       3

#define UNDO_ITEM       1
#define CUT_ITEM        3
#define COPY_ITEM       4
#define PASTE_ITEM      5
#define CLEAR_ITEM      6

#define DRAG_THRESHOLD          30

#define WINDOW_HOME_LEFT        5
#define WINDOW_HOME_TOP         45
#define NEW_WINDOW_OFFSET       20

#define MIN_SLEEP               0L
#define NIL_MOUSE_REGION        0L

#define LEAVE_WHERE_IT_IS       FALSE

#define WNE_TRAP_NUM            0x60
#define UNIMPL_TRAP_NUM         0x9F

#define NIL_STRING              "\p"
#define HOPELESSLY_FATAL_ERROR  "\pGame over, man!"
```

```
Boolean     gDone, gWNEImplemented;
EventRecord gTheEvent;
MenuHandle  gAppleMenu, gEditMenu;
PicHandle   gMyPicture;
Rect        gDragRect;
int         gNewWindowLeft = WINDOW_HOME_LEFT,
            gNewWindowTop  = WINDOW_HOME_TOP;


/****************************** main *********/

main()
{
    ToolBoxInit();
    MenuBarInit();
    LoadPicture();
    SetUpDragRect();

    MainLoop();
}


/******************************** ToolBoxInit */

ToolBoxInit()
{
    InitGraf( &thePort );
    InitFonts();
    FlushEvents( everyEvent, REMOVE_ALL_EVENTS );
    InitWindows();
    InitMenus();
    TEInit();
    InitDialogs( NIL_POINTER );
    InitCursor();
}
```

```
/********************************          MenuBarInit      */

MenuBarInit()
{
    Handle        myMenuBar;

    if ( ( myMenuBar = GetNewMBar( BASE_RES_ID ) ) ==
        NIL_POINTER ) ErrorHandler( NO_MBAR );
    SetMenuBar( myMenuBar );
    if ( ( gAppleMenu = GetMHandle( APPLE_MENU_ID ) ) ==
        NIL_POINTER ) ErrorHandler( NO_MENU );
    if ( ( gEditMenu = GetMHandle( EDIT_MENU_ID ) ) ==
        NIL_POINTER ) ErrorHandler( NO_MENU );

    AddResMenu( gAppleMenu, 'DRVR' );
    DrawMenuBar();
}


/******************************** LoadPicture *********/

LoadPicture()
{
    if ( ( gMyPicture = GetPicture( BASE_RES_ID ) ) ==
        NIL_POINTER ) ErrorHandler( NO_PICTURE );
}


/******************************** SetUpDragRect *********/

SetUpDragRect()
{
    gDragRect = screenBits.bounds;
    gDragRect.left += DRAG_THRESHOLD;
    gDragRect.right -= DRAG_THRESHOLD;
    gDragRect.bottom -= DRAG_THRESHOLD;
}
```

```
/***************************** MainLoop ********/

MainLoop()
{
    gDone = FALSE;
    gWNEImplemented = ( NGetTrapAddress( WNE_TRAP_NUM,
                        ToolTrap ) != NGetTrapAddress
                        ( UNIMPL_TRAP_NUM, ToolTrap ) );
    while ( gDone == FALSE )
    {
        HandleEvent();
    }
}


/*********************************** HandleEvent      */

HandleEvent()
{
    char    theChar;
    GrafPtr oldPort;    /*  This variable is used in
                            updateEvt handling -
                            It is not in the book...    */

    if ( gWNEImplemented )
        WaitNextEvent( everyEvent, &gTheEvent, MIN_SLEEP,
                    NIL_MOUSE_REGION );
    else
    {
        SystemTask();
        GetNextEvent( everyEvent, &gTheEvent );
    }

    switch ( gTheEvent.what )
    {
        case mouseDown:
            HandleMouseDown();
            break;
```

```
          case keyDown:
          case autoKey:
              theChar = gTheEvent.message & charCodeMask;
              if (( gTheEvent.modifiers & cmdKey ) != 0)
              {
                  AdjustMenus();
                  HandleMenuChoice( MenuKey( theChar ) );
              }
              break;
          case updateEvt:
              /*  This code is different than that found in
                  the book -
                  Use this version... */
              if (!IsDAWindow( gTheEvent.message ) )
              {
                  GetPort( &oldPort );
                  SetPort( gTheEvent.message );
                  BeginUpdate( gTheEvent.message );
                  DrawMyPicture( gMyPicture,
                                    gTheEvent.message );
                  EndUpdate( gTheEvent.message );
                  SetPort( oldPort );
              }
              break;
      }
}


/*********************************** HandleMouseDown */

HandleMouseDown()
{
    WindowPtr    whichWindow;
    short int    thePart;
    long int     menuChoice, windSize;

    thePart = FindWindow( gTheEvent.where, &whichWindow );
    switch ( thePart )
```

```
        {
            case inMenuBar:
                AdjustMenus();
                menuChoice = MenuSelect( gTheEvent.where );
                HandleMenuChoice( menuChoice );
                break;
            case inSysWindow:
                SystemClick( &gTheEvent, whichWindow );
                break;
            case inDrag:
                DragWindow( whichWindow, gTheEvent.where,
                            &gDragRect );
                break;
            case inGoAway:
                if ( TrackGoAway( whichWindow, gTheEvent.where ) )
                    DisposeWindow( whichWindow );
                break;
            case inContent:
                SelectWindow( whichWindow );
                break;
        }
}


/*********************************** AdjustMenus */

AdjustMenus()
{
    if (IsDAWindow( FrontWindow() ) )
    {
        EnableItem(gEditMenu, UNDO_ITEM );
        EnableItem(gEditMenu, CUT_ITEM );
        EnableItem(gEditMenu, COPY_ITEM );
        EnableItem(gEditMenu, PASTE_ITEM );
        EnableItem(gEditMenu, CLEAR_ITEM );
    }
    else
    {
```

```
            DisableItem(gEditMenu, UNDO_ITEM );
            DisableItem(gEditMenu, CUT_ITEM );
            DisableItem(gEditMenu, COPY_ITEM );
            DisableItem(gEditMenu, PASTE_ITEM );
            DisableItem(gEditMenu, CLEAR_ITEM );
    }
}


/*************************************** IsDAWindow */

IsDAWindow( whichWindow )
WindowPtr    whichWindow;
{
    if ( whichWindow == NIL_POINTER )
        return( FALSE );
    else /* DA windows have negative windowKinds */
        return( ( (WindowPeek)whichWindow )->windowKind < 0 );
}


/*************************************** HandleMenuChoice */

HandleMenuChoice( menuChoice )
long int    menuChoice;
{
    int theMenu;
    int theItem;

    if ( menuChoice != 0 )
    {
        theMenu = HiWord( menuChoice );
        theItem = LoWord( menuChoice );
        switch ( theMenu )
        {
            case APPLE_MENU_ID :
                HandleAppleChoice( theItem );
                break;
```

```
                    case FILE_MENU_ID :
                        HandleFileChoice( theItem );
                        break;
                    case EDIT_MENU_ID :
                        HandleEditChoice( theItem );
                        break;
            }
            HiliteMenu( 0 );
    }
}


/***************************  HandleAppleChoice ******/

HandleAppleChoice( theItem )
int     theItem;
{
    Str255      accName;
    int         accNumber;

    switch ( theItem )
    {
        case ABOUT_ITEM :
            NoteAlert( ABOUT_ALERT, NIL_POINTER );
            break;
        default :
            GetItem( gAppleMenu, theItem, accName );
            accNumber = OpenDeskAcc( accName );
            break;
    }
}


/****************************** HandleFileChoice ******/

HandleFileChoice( theItem )
int theItem;
{
```

```
    WindowPtr    whichWindow;
    switch ( theItem )
    {
        case NEW_ITEM :
            CreateWindow();
            break;
        case CLOSE_ITEM :
            if ( ( whichWindow = FrontWindow() ) !=
                    NIL_POINTER )
                DisposeWindow( whichWindow );
            break;
        case QUIT_ITEM :
            gDone = TRUE;
            break;
    }
}


/***************************** HandleEditChoice   *******/

HandleEditChoice( theItem )
int     theItem;
{
    SystemEdit( theItem - 1 );
}


/********************************** CreateWindow   */

CreateWindow()
{
    WindowPtr    theNewestWindow;

    if ( ( theNewestWindow = GetNewWindow( BASE_RES_ID,
                          NIL_POINTER, MOVE_TO_FRONT ) )
                          == NIL_POINTER )
        ErrorHandler( NO_WIND );
```

```
    if ( ( (screenBits.bounds.right - gNewWindowLeft)
            < DRAG_THRESHOLD ) ||
         ( ( screenBits.bounds.bottom - gNewWindowTop)
            < DRAG_THRESHOLD ) )
    {
        gNewWindowLeft = WINDOW_HOME_LEFT;
        gNewWindowTop = WINDOW_HOME_TOP;
    }

    MoveWindow( theNewestWindow, gNewWindowLeft,
                gNewWindowTop, LEAVE_WHERE_IT_IS );
    gNewWindowLeft += NEW_WINDOW_OFFSET;
    gNewWindowTop += NEW_WINDOW_OFFSET;
    ShowWindow( theNewestWindow );
}


/****************************** DrawMyPicture *********/

DrawMyPicture( thePicture, pictureWindow )
PicHandle    thePicture;
WindowPtr    pictureWindow;
{
    Rect     myRect;

    myRect = pictureWindow->portRect;
    CenterPict( thePicture, &myRect );
    SetPort( pictureWindow );
    DrawPicture( thePicture, &myRect );
}


/****************************** CenterPict *********/

CenterPict( thePicture, myRectPtr )
PicHandle    thePicture;
Rect         *myRectPtr;
{
```

```
    Rect      windRect, pictureRect;

    windRect = *myRectPtr;
    pictureRect = (**( thePicture )).picFrame;
    myRectPtr->top = (windRect.bottom - windRect.top -
                      (pictureRect.bottom - pictureRect.top))
        / 2 + windRect.top;
    myRectPtr->bottom = myRectPtr->top + (pictureRect.bottom
                                        - pictureRect.top);
    myRectPtr->left = (windRect.right - windRect.left -
                      (pictureRect.right - pictureRect.left))
        / 2 + windRect.left;
    myRectPtr->right = myRectPtr->left + (pictureRect.right
                                        - pictureRect.left);
}


/****************************** ErrorHandler ********/

ErrorHandler( stringNum )
int stringNum;
{
    StringHandle     errorStringH;

    if ( ( errorStringH = GetString( stringNum ) ) ==
          NIL_POINTER )
       ParamText( HOPELESSLY_FATAL_ERROR, NIL_STRING,
                 NIL_STRING, NIL_STRING );
    else
    {
        HLock( errorStringH );
        ParamText( *errorStringH, NIL_STRING, NIL_STRING,
                  NIL_STRING );
        HUnlock( errorStringH );
    }
    StopAlert( ERROR_ALERT_ID, NIL_POINTER );
    ExitToShell();
}
```

wordCount.c

```c
#define MAX_LINE_LENGTH 200

#define C_RETURN     '\n'
#define C_TAB        '\t'
#define C_SPACE      ' '

main()
{
    char    line[ MAX_LINE_LENGTH ], *charPtr, inWord;
    int     numWords;

    printf( "Type a line of text, please:\n" );

    charPtr = line;
    numWords = 0;
    inWord = FALSE;

    while ( ( *charPtr = getchar() ) != C_RETURN )
    {
        if ( (*charPtr != C_TAB) && (*charPtr != C_SPACE) )
        {
            if ( ! inWord )
            {
                inWord = TRUE;
                numWords++;
            }
        }
        else
            inWord = FALSE;

        charPtr++;
    }

    printf( "You just typed %d word", numWords );
```

```
    if ( ( numWords > 1 ) || ( numWords == 0 ) )
        printf( "s." );
    else
        printf( "." );
}
```

C Syntax Summary

The if Statement

syntax:

```
if ( expression )
    statement
```

example:

```
if ( numEmployees > 20 )
    BuyNewBuilding();
```

alternate syntax:

```
if ( expression )
    statement
else
    statement
```

example:

```
if ( temperature < 60 )
    WearAJacket();
```

```
else
    BringASweater();
```

The while Statement

syntax:

```
while ( expression )
    statement
```

example:

```
while ( FireTooLow() )
    AddAnotherLog();
```

The for Statement

syntax:

```
for ( expression1 ; expression2 ; expression3 )
    statement
```

example:

```
int i, myArray[ 100 ];

for ( i=0; i<100; i++ )
    myArray[ i ] = 0;
```

The do Statement

syntax:

```
do
    statement
while ( expression ) ;
```

example:

```
do
    SpendABuck();
while ( StillGotAFew() ) ;
```

The switch Statement

syntax:

```
switch ( expression )
{
    case constant:
        statements
    case constant:
        statements
    default:
        statements
}
```

example:

```
switch ( theYear )
{
    case 1066:
        printf( "Battle of Hastings" );
        break;
    case 1492:
        printf( "Columbus sailed the ocean blue" );
        break;
    case 1776:
        printf( "Declaration of Independence\n" );
        printf( "A very important document!!!" );
        break;
    default:
        printf( "Don't know what happened during this year" );
}
```

The break Statement

syntax:

```
break;
```

example:

```
i=1;

while ( i <= 9 )
{
    PlayAnInning( i );
    if ( ItsRaining() )
        break;
    i++;
}
```

The return Statement

syntax:

```
return;
```

example:

```
if ( FatalError() )
    return;
```

alternate syntax:

```
return( expression );
```

example:

```
int AddThese( int num1, int num2 )
{
    return( num1 + num2 );
}
```

Appendix D

Standard Library Functions Used in This Book

THE STANDARD LIBRARY FUNCTION DESCRIPTIONS IN THIS appendix were taken from the pages of the Standard Libraries Reference that comes with THINK C. They represent only a small part of the Standard Library, limited to those functions that appear in this book. When you get your copy of THINK C, spend some time with the real Standard Libraries Reference, getting to know each and every one of the Standard Library functions. You never know when you'll need one of them. For example, you'll notice that each entry in this appendix includes *See Also*, a reference to related Standard Library functions. Some of the *See Also* functions may not appear in this appendix. You will find them in the THINK C Standard Libraries Reference, though. Remember, if you can't find it in this appendix, don't give up!

clock

Library	ANSI
Syntax	`#include <time.h>` `clock_t clock(void)`
Description	`clock()` determines the elapsed time since power-up, in clock ticks.
	The time in seconds is `clock() / CLOCKS_PER_SEC`. `clock()` is useful for calculating durations.
Returns	The elapsed time since power-up, in clock ticks, if successful.
	`(clock_t)-1`, if that time is not available or its value cannot be represented.

exit

Library	ANSI
Syntax	`#include<stdlib.h>` `void exit (int status);`
Description	`exit()` terminates the program normally.
	`exit()` executes all functions registered with `_atexit()` or `atexit()`, flushes all open output streams, closes all open files, and removes all temporary files.
	The `status` argument is ignored.
See Also	`_exit()`, `abort()`.

fclose

Library	ANSI
Syntax	`#include <stdio.h>` `int fclose(FILE *stream);`
Description	`fclose()` flushes the stream that `stream` points to and closes the file that is associated with that stream. `fclose()` delivers any unwritten buffered data to the host environment and discards any unread buffered data. `fclose()` won't close or deallocate buffers that the program allocated itself (e.g., by handing a buffer to `setbuf()`), but it will close buffers that were allocated automatically (e.g., by `setbuf()`, if the program called `setbuf()` but did not hand it a buffer, or by `fopen()`). The difference between `fclose()` and the Unix Library function `close()` is that `fclose()` takes a file pointer as its argument, while `close()` takes a file descriptor number.
Returns	0 (zero), if successful. `EOF`, if failure.

fgetc

Library	ANSI
Syntax	`#include <stdio.n>` `int fgetc(FILE *stream);`
Description	`fgetc()` reads in the next character from the given stream.
	`fgetc()` returns an unsigned integer in the range 0 - 255 (decimal), or `EOF`.
	Since `fgetc()` returns the integer value of the character, it is useful for getting bytes from binary files.
	To read in multiple characters more efficiently, you can also use `fread()` or `fgets()`. To read text and data directly into variables, use `scanf()`.
Returns	The next character from the input stream, if successful.
	`EOF`, if failure. Also, it sets the file's error indicator if there was a read error, and sets the file's EOF indicator if it reaches the end of the file.
See Also	`fread()`, `fgets()`, `fscanf()`, `getc()`, `gets()`, `read()`, `scanf()`.

fopen

Library	ANSI
Syntax	`#include <stdio.h>` `FILE *fopen(char *filename, char *mode);`
Description	`fopen()` opens the given file. `fopen()` automatically allocates a buffer for the file's stream, creates a new stream, and sets the stream to be fully buffered. `fopen()` clears the error and EOF indicators for the stream.

These are the arguments to `fopen()`:

`filename`	pointer to the name of the file.
`mode`	pointer to a string describing how to open the file.

The three main modes are read, write, and append. Each mode has a similar set of variations: read binary, write binary, append binary, and so on.

These are all the possible modes:

String	Mode
`r`	Open this text file for reading.
`w`	Truncate this text file to zero length, or create a new text file for writing.
`a`	Append to this file. That is, open or create this text file for writing at end-of-file.
`rb`	Open this binary file for reading.
`wb`	Truncate this binary file to zero length, or create a new binary file for writing.
`ab`	Append to this binary file. That is, open or create this binary file for writing at end-of-file.
`r+`	Open this text file for updating (reading and writing).

w+	Truncate this text file to zero length or create a new text file for updating (reading and writing).
a+	Open this text file for updating (reading and writing), but append all writing at the end of the file.
r+b or rb+	Open this binary file for updating (reading and writing).
w+b or wb+	Truncate this binary file to zero length or create a new binary file for updating.
a+b or ab+	Open this binary file for updating (reading and writing), but append all writing at the end of the file.

When opening a file for reading (i.e., mode is r, rb, r+, or r+b/rb+) and there is no file named filename, fopen() fails and returns NULL.

When opening a file for appending (i.e., mode is a, ab, a+, a+b, or ab+), all writing is appended to the end of the file, regardless of intervening calls to fseek().

When opening a file for updating (i.e., + is the second or third character in mode), the program can both read from and write to the associated stream. However, between a read and a write (or vice versa), the program must make an intervening call to fflush() or one of the file positioning functions (fseek(), fsetpos(), or rewind()).

Returns	A pointer to the stream, if successful.
	NULL, if failure.
See Also	open(), fileno(), fclose(), fflush(), fread(), fwrite().
	freopen() opens a file on a specific stream.

fprintf

Library	ANSI
Syntax	`#include <stdio.h>` `int fprintf(FILE *stream, char *format, ...)`
Description	`fprintf()` writes to the given stream. It takes the output from the data arguments, converts them according to the format specifiers in the format argument, and writes the result to the stream that `stream` points to. These are the arguments to `fprintf()`:

`stream`   The stream `fprintf()` writes to.

`format`   Pointer to a string of format specifiers.

`...`   Represents the list of data that `fprintf()` writes.

For more information on the format specifier, refer to Figure D.1 in the entry for printf.

The data `fprintf()` prints must consist of valid expressions.

Returns	The number of characters printed, if successful. A negative value, if failure.
See Also	`fscanf()`, `printf()`, `scanf()`, `sprintf()`, `sscanf()`, `vfprintf()`, `vprintf()`, `vsprintf()`.

fputc

Library	ANSI
Syntax	`#include <stdio.h>` `int fputc(int c, FILE *stream);`
Description	`fputc()` adds a single character c to the output stream `stream`.
	`fputc()` writes the character at the position indicated by the file position indicator that is associated with the stream. It then advances the indicator appropriately.
	If the file cannot support positioning requests, or if the stream was opened with append mode (see `fopen()`), `fputc()` appends the character to the end of the output stream.
Returns	The integer value of the character c, if successful.
	`EOF`, if failure (e.g., file is read only).
See Also	`putc()`, `fputs()`, `fwrite()`, `fprintf()`.

fputs

Library	ANSI
Syntax	`#include <stdio>` `int fputs(char *s, FILE *stream);`
Description	`fputs()` writes the string to which s points to the stream to which `stream` points.
	The string must end in a `NULL ('\0')`, but `fputs()` does not write the `NULL` to the stream.
Returns	0 (zero), if successful.
	`EOF`, if failure.
See Also	`puts()`, `fprintf()`, `fwrite()`, `fputc()`.

free

Library	ANSI
Syntax	`#include <stdlib.h>` `void free(void *ptr);`
Description	`free()` releases the block of memory that `ptr` points to, making the memory available for further allocation.
	Note: Make sure the argument `free()` receives is a pointer returned earlier by `calloc()`, `malloc()`, or `realloc()`. Otherwise, the results are unpredictable.
	`free()` keeps its own internal accounting of how much memory to free.
	If `ptr` is a `NULL` pointer, `free()` performs no action.
See Also	`calloc()`, `malloc()`, `cfree()`.

fscanf

Library	ANSI
Syntax	`#include <stdio.h>` `int fscanf(FILE *stream, char *format, ...);`
Description	`fscanf()` reads from the given stream. It separates the input according to the format specifiers in the format argument and stores the results in the objects pointed to by the data arguments.

fscanf() is the input analog of `fprintf()`. If the format is exhausted while arguments remain, `fscanf()` will evaluate the excess arguments but will otherwise ignore them.

These are the arguments to `fscanf()`:

`stream`   The stream from which `fscanf()` should read.

`format`   Pointer to a string of format specifiers.

`...`   Represents the items into which `fscanf()` will store the data it reads. These items must all be pointers.

For more information on the format specifier refer to Figure D.1 in the entry for printf.

Returns	The number of items successfully assigned, if successful. This can be fewer than the number of items in its argument list or even zero in the event of an early matching failure (i.e., when an input argument does not match what `fscanf()` is looking for).

`EOF`, if an input failure occurs before it performs any data conversion.

See Also	`fprintf()`, `printf()`, `scanf()`, `sprintf()`, `sscanf()`, `vfprintf()`, `vprintf()`, `vsprintf()`.

getchar

Library	ANSI
Syntax	`#include <stdio>` `int getchar(void)`
Description	`getchar()` is a macro that calls `fgetc()`, supplying `stdin` as the argument. This gets the next character from the standard input.
Returns	The integer value of the character, if successful. `EOF`, if error or end-of-file.

malloc

Library	ANSI
Syntax	`#include <stdlib.h>` `void *malloc(size_t size);`
Description	`malloc()` allocates a block of memory for an object. `size` specifies the size of the object. Unlike `calloc()`, `malloc()` does not clear the block of memory. To free the memory that `malloc()` allocates, use `free()`.
Returns	A pointer to the block of space, if successful. `NULL`, if failure.
See Also	`free(), calloc(), realloc().`

printf

Library	ANSI
Syntax	`#include <stdio.h>` `int printf(char *format, ...);`
Description	`printf()` performs the same operations as `fprintf()` except that `printf()` writes its output to `stdout`. For more information on the format specifier refer to Figure D.1.
Returns	The number of characters it wrote to `stdout`, if successful A negative value, if failure.
See Also	`fprintf()`, `fscanf()`, `scanf()`.

Format Character	Type of Corresponding Argument	Output
c	int	a single character
d	int	a signed integer
f	float	a signed float

i	int	a signed integer
		   - Default precision of 1
		   - Pads the result with zeros

p	void *	a pointer, displayed in hexadecimal
s	char *	a zero terminated string
u	unsigned int	an unsigned integer
%	no argument	a single % character

Figure D.1 Table of Format specification characters.

putchar

Library	ANSI
Syntax	`#include <stdio.h>` `int putchar(int c);`
Description	`putchar()` calls the `fput()` function, supplying `stdout` as the output stream. `putchar()` is implemented as a macro rather than a true function.
Returns	The character written, if successful. `EOF`, if failure. It also sets the error indicator for the stream.
See Also	`putc()`, `puts()`, `printf()`.

rand

Library	ANSI
Syntax	`#include <stdlib.h>` `int rand(void);`
Description	`rand()` returns a pseudo-random integer in the range 0 to `RAND_MAX`. Successive calls to `rand()` result in a pseudo-random sequence of numbers. If you set the seed (using `srand()`) to the same number each time you run your program, you'll always get the same sequence of pseudo-random numbers.
Returns	A pseudo-random integer in the range 0 to `RAND_MAX`.
See Also	`srand()`.

scanf

Library	ANSI
Syntax	`#include <stdio.h>` `int scanf(char *format, ...);`
Description	`scanf()` performs the same operations as `fscanf()` except that `scanf()` uses `stdin` as the input stream. For more information on the format specifier, refer to Figure D.1 in the entry for printf.
Returns	The number of items successfully read, if successful. This can be fewer than the number of items in the argument list or even zero in the event of an early matching failure (i.e., when an input argument does not match what `scanf()` is looking for). `EOF`, if an input failure occurs before any data conversion.

srand

Library	ANSI
Syntax	`#include <stdlib.h>` `void srand(unsigned int seed);`
Description	`srand()` initializes the pseudo-random number generator, using its argument as a seed for a new sequence. Use `rand()` to produce a pseudo-random number. Using the same number as the seed for `srand()` will always produce the same sequence of numbers.

strcat

Library	ANSI
Syntax	```#include <string.h>``` ```char *strcat(char *s1, char *s2)```
Description	`strcat()` appends a copy of the string that `s2` points to to the end of the string that `s1` points to.
	The initial character of `s2` overwrites the NULL character at the end of `s1`.
	Make sure there is enough space for string `s2` in the character array after the end of the string `s1`.
Returns	The value of `s1`, after `s2` has been appended.

strchr

Library	ANSI
Syntax	```#include <string.h>``` ```char *strchr(char *s, int c);```
Description	`strchr()` locates the first occurrence of `c` (which it converts to a char) in the string that `s` points to.
	`strchr()` considers the terminating NULL character to be part of the string `s`.
Returns	A pointer to the first occurrence of `c` in the string `s`, if `c` is found.
	The NULL pointer, if `c` is not found.
See Also	`strrchr()`

strcmp

Library	ANSI
Syntax	`#include <string.h>` `int strcmp(char *s1, char *s2);`
Description	`strcmp()` compares the string that `s1` points to to the string that `s2` points to.
	Note that if `s1` is a substring of `s2`, `strcmp()` will return a number greater than zero because the last characters it compares will be the terminating NULL (`'\0'`) character of `s1` against some character in `s2`.
Returns	Positive integer if `s1` is greater than `s2`. 0 if `s1` equals `s2`. Negative integer if `s1` is less than `s2`.

strcpy

Library	ANSI
Syntax	`#include <string.h>` `char *strcpy(char *s1, char *s2);`
Description	`strcpy()` copies the string that `s2` points to (including the terminating NULL character (`'\0'`)) into the array that `s1` points to.
Returns	The value of `s1`.
See Also	`strncpy()`.

strlen

Library	ANSI
Syntax	`#include <strings.h>` `size_t strlen(char *s);`
Description	`strlen()` computes the length of the string that s points to.
Returns	`strlen()` returns the number of characters that precede the terminating NULL character.

strncat

Library	ANSI
Syntax	`#include <string.h>` `char *strncat(char *s1, char *s2, size_t n)`
Description	`strncat()` appends a copy of the string that s2 points to to the end of the string that s1 points to, until it has appended n characters or it has reached the end of string s2. The initial character of s2 overwrites the NULL character at the end of s1. If `strncat()` appends n characters without reaching the end of s2, `strncat()` will add a terminating NULL character (`'\0'`). Make sure there is enough space for s2 in the character array after the end of the string s1.
Returns	The value of s1, after appending the string s2. If n is negative or zero, it returns s1 unchanged.
See Also	`strcat()`.

strncmp

Library	ANSI
Syntax	`#include <string.h>` `int strncmp(char *s1, char *s2, size_t n);`
Description	`strncmp()` compares the string that `s1` points to to the string that `s2` points to, up to a limit of n characters. `strncmp()` does not compare characters that follow the `NULL` character.

Returns	Positive integer	if the first n characters of `s1` are greater than the first n characters of `s2`.
	0	if the first n characters of `s1` are equal to the first n characters of `s2`.
	Negative integer	if the first n characters of `s1` are less than the first n characters of `s2`.

See Also	`strcmp()`.

strncpy

Library	ANSI
Syntax	`#include <string.h>` `char *strncpy(char *s1, char *s2, size_t n);`
Description	`strncpy()` copies characters from `s2` to `s1` until either it has copied n characters or it reaches a `NULL` character in `s2`. If `s2` is shorter than n characters, `strncpy()` will append `NULL` characters to `s1` until it has written n characters there.
Returns	The value of `s1`.

The Complete THINK C Development Environment

NOW THAT YOU'VE WORKED WITH A SCALED-DOWN version of THINK C, you'll want to upgrade to the full version. The complete THINK C development environment lets you take advantage of the powerful features and capabilities that have made the THINK Languages the leading development tools for the Macintosh. This chapter will describe some of those features, including:

- The Project
- The Editor
- Libraries
- Fast turnaround
- Source-level debugging

- Inline assembler
- Object-oriented programming
- The THINK Class Library

You're familiar with some features of the THINK C environment from working with the special version of the product included with this book. In the full version of the product, however, you can take advantage of many additional features, such as an enhanced project window, full source-level debugging capabilities, an inline assembler, and object-oriented programming. Other powerful new features include an optional optimizer for even tighter code, a class browser for object-oriented programming, and full ANSI compatibility. In addition, with the complete version of THINK C, you can build your own double-clickable applications.

Special Upgrade Offer

Symantec will upgrade owners of *"Learn C on the Macintosh"* to the complete THINK C development environment for a special price. You can upgrade to the full version for just $129, almost 50 percent off the price of the retail product. See the back page for further details and an upgrade coupon.

Overview of the THINK C Environment

THINK C is a unique development environment for the Macintosh. It features a very fast compiler, a faster linker, an integrated text editor, an auto-make facility, and a project organizer that holds all the pieces together. Because the editor, the compiler, and the linker are all components of the same application, THINK C knows when edited source files need to be recompiled.

THINK C is a complete, integrated environment, not just a C compiler for the Macintosh. Traditional development environments consist of three separate applications: the editor, the compiler, and the linker. It is up to you to create your source files with a text editor, run each file through the compiler, and finally link all your object files. In THINK C, the three components work in concert as parts of the same application. This way, THINK C knows when you've edited a file. The compiler produces object code that the linker can put together in an instant. Then THINK C can launch your program. And because THINK C is still running, it can launch the source level debugger, so you can debug your program.

You can run your program from THINK C as you work on it. Your program runs exactly as if you had launched it from the Finder, not under a simulated environment. If you use MultiFinder, your program runs in its own partition while THINK C remains active, so you can examine and edit your source files as you watch your program run.

With THINK C you can build Macintosh applications, desk accessories, device drivers, and any kind of code resource. The standard C libraries include all the functions specified in the ANSI C standard, as well as some additional UNIX operating system functions.

Writing a program in THINK C is like writing a program in any other development environment. You create your source files, compile them, then link the object code to create an executable file. The difference is that in THINK C, you use the same application to do all of this.

The Project

The project is at the heart of the THINK C development environment. It takes over the functions of several other files in traditional development environments. The project holds the object code of all your compiled source files and maintains the dependencies and connections among them. It keeps track of files that need to be recompiled or that depend on an edited #include file. If you're using the source level debugger, the project keeps the tables that the debugger needs.

Figure E.1 shows a sample project window. It contains a list of all the files that comprise your program. To the right of each file name is the size of that file's object code. To the left of each file name is the "bug" column that THINK C adds to the project window when you choose the **Use Debugger** command. THINK C generates debugging information for files that have gray diamonds next to them.

Rather than producing a separate binary object code file, THINK C keeps all object code in the project document in ready-to-link form. Because the project document knows all the files that make up your program (including header files), it can keep track of changes. When you edit a source file, the project manager marks it for recompilation. When you edit an #include file, the project manager marks all the files that use it.

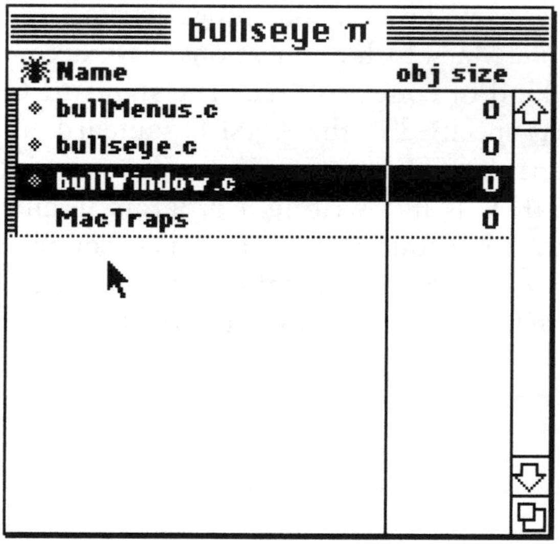

Figure E.1

The Editor

Once you've created a project document, the next step is to add your source files. THINK C source files are standard text files, so you'll be able to use existing source files. The THINK C editor uses standard Macintosh editing techniques, so you're familiar with its basic operation. It also provides some features that help you edit C source code. Its search facilities include a pattern-matching option based on Grep, and a multi-file search that looks for strings in any file in your project.

Figure E.2 shows a sample search dialog from THINK C.

```
┌─────────────────────────────────────────────────────────┐
│  Search for:                    Replace with:            │
│  ┌──────────────────────┐       ┌──────────────────────┐ │
│  │ myWindow│            │       │                      │ │
│  └──────────────────────┘       └──────────────────────┘ │
│      ☐ Match Words        ☐ Grep   ☐ Multi-File Search   │
│      ☐ Wrap Around     ┌────────┐ ┌──────────┐ ┌────────┐│
│      ☒ Ignore Case     │  Find  │ │Don't Find│ │ Cancel ││
│                        └────────┘ └──────────┘ └────────┘│
└─────────────────────────────────────────────────────────┘
```

Figure E.2

You can open as many files as the memory in your Macintosh will allow, and each file appears in its own edit window. Although you usually create and open source or header files, you can also use the THINK C editor to open any text file.

Holding down the Option key as you click in the title bar of the project window brings up a pop-up menu containing the names of all the #include files used in the project. (See Figure E.3.)

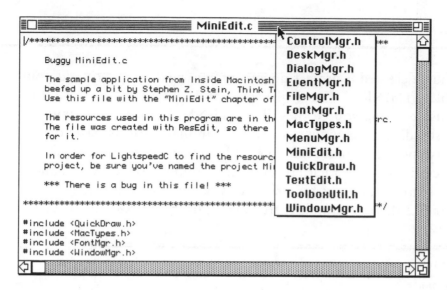

Figure E.3

Libraries

Along with your source files, you must add your libraries to the project document. Virtually every program you write will need to access the Macintosh Toolbox. You can call any Macintosh Toolbox routine exactly as it's described in *Inside Macintosh*. The code for Toolbox routines marked:

```
[Not In ROM]
```

as well as the glue code needed to call some of the other Toolbox routines is in the MacTraps library.

Your THINK C package also includes several other libraries you can use in your programs. The ANSI library contains the standard ANSI functions defined in the ANSI standard. The UNIX library contains UNIX system functions, including memory calls. You can use these libraries when you port code from other systems. You can also create your own libraries in THINK C.

Fast Turnaround

THINK C lets you run your program directly from THINK C. With the single command **Run**, the project manager automatically recompiles the source files that are new or have changed, and loads any unloaded libraries. Then the THINK C linker links all your code together instantly. In this one step you accomplish in seconds what used to take several minutes or longer.

THINK C launches your program as if you had double-clicked on it from the Finder. This way, you know exactly how your program will behave in actual conditions. If you're running under MultiFinder, THINK C launches your program in its own partition. Since THINK C is still running, you can look at your source files while your program is running.

Source-level Debugging

To help get your program working correctly, you can use THINK C's source level debugger. The THINK C debugger lets you debug your code the way you wrote it: in C. You can set breakpoints, step through your code, debug objects, examine variables, and change their values while your program is running. You can set conditional breakpoints that stop execution only when certain conditions are true. And because the debugger runs under MultiFinder, you can edit your source files while you're debugging.

The debugger windows show you the source of your program and the values of your variables. The Source window (see Figure E.4) con-

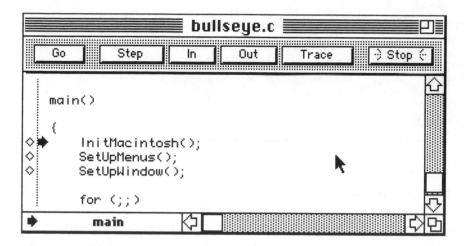

Figure E.4

tains the source text of your program, the debugger's status panel, statement markers, the current statement arrow, and the current function indicator. The title of the Source window is the name of the source file.

The Source window shows the source text of your program. When you start the debugger, this window shows the file that contains the main() routine of your application. The top of the Source window has a six-button status panel. These buttons control the execution of your program. The column of diamonds running along the left side of the source text are **statement markers**. Every line of your program that generates code gets a statement marker. You can set breakpoints at these statement markers. When your program is running, the debugger stops execution just before a breakpoint. You can set three kinds of breakpoints: simple breakpoints, conditional breakpoints, and temporary breakpoints.

The black arrow to the right of the statement markers is the **current statement arrow**. This indicator shows you the **current statement**, the one the debugger is about to execute. When you start your program, the current statement arrow is at the first executable line of your program.

The source debugger uses the space at the lower left of the Source window for the name of the **current function**. When you click here and hold the mouse button down, the debugger displays a pop-up menu that shows the call chain — the names of the functions that were called to get to the current function.

The other debugger window is the Data window. (See Figure E.5.) In this window you can examine and set the values of your variables. The Data window is modeled after a spreadsheet. You can type variable names into the entry field (left column), then press the Return or Enter key. When your program is running, the variable value will appear in the right column.

Figure E.5

Inline Assembler

THINK C lets you use assembly language in your THINK C programs. You can use THINK C's built-in inline assembler for assembly language in your source files, or you can use object files generated by other assemblers. THINK C works within the compiler to produce object code. You can use instructions for the Motorola MC68000 and MC68020 processors and for the MC68881 floating-point coprocessor.

You can refer to C variables and functions within assembly language routines. Your C routines can go to labels in the assembly routines and vice versa.

Object-Oriented Programming (OOP)

The basic distinction between procedural and object-oriented programming is in the way the two disciplines treat data and action. In procedural programming, data and action are two separate things. You define your data structures, then you define some routines to operate on them. For each data structure you define, you need a new set of routines.

In object-oriented programming, action and data are closely coupled. When you define your data— your objects— you also define their actions. Instead of a set of routines that do something to data, you have a set of objects interacting with each other.

Object-oriented programming is a compelling choice for many programmers today and THINK C's built-in OOP capabilities make it accessible to you whether you're a novice or more advanced professional.

The THINK Class Library

Object-oriented programming is not hard to learn, but it requires mastering a few key concepts and a few new words. To make learning object-oriented programming easier, THINK C comes with the THINK Class Library.

The THINK Class Library (TCL) is a collection of classes that implement a standard Macintosh application. The TCL takes care of things like handling menu commands, updating windows, dispatching events, dealing with MultiFinder, maintaining the Clipboard, and so on. The TCL takes care of the common Macintosh interface, so you can concentrate instead on your program's functionalism.

Why Upgrade?

As you can see, the full version of THINK C offers a host of features not included in this special book-version of the product: the project document, libraries, full source-level debugging, inline assembler, object-oriented programming, the THINK Class Library, and more. As you develop your skills as a Macintosh programmer, you'll want the power and flexibility the THINK C development environment offers. Plus, you can upgrade to the complete version for a special price. See the coupon at the back of the book for details.

Why Consider?

Answers to Selected Exercises

Chapter 3

1) 00011010
3) 00001100
5) 01111111
7) 00101111
9) 11111111
11) 11100010
13) 10011101
15) 11110011

Convert these two's complement numbers to decimal:
17) -1
19) -113
21) -64
23) -29

Chapter 4

1) The error message `"invalid declaration"` **appears.**
3) The error message `"syntax error"` **appears.**

Chapter 5

1) a. The text string `"Hello, world"` is missing its double-quote characters.
    c. The += operator is reversed.
    e. The format specifier, %d, is missing.
    g. The left and right sides of the assignment are reversed.
2) a. 70
    c. -1
    e. -8
    g. 14

Chapter 6

1) a. The if statement's expression should be surrounded by parentheses.
    c. The while loop has parentheses, but is missing an expression.
    e. A switch statement cannot switch on a text string. If the variable i is declared as an int, each case should contain a constant. Also, `case default` should be `default`.
    g. The while loop's expression contains an assignment statement instead of a comparative operator. This code is legal, but it doesn't make much sense. The expression:

    ```
    done = TRUE
    ```

    returns the value of done, which is TRUE. Therefore, the while expression will always evaluate to TRUE, and the while loop will continue ad infinitum.

Chapter 7

1) a. Final value is 25.
   c. Final value is 1.

Chapter 8

1) a. The for loop will never exit. c is declared as a char and has a range from -128 to 127. If c has a value of 127 and you add 1 to it, c will have a value of -128. Try it yourself...

   c. The text string "a" represents two characters, both 'a' and a character with a value of 0. You can't assign a text string to a char variable.

   e. The #define of MAX_ARRAY_SIZE must come before the first reference to it.

   g. This code is legal, but it doesn't make much sense. The problem occurs in the line:

   ```
   cPtr++ = 0;
   ```

   This line assigns the pointer variable cPtr a value of 0, then increments it to 1. These two lines make more sense:

   ```
   *cPtr = 0;
   cPtr++;
   ```

   With this change in place, the for loop will initialize each element of the array c to 0.

Chapter 9

a. There's one tiny problem with this declaration and explicit initialization. The array line is allocated only 5 bytes, but the text string "hello" needs 6 bytes, 5 for the letters in the word hello, and 1 byte for the 0 that terminates the text string.

c. The declaration of the field employeeNumber should be terminated by a semicolon.

e. The file name "stdio.h" should appear as <stdio.h>.

g. The fields next and prev should be declared as pointers. Also, a semi-colon should follow the struct declaration.

Chapter 10

1) a. The arguments to fopen() appear in reverse order.

c. line is declared as a char pointer, yet no memory was allocated for line to point to. Also, since line is already a pointer, the & in the call of fscanf() should not be used. Finally, since the file was opened for writing, an fscanf() is inappropriate.

e. This code has one problem. Once again, line is declared as a char pointer, yet no memory has been allocated for it to point to.

Chapter 11

1) a. The problem with this code is in this line:

```
myDog.next = &myCat;
```

Since myDog.next is declared as a Dog pointer, some typecasting should be added to this line. Here's the corrected version:

```
myDog.next = (struct myDog *)(myCat.next);
```

c. The declaration of myUnion is missing the keyword union. Here's the corrected declaration:

```
union Number    myUnion;
```

e. A pair of parentheses has been left out of the function pointer declaration and the call of the function pointer. Here's the corrected code:

```
int        (*myFuncPtr)( int );

myFuncPtr = main;
(*myFuncPtr)();
```

g. The parameters in `strcpy()` appear in reverse order.

Next on your reading list from Addison-Wesley...

Macintosh® C Programming Primer, Volume I: Inside the Toolbox Using THINK C™, by Dave Mark and Cartwright Reed, 672 pages, $26.95, ©1992.

Macintosh® C Programming Primer, Volume II: Mastering the Toolbox Using THINK C™, by Dave Mark, 496 pages, $26.95, ©1990.

Macintosh® Pascal Programming Primer, Volume I: Inside the Toolbox Using THINK Pascal, Dave Mark and Cartwright Reed, 544 pages, $24.95, ©1991.

These and other Addison-Wesley computer titles are available wherever computer books are sold, or by calling Addison-Wesley's order department at (617)-944-3700, 9 a.m. to 5 p.m., EST.

Appendix G

Bibliography

EACH BOOK ON THIS LIST OFFERS INSIGHT INTO SOME part of the C development process. At one end of the spectrum, *The C Programming Language* is an extremely popular reference guide to C programming. It offers a complete specification of the C programming standard.

The first two volumes of the *Macintosh Primer* series take you beyond C programming into the world of Macintosh programming. The *Inside Macintosh* series contains Apple's detailed technical specifications for the Macintosh. If you plan on programming on the Macintosh, you'll want to pick up each of these.

The *THINK C™ User's Guide* comes with your purchase of the THINK C compiler. THINK C is *the* compiler for the Macintosh computer. Get yourself a copy.

The final two books provide a high-level technical view of the Macintosh. If you don't have the cash to buy these, try to find a copy you can borrow for a weekend. They're worth checking out.

1. *Macintosh C Programming Primer,* Volume I, Second Edition, Dave Mark and Cartwright Reed, 1992, Addison-Wesley Publishing Company, Reading, MA.

2. *Macintosh C Programming Primer,* Volume II, Dave Mark, 1990, Addison-Wesley Publishing Company, Reading, MA.

3. *Inside Macintosh,* Volumes I-V, Apple Computer Inc., 1985–88, Addison-Wesley Publishing Company, Reading, MA.

4. *Inside Macintosh,* Volume VI, Apple Computer Inc., 1991, Addison-Wesley Publishing Company, Reading, MA.

5. *Inside Macintosh, X-Ref,* Revised Edition, Apple Computer Inc., 1991, Addison-Wesley Publishing Company, Reading, MA.

6. *The C Programming Language,* Brian W. Kernighan and Dennis M. Ritchie, ©1988, Prentice Hall, Englewood Cliffs, NJ.

7. *THINK C™ User's Manual,* Symantec Corporation, 1989, Cupertino, CA.

8. *THINK C™ Standard Libraries Reference,* Symantec Corporation, 1989, Cupertino, CA.

9. *Technical Introduction to the Macintosh Family,* Apple Computer, Inc., 1987, Addison-Wesley Publishing Company, Reading, MA.

10. *Programmer's Introduction to the Macintosh Family,* Apple Computer, Inc., 1988, Addison-Wesley Publishing Company, Reading, MA.

Index

& (address of) operator, 150, 163
* (multiplication) operator, 77
*= (multiplication) operator, 77
+ (addition) operator, 74
++ (increment by 1) operator, 74-75, 89-91
+= (increment by value) operator, 76
- (subtraction) operator, 74
-- (decrement by 1) operator, 74-75, 89
-= (decrement by value) operator, 76
{ } (curly braces), 46, 116
/ (division) operator, 77-78
/= (division) operator, 77
32-bit addressing, 153
= (equals) operator, 71-72
\ (cancel character), 93
\" (quotation mark character), 93
\a (beep character), 93
\b (backspace character), 93
\n (newline character), 87, 92, 133
\r (carriage return no line feed character), 92
\t (single tab character), 93
#define, 221-224, 226, 236, 248, 258, 311
#include file, 257-258, 269

A

About WindowMaker menu item, 345-346
addThese.c file, 361
AddTheseNumbers() function, 168-169, 171
AddToList() function, 260, 266, 295
AddTwo() function, 155
Algorithms, 47-49, 131, 351
Alphabetic characters, 193-194
and (&&) logical operator, 111
AnotherFunction() function, 49
ANSI C (American National Standards Institute C), 51, 351
ANSI.lib file, 17-19, 34, 285
Append, 351
Applications, checking memory size, 35
Arguments, 351
Arithmetic pointers, 356
Arrays, 200-212, 235-247, 351
    dimensions, 201-202, 236-238
    elements, 200, 351
    exceeding bounds, 211-212
    explicit initialization, 261
    index, 200
    multi-dimensional, 236-238, 356
    names as pointers, 208
    one-dimensional, 236, 356
    stepping through, 202
    struct, 246
ASCII (American Standard Code for Information Interchange), 194
ASCII character set, 194, 199, 351
    unprintable characters, 198
    uppercase and lowercase letters, 197
ASCII.π file, 195-197

ASCII.c file, 199-200, 362
ASCII program, 195-197, 199-200
Assignment statements as expressions, 107

B

Back-up copy of THIN C, 15
Backslash (\) key, 87
Backslash sequence, 87, 351
Backspace character (\b), 93
Balanced tree, 323, 352
Base, raising to exponent power, 175-176
Beep character (\a), 93
Bell curves, 203, 352
Binary
    numbers, 37, 39-40, 352
    operators, 111
Binary trees, 319-328
    balanced tree, 323
    comparative relationship, 320
    in-order search, 325-327
    leaf node, 320
    postorder search, 326-327
    recursion, 324-328
    root node, 320
    searching, 324
    struct, 320
Bits, 37, 352
break statement, 126-127, 129
    syntax, 404
Buffers
    input, 216-219, 355
    output, 284-285
Bytes, 35, 37-38
    as negative number, 38

443

two's complement notation, 38-39

C

C programming language, 4
  functions, 45-52
Calling functions, 49, 50
Cancel character (\), 93
Carriage return no line feed character (\r), 92
case, 127-128
Case sensitivity, 58, 352
Cast, 306, 352
cdData file, 285-287
cdFiler.π file, 285, 287-290
cdFiler program, 285-298
cdFiles.c file, 285, 291-298, 362-366
cdMain.c file, 285, 366-370
cdMain file, 290-291
cdTracker.π file, 254-256
cdTracker.c file, 256-269, 370-375
cdTracker program, 254-269
Central Processing Unit (CPU), 29, 352
char variable type, 192-200
Characters, 193-200
Chicago font, 343
Child, 352
Clear menu item, 21
clock() function, 205, 406
Close menu item, 20, 22, 89, 91, 346
Command-key equivalent, 352
Comments, 96-97
Comparative operators, 108-109, 352
  != (not equal to), 109
  < (less than), 109
  <= (less than or equal to), 109
  == (equal to), 109
  > (more than), 109
  >= (more than or equal to), 109
Comparative relationship, 320, 352
Compilers, 14, 32, 352
Complex statements, 117, 352
Compound expressions, 113
Computers, parts of, 29-31
  console, 30
  input devices, 30

memory, 30-31
motherboard, 29
operation, 28-29
output devices, 30
storage devices, 30
Console, 30, 352
Console window, 80, 82
Constants, 128
Control Manager, 344, 353
Copy menu item, 21
CountCDs() function, 297-298
Counters, 353
Curly braces, 46, 116
Current function, 430
Current statement, 430
Current statement arrow, 430
Cut menu item, 21

D

Data structures in linked list, 251-269
Data types (see Type)
DealTheCards() function, 328-329
Declaration, 353
Declaring variables, 68
Decrement, 353
default case, 127-128
Dereferencing, 154, 353
Development folder, 15
Devices
  input, 355
  output, 356
dice.π file, 203
dice.c file, 204-208, 210-211, 375-376
dice program, 203-208, 210-211
Dimension, 353
do statement, 125
  syntax, 402-403
Doping, 353
DoPower() function, 175-176, 178-180
double variable type, 192
DrawDots() function, 157-161
drawDots.π file, 158
drawDots.c file, 376

E

Edit cursor, 57
Edit menu, 21-22

Editing windows, 18
Elements of arrays, 351
Equal to (==) comparative operator, 109
Error messages
  link failed, 58
  syntax error, 57
Exceeding the bounds, 353
exit() function, 263, 406
Explicit initialization, 260-261, 353
  arrays and global variables, 261
Expressions, 106-113
  assignment statement as, 107
  comparative operators, 108-109
  compound, 113
  literals as, 107
  translating values to another type, 306-307
  TRUE and FALSE, 107-109
  variables as, 106

F

factorial() function, 316-319
FALSE expressions, 107-109
FALSE literal, 110
fclose() function, 282, 407
fgetc() function, 278-283, 295-296, 408
File menu, 20, 35, 345-346
File mode, 353
File name, 353
File pointers, stdin and stdout, 282-283
Files, 275-298, 353
  See also programs, program listings, projects, and individual
program names
  #include, 269
  addThese.c, 361
  ANSI.lib, 17-19, 34, 285
  ASCII.π, 195-197
  ASCII.c, 362
  appending, 277
  cdData, 285-287
  cdFiler.π, 285-290
  cdFiles.c, 285, 291-298, 362-366
  cdMain.c, 285, 366-370
  cdMain, 290-291

cdTracker.π, 254-256
cdTracker.c, 256-269, 370-375
dice.π, 203
dice.c, 204-208, 210-211, 375-376
drawDots.π, 158
drawDots.c, 376
float.π, 190-191
float.c, 377
funcPtr.c, 377
hello.π, 15-17, 19
hello.c, 15-18, 34, 378
hello2.π, 55
hello2.π, 52-53
hello2.c, 53, 378
isOdd.π, 130-134
isOdd.c, 130, 378-379
iterate.c, 379
listPrimes.π, 172-175
listPrimes.c, 379-380
mode, 276-277
My Data File, 279
name, 276
name.π, 214-216, 219-221
names.c, 380
nextPrime.π, 134
nextPrime.c, 135-138, 380-381
opening, 276-284, 356
operator.π, 79
operator.c, 79-81, 83-84, 86-88, 381-382
postfix.π, 89
postfix.c, 89-91, 382
power.π, 175-177
power.c, 382-383
printFile.π, 279
printFile.c, 279-284, 383-384
project, 16, 357
reading, 277-283, 357
recurse.c, 384
slasher.π, 91
slasher.c, 92-93, 385
source code, 16
squareIt.c, 385
stdio.h, 257-259
stdlib.h, 257
structSize.π, 242-243
structSize.c, 243-246, 386

sumFive.c, 386-387
windowMaker.π, 344-346
windowMaker.c, 387-398
wordCount.π, 224-230
wordCount.c, 225, 399-400
writing to, 277, 283-284, 359
Find Text... menu item, 22
Finder, 35, 343, 353
float.π file, 190-191
float.c file, 377
float program, 190-191
float variable type, 189-190, 192
Floating-point numbers, 189-192, 353
Floppy disk system, running THIN C, 15
Flow charts, 48
Flow control, 104-106, 353
Flush() function, 261, 264, 266
FlushFile() function, 293, 295
Fonts
    Chicago, 343
    setting for source code files, 21
fopen() function, 276-279, 281, 297, 409-410
for loop, 122-124, 131-132, 135-136, 160
for statement, 121-124
    syntax, 402
Format specifications table, 416
Format specifiers
    %c (character), 199
    %d (integer), 190, 215
    %f (float), 190, 192
    %s (0 terminated string), 220, 238, 267
fprintf() function, 283-284, 297, 411
fputc() function, 283-284, 412
fputs() function, 283-284, 412
Fractional part, 354
free() function, 250-251, 413
fscanf() function, 278, 293-295, 414
funcPtr.c file, 377
Functions, 45-47, 49-52, 354
    AddTheseNumbers(), 168-169, 171
    AddToList(), 260, 266, 295
    AddTwo(), 155
    AnotherFunction(), 49

arguments, 84-86
body, 46-47, 354
built-in, 50
calling, 49-50
case sensitivity, 58
clock(), 205, 406
CountCDs(), 297-298
DealTheCards(), 328-329
declaring variables within, 72
DoPower(), 175-180
DrawDots(), 157-161
exit(), 263, 406
factorial(), 316-319
fclose(), 282, 407
fgetc(), 278-283, 295-296, 408
Flush(), 261, 264, 266
FlushFile(), 293, 295
fopen(), 276-279, 281, 297, 409-410
fprintf(), 283-284, 297, 411
fputc(), 283-284, 412
fputs(), 283-284, 412
free(), 250-251, 413
fscanf(), 278, 293-295, 414
getchar(), 227, 265-266, 278, 283, 415
GetCommand(), 259-260, 262
IsItPrime(), 173-175
ItsRaining(), 129
left-curly bracket ({), 46
naming, 96
ListCDs(), 260, 266-267
main(), 46-47, 49-50, 54, 65, 131, 160, 167, 173-175, 178, 200, 204-206, 210, 244, 259, 262, 268-269, 280, 292
MakeWindow(), 84
malloc(), 249-252, 257, 263-264, 294, 415
MyFunction(), 49
parameters, 46, 84-86, 155-163, 354
    passing, 84, 161-163
PassAlong(), 166
pointers, 328-329, 354
print.f(), 257
PrintChars(), 199-200
printf(), 47, 50-51, 54, 80,

83-86, 90-93, 114, 131-132, 138, 175, 190-191, 199, 220, 227, 229, 245-246, 265, 267, 281-282, 416
printf, 213
PrintMyVar(), 167
PrintRolls(), 206, 208, 210-211
PrintX, 211
putchar(), 281-282, 417
Rand(), 207, 417
ReadALine(), 268-269
ReadFile(), 285, 290, 293, 295
ReadFileLine(), 294, 296
ReadLine(), 264-265
ReadStruct(), 260, 262-263
recursion, 314-319
return(), 168-169
return values, 168, 354
returns, 164, 168-171
right-curly bracket (}), 46
RollOne(), 205, 207
RowOfDots(), 160
SayHello(), 52-54
scanf(), 214-215, 217-220, 261, 264, 278, 418
Searcher(), 325-326
sharing variables, 164
sizeof(), 245-246, 249
source code in, 54-55
SquareIt(), 162-163
srand(), 205, 418
Standard Library, 51-52
statements, 47
strcat(), 331, 419
strchr(), 419
strcmp(), 331, 420
strcpy(), 330, 420
strlen(), 221, 332, 421
strncat(), 421
strncmp(), 422
strncpy(), 422
text string, 84
titles, 46, 354
types, 262
uninitialized return values, 170-171
variables, 84, 156, 159
VisitNode(), 325
WriteFile(), 285, 291, 296

G
Get Info menu item, 35
getchar() function, 227, 265-266, 278, 283, 415
GetCommand() function, 259-260, 262
gIsColor global variable, 181
Global variables, 164-167, 354
  adding to programs, 166-167
  explicit initialization, 261
  gIsColor, 181
  gPrintExtraInfo, 175-180
  memory and, 167
Global struct, 244
gPrintExtraInfo global variable, 175-180
Graphical user interface (GUI), 342-344, 354

H
Hard disk system running THIN C, 14-15
Hardware requirements, 5
hello.π file, 15-17, 19
hello.c file, 15-18, 34, 378
hello2.π file, 52-53, 55
hello2.c file, 53, 378
hello2 program, 54-55
  saving after correcting errors, 58
  source code errors, 56-57
[c]hello[c] folder, 15
hello program, 15-16, 49, 54

I
if-else statement, 106
if keyword, 104
if statement, 104-105, 108, 114-115, 117
  syntax, 401, 402
In-order search, 325-327, 354
Increment, 354
Index, 354
Initialization, 354
  explicit, 260-261, 353
  variables, 83
Initialized, 354
Input buffer, 216-219, 355
Input devices, 30, 355
Inside Macintosh, 347-348
Installing THIN C, 13-15

int variable type, 188
int variables, 68-79
  size of memory, 69
Integer part, 355
Integers, 71, 355
Integrated Circuits (ICs), 28-29, 355
IsItPrime() function, 173-175
isOdd.π file, 130-134
isOdd.c file, 130, 378-379
isOdd program, 130
iterate.c file, 379
Iteration, 314-315, 355
ItsRaining() function, 129

K
Key, 355

L
Leaf node, 320, 355
Less than (<) comparative operator, 109
Less than or equal to (<=) comparative operator, 109
Link Errors window, 58
link failed dialog box, 58
link failed error message, 58
Linked list, 251-269, 288-290, 355
  master pointer, 252
ListCDs() function, 260, 266-267
listPrimes.π file, 172-175
listPrimes.c file, 379-380
listPrimes program, 172-175
Literals, 71, 355
  as expressions, 107
  FALSE, 110
  TRUE, 110
Logical operators, 110-112
  ! (switch TRUE/FALSE), 110-111
  && (and), 111
  || (or), 112
Loops, 121-129, 355
  counters, 120
  for, 131, 132
  initialization, 119
  modification, 119-120
  termination, 119-120

M

Machine code, 14, 22, 32, 34, 355
Macintosh C Programming Primer, 348-349
Macintosh Programming Secrets, 349
Macintosh Toolbox, 342-344
  Control Manager, 344
  Menu Manager, 343
  using in your programs, 346-347
  Window Manager, 344
Macintosh user interface, 341-342
Macros, 224, 355
main() function, 46-47, 49-50, 54, 65, 131, 160, 167, 173-175, 178, 200, 204-206, 210, 244, 259, 262, 268-269, 280, 292
MakeWindow() function, 84
malloc() function, 249-252, 257, 263-264, 294, 415
  address, 250-251
Master pointer, 252, 355
Memory, 30-31, 355
  allocating, 248-249
  checking for applications, 35
  deallocating, 250-251
  global variables and, 167
  Model A program usage, 239-240
  RAM (Random Access Memory), 35-39
  size for variables, 69-70
  text strings, 213-216, 219-221
Menu Manager, 343, 356
Menus, 20-23
  Edit, 21, 22
  File, 20, 35, 345-346
  Project, 22-23, 35, 49, 55, 79, 89, 91
Model A program, 236-238
  memory usage, 239-240
Model B program, 240-242
More than (>) comparative operator, 109
More than or equal to (>=) comparative operator, 109
Motherboard, 29, 356
Multi-dimensional arrays, 236-238, 356

My Data File file, 279
MyFunction() function, 49

N

name program, 214-216, 219-221
name.π file, 214-216, 219-221
names.c file, 380
Naming
  functions, 96
  variables, 69, 96
New menu item, 14, 20, 345
Newline character (\n), 87, 92, 133
nextPrime.π file, 134
nextPrime.c file, 135-138, 380-381
Not equal to (!=) comparative operator, 109
Notation
  postfix, 356
  prefix, 357
Numbers
  checking odd and even, 130-133
  dividing by zero, 115-116
  floating-point, 189-192, 353
  prime, 134-138, 172-175, 314
  raising base to exponent power, 175-176
  squaring, 162
  whole, 188
Numerical constants, 71

O

Object code, 22, 34, 356
  deleting, 35
One-dimensional arrays, 236, 356
Open... menu item, 14, 20, 22
Opening files, 356
Operating system requirements, 5
operator.π file, 79
operator.c file, 79-88, 381-382
  source code, 83-88
Operators, 71-81, 83-84, 356
  See also comparative operators *and* logical operators
  & (address of), 150, 163
  * (multiplication), 77
  * (star), 151-152, 154, 161
  *= (multiplication), 77
  + (addition), 74
  ++ (increment by 1), 74-75, 89-91

+= (increment by value), 76
- (subtraction), 74
-- (decrement by 1), 74-75, 89
-= (decrement by value), 76
/ (division), 77-78
/= (division), 77
= (equal), 71-72
  binary, 111
  comparative, 108-109, 352
  defining precedence with (), 78-79
  logical, 110-112
  postfix notation, 75-76, 89-91
  precedence, 78
  prefix notation, 75-76, 89
  unary, 111
Or (||) logical operator, 112
Output
  buffers, 284-285
  devices, 30, 356

P

Page Setup... menu item, 20
Parameters, 356
  functions, 354
  passing, 84
Parent pointer, 208-211, 356
PassAlong() function, 166
Passing, 356
Paste menu item, 21
Pointer variable, 150-154
  declaring, 151-154
Pointers, 138, 144-163, 356
  adding level of indirection, 147
  arithmetic, 229, 356
  array names as, 208
  dereferencing, 154
  functions, 328-329, 354
  master, 355
  parent, 208-211, 356
  struct and, 247
  typecasting, 308-309
  variables, 356
Postfix notation, 75-76, 89-91, 356
postfix.π file, 89
postfix.c file, 89-91, 382
  source code, 90-91
Postorder search, 326-327, 356
power.π file, 175-177
power.c file, 382, 383
power program, 175-181

source code, 177-181
Prefix notation, 75-76, 89, 357
Preorder search, 357
press <<return>> to exit window, 80
Prime numbers, 134-138, 172-175, 314
Print... menu item, 20
print.f() function, 257
PrintChars() function, 199, 200
printf() function, 47, 50-51, 54, 80, 83-86, 90-93, 114, 131-132, 138, 175, 190-191, 199, 220, 227, 229, 245-246, 265, 267, 281-282, 416
    parameters, 84-86
    quoted text string, 85
    variable value in text string, 85
printFile.π file, 279
printFile.c file, 279-284, 383-384
printFile program, 279-284
printf function, 213
PrintMyVar() function, 167
PrintRolls() function, 206, 208, 210-211
PrintX function, 211
Program listings. See also files, programs, and individual program names
    addThese.c, 361
    ASCII.c, 362
    cdFiles.c, 362-366
    cdMain.c, 366-370
    cdTracker.c, 370-375
    dice.c, 375-376
    drawDots.c, 376
    float.c, 377
    funcPtr.c, 377
    hello.c, 378
    hello2.c, 378
    isOdd.c, 378-379
    iterate.c, 379
    listPrimes.c, 379-380
    location, 15
    names.c, 380
    nextPrime.c, 380-381
    operator.c, 381-382
    postfix.c, 382
    power.c, 382-383

printFile.c, 383-384
recurse.c, 384
slasher.c, 385
squareIt.c, 385
structSize.c, 386
sumFive.c, 386-387
windowMaker.c, 387-398
wordCount.c, 399-400
Programming basics, 27-28
Programs, 16, 28, 31-33
    See also files, program listings, and individual program names
    adding global variables, 166-167
    algorithm, 131
    allocating memory for variables, 148
    ASCII, 195-197, 199-200
    cdFiler, 285-298
    cdTracker, 254-269
    compiling then running, 19
    controlling order of statement execution, 104
    dice, 203-211
    float, 190-191
    hello2, 54-58
    hello, 15-16, 49, 54
    isOdd, 130
    listPrimes, 172-175
    Model A, 236-240
    Model B, 240-242
    name, 214-216, 219-221
    power, 175-181
    printFile, 279-284
    running, 23, 32
        THINK C, 429-431
    source code, 31-33
    structSize, 242-246
    using Macintosh Toolbox, 346-347
    windowMaker, 344-346
    wordCount, 224-230
Project menu, 22-23, 35, 49, 55, 89, 91
Project window, 19, 79
Project files, 16, 33-35, 357
    compacting, 22
Project windows, 17-18, 33-34, 357
    title, 17
Projects, 16
    See also files

opening and closing, 22
Projects folder, 15, 52
Prompts, 216, 357
Pull-down menus. See menus
putchar() function, 281-282, 417

Q
Quit menu item, 20, 346
Quotation mark character (\"), 93
Quoted text string, 85

R
rand() function, 417
Random Access Memory (RAM), 35-39, 357
Read-only memory (ROM), 342, 357
ReadALine() function, 268-269
ReadFile() function, 285, 290, 293, 295
ReadFileLine() function, 294, 296
ReadLine() function, 264-265
ReadStruct() function, 260, 262-263
recurse.c file, 384
Recursion, 357
    binary trees, 324-328
    functions, 314-319
Remove Objects menu item, 22-23, 35
return() function, 168-169
return statement, 174
    syntax, 404
Return value in functions, 354
Revert menu item, 20
RollOne() function, 205, 207
Root node, 320, 357
Root struct, 357
RowOfDots() function, 160
Run menu item, 19, 23, 49, 55, 79, 91
Running, 357

S
Save menu item, 14, 20
Save As... menu item, 20
SayHello() function, 52-54
scanf() function, 214-215, 217-220, 261, 264, 278, 418

Searcher() function, 325-326
Searching, 357
    in-order, 325-327, 354
    postorder, 326-327, 356
    preorder, 357
Set Tabs & Font... menu item, 21
Signed, 357
    variables, 70, 193
Simple statements, 116, 358
    semicolon (;) and, 116
Single tab character (\t), 93
sizeof() function, 245-246, 249
slasher.π file, 91
slasher.c file, 92-93, 385
Source code, 14, 31-34, 358
    #define, 221-224, 226
    algorithms, 47-49
    ASCII program, 199-200
    cdFiler program, 290-298
    cdTracker program, 256-269
    comments, 96-97
    dice program, 204-208, 210-
        211
    documenting, 96-97
    editor, 32, 358
    errors in hello2 program, 56-
        57
    functions, 54-55
    nextPrime program, 135
    operator program, 83-84, 86-
        88
    parentheses, 96
    postfix program, 90-91
    power program, 177-181
    printFile program, 279-284
    recompiling, 23
    saving after correcting errors,
        58
    spacing, 94-96
    substituting text for text, 221-
        224, 226
    syntax errors, 47
    viewing, 18
Source code files, 16
    opening and closing, 20
    printing, 20
    saving, 20
    searching for text string, 22
    setting tabs and fonts, 21
SquareIt() function, 162-163
squareIt.c file, 385

srand() function, 205, 418
Standard Library, 51-52, 358
    functions, 405-422
Star (*) operator, 151-152, 154,
    161
Statement markers, 430
Statements, 47, 114-129, 358
    break, 126-127, 129
    complex, 117, 352
    curly braces ({}) and, 116
    do, 125
    for, 121-124
    grouping, 116
    if, 108
    return, 174
    semicolon (;) and, 117
    simple, 116, 358
    switch, 126-128
    typedef, 332
    while, 118-121, 124
stdin file pointer, 282-283
stdio.h file, 257, 259
stdlib.h file, 257
stdout file pointer, 282-283
Stepping through, 358
Storage devices, 30
strcat() function, 331, 419
strchr() function, 419
strcmp() function, 331, 420
strcpy() function, 330, 420
String constant, 358
Strings
    appending, 331
    comparing, 331
    copying, 330
    length, 332
    manipulation, 330-332, 358
    printing text on-screen, 50-51
strlen() function, 221, 332, 421
strncat() function, 421
strncmp() function, 422
strncpy() function, 422
structSize.π file, 242-243
structSize.c file, 243-246, 386
structSize program, 242-246
struct, 242, 251-254, 312-314,
    319-320
    arrays, 246
    global, 244
    linking different types, 308-309
    pointers and, 247

struct types, 241-242, 244, 258
Structures, 235-247
sumFive.c file, 386, 387
switch statement, 126-128
    syntax, 403
    case, 127-128
    default case, 127-128
Switch TRUE/FALSE (!) logical
        operator, 110-111
syntax error message, 57
Syntax errors, 47, 358
System 7 running THIN C, 15

T
Tabs, setting for source code files,
    21
Tech block, 358
Terminal node, 358
Text, printing strings, 50-51
Text editor, 14, 358
Text strings, 212-223, 224, 358
    functions, 84
    memory, 213-216, 219-221
    quoted, 85
    searching source code files, 22
Text window, 50-51, 56
THIN C, 3
    as compiler, 32
    back-up copy, 15
    case sensitivity, 58
    compiler, 14
    compiling then running
        programs, 19
    edit cursor, 57
    exiting, 20
    features, 20-23
    floppy disk system, 15
    hard disk system, 14-15
    installing, 13-15
    project files, 33-35
    running under System 7, 15
    Standard Library, 51
    testing, 15-19
    text editor, 14
THINK C, 4, 346-347, 423-433
    #include files, 426-427
    ANSI library, 428
    current function, 430
    current statement, 430
    current statement arrow, 430
    Data window, 431

editor, 427
inline assembler, 431-432
libraries, 428-429
Macintosh Toolbox routines, 428
object code, 426
object-oriented programming (OOP), 432
overview, 424-425
projects, 425-426
running programs, 429
source files, 427
Source window, 429-430
source-level debugging, 429-431
statement markers, 430
THINK Class Library (TCL), 432
UNIX library, 428-429
upgrade policy, 424
Toolbox, 342-344, 359
Traversal, 359
TRUE expressions, 107-109
TRUE literal, 110
Truncating values, 77-78
Two's complement notation, 38-39
Type, 359
Typecast, 306, 359
Typecasting, 306-309, 359
pointers, 308-309
typedef statement, 332
Typos, 47, 359

U
Undo menu item, 21
Unary operators, 111
Uninitialized variables, 83
Unions, 310-314
Unsigned, 359
Unsigned variables, 70, 193
User interface, 341-342, 359

V
Values, truncating, 77-78
Variables, 36, 66-84, 144, 156, 359
addresses, 148-150
allocating memory, 148, 248
as different data types, 310-314
as expressions, 106

assigning values, 71, 73-75, 89
declaring, 68
within functions, 72
functions and, 84, 156, 159
global, 164-167, 354
initialization, 83
naming, 69, 96
pointer, 150-154
scope, 156-157, 359
sharing between functions, 164
signed, 70, 193
types, 68-71, 359
char, 192-200
double, 192
float, 189-190, 192
int, 68, 70-79, 188
memory size, 69-70
uninitialized, 83
unsigned, 70, 193
VisitNode() function, 325

W
while loop, 118, 122, 135-137
while statement, 118-121, 124
syntax, 402
White space, 94, 97, 359
Whole numbers, 188
Window Manager, 344, 359
windowMaker.π file, 344-346
windowMaker.c file, 387-398
windowMaker program, 344-346
Windows
press <<return>> to exit, 80
console, 80, 82
project, 357
wordCount.π file, 224-230
wordCount.c file, 225, 399-400
wordCount program, 224-230
WriteFile() function, 285, 291, 296

You can have it all!

Special reader offer:
Upgrade to the full version of THINK C for just $129.

The complete THINK C environment gives you the powerful features that have made THINK C the #1 tool for Macintosh development.

You're now familiar with THINK C, and the full version offers even more. Plus, you can build your own double-clickable applications!

As you develop your skills as a Macintosh programmer, you'll want the power and flexibility of THINK C. So act now to take advantage of this special upgrade offer.

Call Symantec Corporation at 1-800-228-4122 Ext. 807 to order your upgrade. Because you *can* have it all!

Limit one upgrade per coupon.

Powerful projects ... Enhanced editor ... Source-level debugging ... Inline Assembler
Libraries ... Object-oriented programming ... THINK Class Library ... Class browser

№ 023186